This copy of

SAN ANTONIO DE BÉXAR

is inscribed for

Mary

With best wishes,

Jesús F. de la Teja

2/27/04

Mision de S Ant.

SAN ANTONI'

University of
New Mexico
Albuquerque

Río de san Pedro

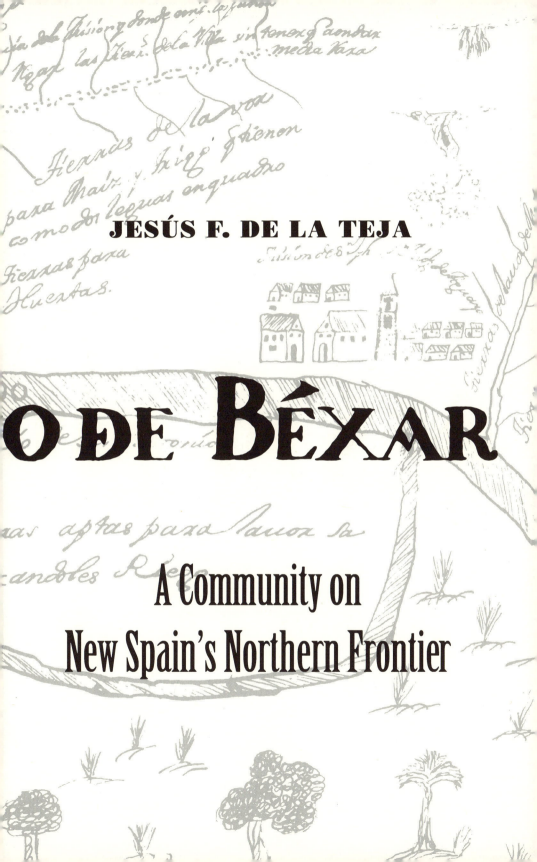

JESÚS F. DE LA TEJA

O DE BÉXAR

A Community on
New Spain's Northern Frontier

Library of Congress
Cataloging-in-Publication Data

Teja, Jesús F. de la, 1956–
San Antonio de Béxar : a community on
New Spain's northern frontier /
Jesús F. de la Teja.
p.   cm.
Includes bibliographical references and index.
ISBN 0-8263-1613-1.—ISBN 0-8263-1751-0 (pa)
1. San Antonio (Tex.)—History.
2. Spaniards—Texas—San Antonio—History.
3. Mexicans—Texas—San Antonio—History.
4. Community life—Texas—San Antonio—History.
5. San Antonio (Tex.)—Social conditions. I. Title.
F394.S2T4 1995
976.4'351—dc20   94–18727
CIP

Design by Stephanie Jurs

Visit the University of New Mexico Press website at www.unmpress.com

For Eduardo and Julia

Contents

Figures

Preface

This work examines community formation on the northern periphery of Spain's colonies in the Americas. As a military extension of a settlement frontier still hundreds of miles to the south, San Antonio de Béxar developed in isolation and sometimes in neglect. Yet this outpost was founded upon institutions already centuries old by settlers who were themselves the products of other frontier areas. As a result of the Spanish Crown's efforts to populate Texas's vast expanses, a small group of Canary Island colonists was added to the Mexican pioneer stock. Despite early conflicts between Isleño (Canary Islander) immigrants and Mexican settlers, economic and political forces shaped them into a single community by the latter part of the eighteenth century.

The importance of Mexican settlers, indeed the importance of civilian settlers on the Spanish borderlands has not always been fully appreciated or understood. Beginning in the late nineteenth century and continuing until the present day, many popular writers and scholars have focused on the "Spanish" in the borderlands. Spanish governors, Spanish missionaries, Spanish irrigation practices, Spanish law and government have all been stressed.[1] This historiographical tradition, focusing on the institutional and political development of the borderlands, has been expressed largely in the work of Herbert E. Bolton and his students and those influenced by the Boltonians.[2] While these authors produced important and enduring works, they tended to write not about communities or regional societies, except as they reflected Spanish norms. For instance, in 1988 Gilbert R. Cruz published a book on town-founding in the borderlands that stressed the Iberian institutional characteristics of the municipalities.[3]

In the last three decades other perspectives on the Spanish borderlands have emerged. The growing interest in ethnic and gender studies and a renewed interest in social history have combined to produce works that emphasize the distinctiveness of borderlands society as a blend of Old and New World cultural, economic, and religious institutions. Numerous journal articles as well as some important books have appeared which point to the richness of the Spanish frontier experience. In 1979 David J. Weber published an anthology on the Spanish borderlands which brought together then recent scholarship with some classic writings in the field. Weber remarked that the selection of articles in some subjects was made more difficult by their sheer numbers, while in other areas the problem was a lack of treatment: "Historians have just begun to explore the social history of New Spain's far northern frontier, for example, and they have largely ignored activities of women. . . . Few historians have compared aspects of the Spanish-Mexican experience in the various frontier provinces."[4] In that same year, Oakah L. Jones published a book which took for its subject the civilian settlers of a borderlands region that included both sides of the United States–Mexico border. In a direct challenge to those writers who stressed things Spanish, Jones asserted that the colonial culture he examined "became the nucleus of the present Mexican society in the northern states of that republic and of the Spanish-speaking life style in the southwestern states of the United States of America."[5] More recently, books by Douglas Monroy on Hispanic California and Ramón Gutiérrez on Hispanic New Mexico have received critical attention for their innovative conceptualizations and methodologies.[6] For instance, although their approaches are very different, both works are concerned with telling the Native American side of the story of contact and incorporation into Spanish colonial society. While Gutiérrez looks at New Mexican society from the perspective of social relations as expressed through sexual behavior and mores, Monroy looks at the same topic from the viewpoint of labor. The absence of an in-depth study of a single *colonial* borderlands community is all the more noticeable in light of the considerable volume of social history for the region which has emerged in the last twenty years.

Recent local histories have looked at frontier settlements across time and sovereignties (in some instances, all the way to the present day). All have paid some attention to social and economic questions for the colonial period. In their chronologically comprehensive histories of Albuquerque and El Paso, Marc Simmons and W. H. Timmons have incorporated demographic and economic material into narratives that stress the formation of Hispanic communities in the face of Indian hostilities and the exigencies of royal officials.[7] Two more chronologically limited local histories, one on Los Angeles by Antonio Ríos-Bustamante and one on Laredo by Gilberto Hinojosa, offer more in-depth views of life in the two communities during the colonial period.[8] Hinojosa, looking at Laredo's history from the viewpoint of demographic change, concentrates on how the town's population responded to major events in the region's history. Ríos-Bustamante's study of Los Angeles is particularly strong on describing the ethnicity of the population, race relations between Californios and the local Indian population, and the general economic characteristics of the community. Both books also deal effectively with the socio-racial structures of their respective communities. None of these works attempt to portray the day-to-day evolution of the community in both the physical and economic spheres.

In recent years, two histories of colonial San Antonio have appeared. One, a collection of essays on eighteenth century San Antonio edited by Gerald E. Poyo and Gilberto M. Hinojosa, looks at the emerging community from the perspective of the various groups that influenced it. Similarly organized, María Esther Domínguez's work treats the San Antonio area from its Spanish occupation until Mexican independence.[9] Both books give considerable attention to missions, and both are strongest in providing a demographic profile of the settlement. Again, although there is material on economic, political, and social aspects of town life, no unified picture of the community as a whole emerges.

None of these works gives a complete picture of the mechanics of community formation. This is in large part because the authors treat their respective subjects over spans of time during which the political and ethnic cultures underwent radical transformations. They all deal with one or more issues such as the demographic and social structure of the community, physical growth of the urban landscape, the predominant economic activities and land tenure questions, the role of religion in the community, the extent of local government, and relations with royal authorities. None, however, deals systematically with all of these issues. How these aspects of local life operated on a day-to-day basis and helped mold a sense of community is not clear.

Important in understanding community building in San Antonio de Béxar, or anywhere, is agreement on the meaning of the term community. For most scholars, the term community is little more than a synonym for settlement or town. At its simplest, community refers to place, but place can exert a powerful force on an individual's and a group's sense of identity.[10] A "profound attachment to the homeland appears to be a worldwide

phenomenon.""[11] As people clear forest and jungle and rearrange the landscape to meet human needs, they create a unique identity for the place and
for themselves. They express and reinforce that unique identity through
public ceremony that is often of a religious nature; and they create criteria,
often based on descent from those who originally brought the place into
being, by which they judge themselves and others.[12]

It is also necessary to define community by reference to characteristics
other than space. Common attitudes and experiences, or shared cultural or
economic values among individuals, are additional traits that serve to identify community. Whether individuals consciously choose to bind themselves to a common set of rules and goals, or subconsciously adhere to
expected norms of behavior, people need and strive to form a community
of the like-minded. This societal binding does not mean that the community is an association of equals or is free from conflict among members;
often, it is quite the contrary. Rather, everyone in the community shares
in an overall sense of belonging based on a broad range of characteristics,
no single one of which may be shared by all members.[13]

Some communities are so closely knit that they exercise political decision making, land owning, and social welfare functions over all members.
In a recent work, John R. Van Ness has discussed how such corporate
communities, mirroring practices in peripheral areas of Old Spain, developed in the area around Santa Fe, New Mexico.[14] It is evident that a
community does not spring up wherever people congregate. Thomas
Bender's observation concerning early New England towns is just as per-
tinent to the world of the Spanish frontier. He noted that as many as half
the settlers tried two or three settlements before finding one made up of
like-minded men and women.[15] New Spain's large floating population,[16]
especially in the land-rich but population-poor north, demonstrates that it·
was difficult to find a place to call home.

The emergence of community does not preclude social and economic
differences within the local society. Judged by local standards, San Antonio contained both prosperous and poor families (although to the outside
world there seemed to be little other than unrelenting poverty). It was
precisely this characteristic of the community that prevented the formation of static social strata. Consequently, many families included members
at opposite ends of the economic spectrum. The community's size, limited
economic opportunity, and the presence of a substantial military establishment, itself a type of "sub-community," created a somewhat fluid
social hierarchy.

The emergence of "community" at San Antonio de Béxar, therefore, is described in this study within both social and economic contexts.[17] The documentation for these themes—population growth, land and water distribution, farming and ranching, commercial activity, politics and public ritual—is abundant, but the documents are often vague and incomplete. Yet, from these records the web of community in the late eighteenth century may be discerned. And, through study of the various aspects of community, there emerges a picture of the degree to which San Antonio de Béxar both represented Spanish colonial society in general and was unique. In the face of isolation, neglect, and danger, the people of San Antonio de Béxar created not only a permanent settlement but a sense of community that survived the test of the wilderness.

This book has been a long time in the making. I would like to single out a handful of the most important contributors to its final form. Erik Mason, my editor on a previous project, helped me whip the final draft into shape. Jerry Poyo, with whom I have also worked on a number of projects, has made valuable suggestions to my work over the years and his observations have found their way into the book. My introduction to the Bexar Archives, window to colonial San Antonio, came from John Wheat, who has been ever willing to attempt to answer even the strangest questions. For suggestions and observations, the importance of which he may not realize, I owe thanks to Ross Frank. My wife Magdalena, who has had to suffer through reading just about everything I write, helped keep my language clear and accessible. The staff of the Center for American History, formerly the Barker Texas History Center, has always been helpful beyond the call of duty, particularly with regard to access to the original manuscripts. Finally, to all those who have shown an interest in my work and who continually prodded me to publish it, my sincere thanks.

SAN ANTONIO DE BÉXAR

1

Wilderness Outpost

*For through observation and exploration of those lands and coasts,
both by land and sea, it must be recognized that these settlements
must be the rampart, fortress, and defense of all this New Spain.*

—INSTRUCTIONS TO GOVERNOR MARTÍN DE ALARCÓN,
1718[1]

The ascent in 1700 of Louis XIV's grandson to the Spanish throne as
Philip V did not signal an end to the rivalry between Spain and France in
the New World. The last three decades of the seventeenth century had
seen the French probings into the interior of North America reach the
mouth of the Mississippi River. Already concerned that French Canadians
might gain access to the silver country of northern New Spain by way of
New Mexico, the Spanish Crown now had to contend with a seaborne
threat from the Gulf of Mexico. The French threat was overshadowed,
however, by an even more serious one in the form of Plains Indians
seeking to trade with, or take what they wanted from, Spanish settlements
along the northern frontier. Against the background of these European
rivalries and borderland concerns, San Antonio de Béxar was born and
grew during the eighteenth century.[2]

I

The role that Texas, Béxar in particular, played within the northward-
expanding Mexican colonial frontier can best be understood within the
context of its neighboring provinces. Extending across the semiarid lands
of today's West Texas—known during the colonial period as Apachería

and Comanchería—Spanish New Mexico seemed at times farther away
than the moon. The oldest of New Spain's frontier provinces was itself
getting back on its feet at the end of the seventeenth century, having
suffered through a revolt of the Pueblo Indians in 1680 that left only El
Paso del Norte in Spanish hands. Reconquest of the province began in
earnest in 1693 with the refounding of Santa Fe, followed by establishment of two other towns, Santa Cruz (1695) and Albuquerque (1706). In
time Spanish settlers, Pueblo Indians, and other Hispanicized Indians
formed other communities in the many valleys of the Rio Grande and
Pecos rivers.

The settled Indian population in New Mexico, which remained stable
for most of the eighteenth century at approximately 10,000, was crucial to
the limited economic prosperity the province's growing Spanish population enjoyed. From only a few hundred settlers in 1700, New Mexico's
Spanish population grew to about 25,000 a century later. In large measure,
these people lived by raising livestock, mostly sheep, and from the production of crude woolens, along with piñon nuts and turquoise, which
found markets in Nueva Vizcaya. Efforts to bring New Mexico into regular contact with Texas for mutual development purposes were discussed
by provincial and viceregal authorities at various times, and in the 1780s
small exploratory expeditions were undertaken from both provinces. Although successful in reaching their destinations—Santa Fe and San Antonio—the magnitude of the effort involved in making the transit
discouraged further attempts after the mid-1790s.[3]

Although until 1787 New Spain's northern province of Coahuila extended geographically from south of Monclova to the Medina River, just
below San Antonio, its northernmost settlement was the presidio-mission
complex at San Juan Bautista del Río Grande, which had been founded in
1700. Coahuila's early history was marked by abortive efforts to found
Spanish settlements. Two early efforts at settlement based on mining in
the Monclova area had floundered, but by the late seventeenth century
new forces were at work. Missionaries wishing to work among the non-
sedentary Indians of the region and government fears of French incursions
combined to bring about the resettlement of Monclova in the 1680s and
the opening of numerous missions.

Population growth in Coahuila was slow, both because it was remote
and hazardous and because it soon became dominated by large haciendas.
A century after its founding in the 1670s the province counted only approximately 8,300 Spanish residents. But in 1787 it received an important
reinforcement when the Saltillo and Parras districts, with over 15,000
residents, were annexed to Coahuila. By the turn of the century about

40,000 inhabitants worked wheat, cotton, grapes, wineries, and textiles in the south and sheep and wool in the north, while cattle and corn were grown throughout.

To the south, along the Gulf of Mexico coast north of Tampico, Spanish settlement did not occur until the late 1740s, when the ambitious José de Escandón, a successful military officer who had proven his capacity for getting the job done, was granted the right to settle a region marked by imposing mountain ranges to the west, semiarid coastal plains to the east, and uniformly unfriendly Indian groups throughout. Beginning in 1748 and throughout the next decade, Escandón brought large numbers of settlers, most of them poor landless farmers from neighboring provinces, into the region. Through careful planning, effective management of local Indians, and a generous immigration policy, Escandón managed to found twenty-three settlements containing approximately eight thousand inhabitants by 1757.

The province of Nuevo Santander stood in marked contrast to Texas at the end of the colonial period. Its 30,450 Spanish residents and 1,434 Christianized Indians occupied 1 city, 25 towns, 3 mining districts, 17 haciendas, 437 ranchos, and 8 missions. Livestock was the principal commercial activity, while farming remained on the subsistence level. The northern extension of Nuevo Santander, between the Rio Grande and the Nueces River, however, remained largely the realm of non-sedentary Indians at the start of the nineteenth century, with the exception of a few scattered, enormous ranches that were occupied on a part-time basis.

Texas had to compete with its neighboring provinces for scarce human and financial resources. All of the northern provinces lacked the mineral resources that had brought huge investments farther south from both private sources and the Crown. Texas had an abundance of land suitable for grazing livestock, but it was also inhabited by Indians who resisted assimilation. The absence of navigable (and manageable) streams, combined with shallow bays and dangerous sand bars, made its coast unattractive to seaborne trade. The one constant in the history of colonial Texas was the Crown's need for at least a nominal military presence there. Born of imperial strategic needs, Texas remained a bastion against intruders, Indian and European, throughout the colonial period.

II

The worst fears of Madrid and Mexico City regarding colonial security against French encroachment came true in February 1685, when René

Robert Cavelier, Sieur de La Salle, landed at Matagorda Bay on the Texas coast with colonists and trade goods. Overnight, Texas, which had remained little more than the vague and distant goal of martyrdom-seeking missionaries, took on a strategic importance that eventually led to its permanent settlement. Unaware of the French colony's self-destructive nature—disease, Indian attack, and internecine conflict quickly engulfed Fort St. Louis—Spanish authorities launched a concerted effort to discover and destroy the intruders.

Finding the French was no easy task, however.[4] The Spanish had almost totally ignored the region east of the Rio Grande since the mid-sixteenth century. After the Coronado and de Soto expeditions failed to turn up great Indian kingdoms to conquer or precious metals to exploit, interest in the North American interior had waned. The geographically confused Spaniards had established New Mexico at the end of the sixteenth century as their listening post against European intruders and could count on thousands of miles of unexplored wilderness for added protection. The northwestern Gulf of Mexico remained a great unknown, sailed only by force of storms that occasionally wrecked a ship off the Texas coast.

It was the land expeditions in search of La Salle that first brought the Spanish into contact with the river valleys of central Texas. Alonso de León led expeditions through the region in 1689 and 1690 and came away with the impression that the upper Guadalupe River would make an ideal site for a presidio to help link any settlement made in East Texas with the interior. Domingo Terán de los Ríos, who passed through the region on his way to East Texas in 1691, considered the upper San Antonio River valley, with its abundant water supply, woods, and agricultural land, the ideal site for missions and towns.[5] La Salle's murder, the complete geographic confusion of both Frenchmen and Spaniards, and the growing antipathy of the Caddoan Indian villagers to the Franciscan missionaries sent to East Texas in 1690 led to the quick abandonment of Texas and, along with it, any idea of settling the San Antonio River valley.

While Spanish attention in the 1690s turned to the new French threat from the Mississippi River eastward, the Franciscans who had been forced to abandon the Caddoan mission in 1693 sought some means of returning there. Among the most vocal were Fray Antonio San Buenaventura Olivares and Fray Francisco Hidalgo, both of whom crossed the Rio Grande on occasion in search of Indian recruits (or conscripts) for the missions south of the river. Fray Hidalgo eventually managed to make contact with the French in Louisiana through correspondence transmitted by way of the natives. In 1714 Louis Juchereau de St. Denis, a Louisiana trader, arrived at the Rio Grande outpost of San Juan Bautista. The trade goods he had with him indicated more than a mere interest in helping the missionaries do their good work among the Caddos. It was clear to Mexico City that the Texas wilderness no longer afforded protection from commercial rivals. The frontier of New Spain must be pushed northward.

III

When the process of reoccupying Texas began in 1716, the San Antonio–Guadalupe rivers region was again recommended for settlement because of its natural advantages. Domingo Ramón declared San Pedro Creek, a tributary of the San Antonio River, capable of providing water for a city.[6] The San Antonio area had also made a deep impression on Fray Olivares, who had seen it in 1709.[7] He lobbied for its occupation when the settlement of Texas was being reconsidered in 1716, arguing that the fertile soil, agreeable climate, and friendly and intelligent natives made Texas an ideal field for Spanish expansion. Knowing where most would-be settlers' interests lay, he commented on Indian stories of a mountain of silver and their use of green pigments that appeared to be derived from silver and copper.[8] As for the San Antonio area, Fray Olivares advocated joint Spanish settlement, "for an entire province will fit in the said river [valley]."[9]

Martín de Alarcón, newly named governor of Texas, received instructions based on these glowing reports. Optimism ran high at first that the new province bordering the French would prove to be a quick success. The viceroy ordered Alarcón to take as settlers families, artisans, and livestock, not just missionaries and soldiers. The missions to be founded between the San Antonio and Colorado rivers were to leave enough room for the founding of two towns or cities, to serve as "metropolises and capitals of those provinces, and for observation and defense from seaborne invasions," as well as to provide communication and aid to the province of Texas.

The first of the towns would be located on the San Antonio River and was typical of the paramilitary settlements that dotted the frontier. At least thirty Spanish[10] families would found the colony, including soldiers from the expedition. The settlers were to receive all the grants and privileges provided by royal laws, but enough land was to be left vacant for a further seventy families. Because the colony would occupy hostile Indian country, each settler was to receive a salary of 450 pesos, livestock, and other supplies.[11]

The response to the viceroy's directives for settlement was, however, less than enthusiastic. The available pool of settlers was extremely limited, for the Spanish populations of Coahuila and Nuevo León were small, and the government's recruitment efforts suffered from fiscal constraints. The Crown's straightened finances even led a member of the viceroy's council to suggest reducing garrisons in Nueva Vizcaya by a figure equivalent to the number of men sent to Texas.[12] Difficulties in recruitment and Fray Olivares's complaints about the low quality and moral character of the prospective colonists drew the sarcastic remark from Governor Alarcón that there were no apostolic colleges in the province of Coahuila from which to obtain settlers.[13]

The colonization expedition that was finally organized included an engineer, a stone mason, a blacksmith, and a number of women and children. They arrived in the vicinity of San Antonio on 25 April 1718. Fray Olivares and his small party, responsible for the mission, arrived soon thereafter. On 1 May, Alarcón designated a spot on the west bank of the river for Mission San Antonio de Valero. He selected a site on San Pedro Creek, approximately three-quarters of a league from the river, for the town. There, on 5 May, he performed the necessary ceremonies for founding the "Villa de Béxar."[14]

Fray Francisco Celiz, chronicler of the Alarcón expedition, provides the only account of the settlement's beginnings. The first crops planted—maize and vegetable gardens—were lost, the latter eaten by rodents. The settlers' early attempts to locate sites on the river where water could be diverted for crops proved unsuccessful. However, by the following January at least one appropriate site on the river and one on the creek had been found, and work on *acequias* (irrigation ditches) for the town and mission began. The settlers and Indians completed the work successfully and expected a large crop of maize, beans, and other produce.[15]

IV

Peace at Béxar was shattered in 1720 when Lipan Apache scouts attacked two of the early settlers, who were looking for missing horses. Apache depredations, the result of pressures exerted on these semi-sedentary people by the advancing Comanches, proved to be a chronic problem throughout the century. As the original inhabitants of the southern plains, the various Apache groups had led partly sedentary lives: planting crops in the spring and following the buffalo in the autumn and winter.

Beginning in the late seventeenth century and throughout the next century, Comanche groups encroached on Apache territory. Cut off from Spanish markets in New Mexico and prevented from establishing their spring farming camps by Comanche raiders, the Apache turned to plundering and warfare in their struggle for survival. The Spanish contributed to hostilities by befriending the Apaches' traditional enemies, the Indian peoples of northeast Texas, and by aiding in their campaigns against the Apaches.[16]

This first cycle of Apache depredations at Béxar lasted until 1726. They were at their destructive peak in 1723 when, in response to the plunder of eighty horses from the presidio's herd, Captain Nicolás Flores y Valdez led a force composed of soldiers and mission Indians on a two-month punitive expedition whose success was marked by the death of more than thirty Apache warriors, the capture of twenty women and children, and plunder in the form of 120 horses and other booty. The arguments of Béxar's missionaries that gentle means would accomplish more than retaliation led the viceroy to prohibit a similar campaign in 1725 and brought a temporary cessation of hostilities the following year.[17]

Even as the Apaches were intruding themselves on the life of the new community, the brief 1719 French invasion of East Texas had repercussions for Béxar's development. The Marqués de San Miguel de Aguayo, appointed governor of both Coahuila and Texas after volunteering to drive the French out of the latter, reinforced San Antonio by more than twenty soldiers in 1722, bringing the presidio's strength to fifty-four.[18] At the same time, Fray Antonio Margil de Jesús, who headed the Zacatecas[19] missionaries in Texas, petitioned the Marqués de Aguayo for a new Franciscan mission to serve the needs of uncongregated central Texas Indians. Aguayo's authorization for a new mission at Béxar was celebrated in its name, San José y San Miguel de Aguayo.[20]

By the time Inspector General Pedro de Rivera arrived at Béxar in December 1727, a certain stability had settled over the area. The garrison was well armed, disciplined, and effective in combating Apache depredations. "This presidio is garrisoned by a captain and fifty-three soldiers, but a smaller number would easily suffice. The only enemies in the area are a few Apaches living in the Lomería Grande, who know from experience how efficiently the soldiers perform their duty."[21] This recommendation was incorporated into regulations issued in 1729 for the operation of the presidial system on the northern frontier.

The hard-fought peace on which Rivera's calculations rested proved illusory, however. In 1731 a second cycle of Indian hostilities began that lasted until 1749. The renewed and increased depredations were the result of the growing ineffectiveness of the Apaches against their Comanche and other enemies. Although horses were the main target of the raiders, other livestock, guns and ammunition, and metal goods were soon added to their list of desirable plunder. Efforts to deprive settlers of the latter items required closer contact with the Spanish and, therefore, produced greater loss of lives. Spanish settlements and Franciscan missions along the entire frontier were easy and necessary prey if the Apache were to acquire the means to defend themselves against their Plains enemies. San Antonio de Béxar, isolated and containing five missions inhabited by Coahuiltecan Indian bands, many of whom had been Apache enemies, made a particularly attractive target. In response, presidio commanders and provincial governors led campaigns that often captured Indian women and children, thus exacerbating the situation.[22]

Efforts at peace by missionaries, particularly by Fray Benito Fernández de Santa Ana, who championed the Apaches as victims of Spanish greed and advocated a mission for them, failed until the mid-1740s. After Captain Toribio de Urrutia led a campaign against the Apaches in the spring of 1745, the Indians were so enraged that they made a direct attack on the presidio in June. Only a rescue party of Valero Mission Indians saved the settlement from destruction. Following the engagement, however, both sides signaled for peace and calmer times prevailed.[23]

Ironically, the Apaches' 1731 return to hostilities came at the same time the settlement was having to make room for newcomers. First, three missions, Nuestra Señora de la Purísima Concepción, San Juan Capistrano, and San Francisco de la Espada, were relocated from East Texas.[24] The abolishment in 1729 of the presidio located near these missions, part of Rivera's reform plan, had left these missionaries without the coercive force necessary to control area Indians. Transfer to the San Antonio River valley afforded these missions the renewed support of a presidio and an opportunity to make converts among the less developed tribes of the region. On 5 March 1731 the new missions were placed in possession of lands on both banks of the San Antonio River south of Mission San José.[25]

Second, just four days later, a group of Canary Island colonists sent to Texas at royal expense founded the town of San Fernando de Béxar adjacent to the presidio. Colonists from the Canary Islands, seeking escape from harsh economic conditions there, had successfully been sent to other parts of the empire. The Marqués de Aguayo, apparently aware of their worth as immigrant stock, recommended settlement of a large number of families in Texas.[26] Although they were to be settled separately from the presidio and missions, the availability of cleared land and the advent of the growing season led Captain Juan Antonio Pérez de Almazán to give the Canary Islanders control of the area adjacent to the garrison.[27] The colonization project proved to be so costly, however, that it was abandoned after the first group was introduced. None of the other four hundred Islander families envisioned for Texas was ever recruited.[28]

Bickering among the disparate elements of the growing Béxar community marked the two decades following the founding of the town. The Canary Islanders proved to be a particular source of contention. Not only did they quarrel with neighboring missionaries, soldiers, and already established civilian settlers, they divided into factions and quarreled among themselves. As one frustrated Mexico City official complained:

> The fourteen families from the Canary Islands complain against the reverend fathers of the five missions, against the Indians that reside therein, against the captain of the presidio, and against the other forty-nine families settled there, so that it seems they desire to be left alone in undisputed possession. Perhaps even then they may not find enough room in the vast area of the entire province.[29]

The most ominous threat to the community, however, continued to be mounted raiders from the north and west.

V

Despite the truce reached in 1745, the Spanish at Béxar continued to experience problems with the Apaches. In part, the problem stemmed from the Indians' own social organization. Although the Spanish tried to treat them as one nation, the Indians operated as independent tribes—and often as individuals. Signing a truce with one chief did not mean all bands in the region would comply with the agreement. By 1748 it had become the opinion of Captain Urrutia that bloody retaliatory expeditions would be required to solve the problem. He used a campaign in early 1749 to try a new strategy: taking a large number of captives, whom he treated well, he launched a broad round of negotiations with four Apache chiefs, who were treated like royalty and lodged at Urrutia's house. Their warriors were fed and entertained at a large building especially erected for the purpose. To seal the quickly negotiated treaty, a large hole was dug in the

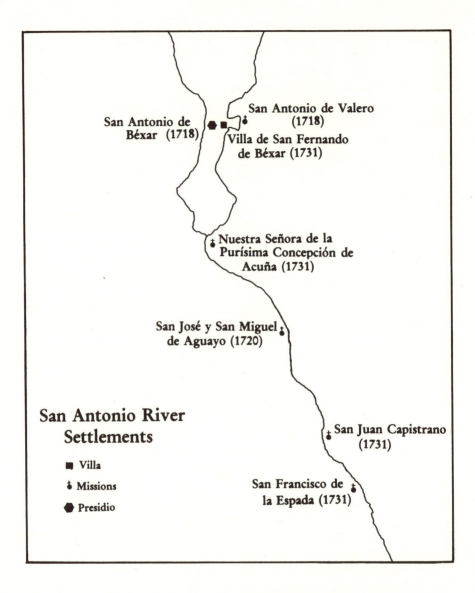

San Antonio de Valero
(1718)

San Antonio de
Béxar (1718)

Villa de San Fernando
de Béxar (1731)

Nuestra Señora de la
Purísima Concepción de
Acuña (1731)

San José y San Miguel
de Aguayo (1720)

San Antonio River
Settlements

■ Villa

♦ Missions

⬡ Presidio

San Juan Capistrano
(1731)

San Francisco de
la Espada (1731)

THE SAN ANTONIO AREA IN THE EIGHTEENTH CENTURY.
(Cartography by Caroline Castillo Crimm.)

military plaza to receive the frontier symbols of war—a horse, hatchet, lance, and arrows—as military recruits, civilians, missionaries, and visiting Indians danced about before filling it in. For the Apaches, the ceremony signaled the acquisition of a potential ally against the Comanches and their other enemies. For the Spaniards, it meant a decade of relative peace, but also an association with the Apaches that would cost them dearly thereafter.[30]

The Apaches' enemies included almost all the other Indian groups of Texas and the Plains. Collectively known as Norteños, because they were found to the north and east of the Apaches and Spanish, these groups included, among others, the Hasinai tribes of eastern Texas, the Tonkawa of present-day central Texas, and most feared of all, the Comanches. This last group was an offshoot of the Northern Shoshones of Colorado and Wyoming that had been introduced to the horse in the course of the seventeenth century. The horse allowed these foragers to move onto the Plains and become nomadic warriors and buffalo hunters. By the early 1700s various Comanche bands had moved into Apache territory, pushing the older tribe ahead of them. The first report from Texas on the Comanches was sent to the viceroy in 1743.[31]

Hostilities between Norteños and Tejanos (Spanish settlers of Texas) began in 1758 with an attack against a recently established mission for Lipan Apaches on the San Sabá River. The following January a war council, consisting of the governors of Texas and Coahuila and the provinces' presidio commanders, convened at Béxar, and the settlement became the staging point for a retaliatory expedition against the Norteños in the summer of 1759. The Béxar settlers were now caught in the middle of the continuing war between Apaches and Norteños. At first, the Comanches and other northern tribes did not attack Béxar, but their growing perceptions of Spanish friendship with the Apaches eventually led to depredations on the town and missions. A manpower shortage caused by the transfer of twenty men to the presidio at San Sabá and the ineffectiveness of expeditions against the swift-moving raiders, left Béxar's military little alternative but to assume a largely defensive position.[32] By the mid-1760s Béxar had become the northeastern linchpin of defense against the Plains Indians, while it continued to serve as a way station to Spanish East Texas.

VI

In 1763 France's transfer of Louisiana to Spain at the end of the Seven Years' War called for a thorough reevaluation of New Spain's northern frontier. The task fell to the Marqués de Rubí, whose inspection tour carried him from the Gulf of California to the Gulf of Mexico. In Texas he found only Béxar and La Bahía worth retaining. He recommended that San Antonio de Béxar should become the capital and point of contact between the Spanish and Plains Indians at the eastern end of the northern frontier; and that in order to carry out this function it should be reinforced with soldiers and settlers from the presidios being closed.[33]

By the time Rubí's recommendations were carried out in the early 1770s, the settlement had been under almost constant attack for five years. When, in 1768, the garrison at San Sabá abandoned the area for a safer area farther south, Béxar had become the primary target of Norteño raids. That summer, Governor Hugo O'Conor forwarded representations from Captain Luis Antonio Menchaca and Béxar's *cabildo* concerning the desperate situation. O'Conor's endorsement to the viceroy was unequivocal: the situation would remain critical until Mexico City decided to make serious war on these nations. "Only in this way will the presidio of Béxar and the town of San Fernando, which are the key to this province and the only good thing it has, achieve peace."[34]

Even during lulls in the depredations, only the settlements adjacent to the mission compounds were relatively safe. Rural property, particularly livestock, and lone ranch hands were always at risk, and the outlying ranches were largely abandoned in the late 1760s. In an effort to provide some security to stockmen, the new governor, Juan María, Barón de Ripperdá, built and manned an outpost on Cíbolo Creek, at an intermediate distance between Béxar and La Bahía. The post remained in operation until 1782, when it was ordered closed as being largely ineffective.[35] Throughout the 1770s and into the 1780s Béxar remained exposed to chronic Apache and Norteño depredations that affected all aspects of life.

Notwithstanding formal peace treaties with the Comanches and other Norteño tribes in the mid-1780s, total peace remained elusive. Resettlement of ranches abandoned during periods of aggression resulted in livestock slaughters by Indians supposedly at peace with Béxar. The Indians' chronic demand for horses, and the slaughter of cattle that usually accompanied their raids, sometimes resulted in the murder of ranch hands or residents. In the period 1795–1796, the destruction grew to alarming proportions. Béxar's citizens accused Governor Manuel Muñoz of indifference toward the settlers' losses and undue laxity in dealing with the Norteños visiting Béxar.[36]

VII

Despite the precariousness of life beyond the immediate confines of the town, at the end of the eighteenth century San Antonio de Béxar stood preeminent as the most developed of the three settlements that represented Spanish Texas. Geographically isolated and economically marginal, the province's sole reason for existence was as a buffer against alien encroachments, whether from European rivals or hostile Indians, into the more valuable interior of the viceroyalty. The effective line of Spanish settlement, which in 1716 had been leapfrogged to the area in response to French incursions to the Rio Grande, remained hundreds of miles from Béxar.[37]

Yet, despite its isolation and exposure to Indian depredations, Béxar was a well-established and growing community. The Crown's interest in maintaining a presence in Texas required a military establishment at Béxar that proved to be the community's backbone. They worked around the insecurity of life on an often hostile frontier to fashion strategies for survival that provided continuity for the settlement. Most importantly, the people of San Antonio de Béxar had by the beginning of the nineteenth century formed a sense of community. They understood themselves to be unique members of the empire and deserving of the King's mercies. It is to the various elements of "community", and the processes by which these elements came together in Béxar, that we now turn.

2

The People of Béxar

*It is necessary to seek recruits outside the province because here
there is no population whatever; and some time is needed to court
them, and they must be given some assistance for their costs besides
their salaries, because of the resignation with which they all come
to this country.*

—GOVERNOR FERNANDO PÉREZ DE ALMAZÁN, 1724[1]

San Antonio de Béxar experienced sustained growth during its first eighty
years of existence. As the settlement's mission diversified and its importance to the occupation of Texas grew, the town's population increased
proportionately. Those who came to Béxar were not Spaniards but sons
and daughters of New Spain's northern frontier. To this pioneer population was added a small group of Isleños (Canary Islanders) whose own sons
and daughters quickly melded into frontier society. The presence of these
immigrants gave a unique flavor to the mix of Indian, African, and Iberian
blood common throughout the borderlands. The intricate web of families
that characterized Béxar colored every aspect of community life.

I

The settlers who followed Martín de Alarcón to the San Antonio River
in 1718 were not the number that the viceroy instructed him to raise, nor
were they—if the accompanying missionary is to be believed—the proper
type. Alarcón's expedition consisted of seventy-two persons, including
thirty-four soldiers (seven of whom brought their families) and some muleteers. Some of these people moved on to East Texas and others returned

to Coahuila, leaving only a small group behind when Alarcón departed. It was these "mulattoes, lobos, coyotes, and mestizos, people of the lowest order, whose customs are worse than those of the Indians,"[2] as Fray Antonio Olivares described them, who became Béxar's founders.

The unsettled situation of Texas during its first years, particularly on its eastern border, kept the population in flux. When the French raided Spanish East Texas in 1719, the recently established Spanish settlers there fled to Béxar. The Marqués de Aguayo's efforts to expel the French likewise brought large numbers of people to San Antonio.[3] Aguayo increased the garrison to fifty-four men, including the captain, before he returned to Coahuila in 1722. Of the expanded complement approximately twenty members of the original military contingent remained.[4] The number of families substantially increased, as many soldiers brought wives and children to their new station. Governor Fernando Pérez de Almazán calculated a total of two hundred inhabitants consisting fifty-four officers and men of the presidio and four civilian residents.[5]

Béxar's population continued to grow in the last half of the 1720s despite the garrison's reduction. Inspector General Pedro de Rivera's 1728 review of conditions at Presidio de Béxar resulted in the elimination of ten positions (bringing the number of officers and men to forty-four) the following year.[6] Many, perhaps all, of those discharged had made homes in the developing community and remained as settlers. When the Canary Islanders arrived then, Béxar already had about twenty-five civilian households, including these former soldiers, and a total population of about three hundred.[7]

Even as the small military community began to grow on its own, efforts to more effectively occupy Texas drew the concern of various higher-level Spanish authorities. Fears of the French and the expense of maintaining a large military force provided impetus to colonization efforts. The idea of bringing Canary Island or other Old World settlers to Béxar, first proposed by the Marqués de Aguayo in 1723, was reiterated by other Crown officials. After two abortive attempts, a royal order of 1729 succeeded in procuring a few families in the Canary Islands. However, the project's high cost guaranteed that the effort would not be repeated, and no more than the first ten of four hundred scheduled families came to Texas.[8] The Isleños' arrival increased Béxar's population by 20 to 25 percent and resulted in the establishment of a clearly defined civilian settlement at Béxar.[9]

During the 1730s and 1740s there was little growth in the size of the garrison. There is also no evidence that significant numbers of new settlers arrived in Béxar during this time, but, as was the case in other frontier areas, females and children of hostile Indian groups were subject to enslavement in Texas. The military campaigns conducted against the Apaches through 1745 yielded women and children captives who were distributed among the settlers.[10]

At the end of the 1740s Pedro del Barrio y Espriella, the new governor, carried out a provincial inspection that included an assessment of the civilian population's military readiness. He found fifty-seven vecinos who were capable of bearing arms; of these six were unmarried, and other sources reveal the presence of an additional twenty-five adult males at the time. Including the presidio's fighting force of forty-three men, San Antonio de Béxar's total Spanish population in 1749–1750 was therefore approximately 560 men, women, and children.[11]

The 1750s were a period of tentative expansion for the Spaniards in Texas. Beginning in 1749 a decade of peace with the Apaches allowed missionaries to open up new mission fields, and civilians to occupy new areas of the province, but these efforts drained Béxar's population as families were drawn off to found the military posts that accompanied the new missions. At mid-century, the reduction of twenty-two men from Béxar's garrison in order to form the new presidio at San Sabá meant not only the loss of fighting men but also the loss of their families to the Béxar community.[12]

Syphoning off population from older frontier settlements to found new outposts was an established Spanish colonial practice, but it was not uncontroversial. The constant Indian menace and limited economic opportunities made civilians resentful of any loss to their community of fighting men, laborers, and their families, all of whom represented both added safety and a market for local produce. During the 1750s and 1760s Béxar's leaders, both civilian and military, made numerous requests on both economic and military grounds for the restoration of the lost fighting men. Making matters look as bad as possible so as to protect the town's interests, the 1762 *cabildo* claimed to have only forty-three householders. Of these, only twenty-five or so could be counted on at any one time, the council declared, arguing that the presidial commander's higher total included vagabonds and dependents without homes or lots. While the town council's claims in 1771 were certainly exaggerated—fifty families taken for San Xavier in 1751, the same number for Orcoquisac in 1756, and a large number recruited for San Sabá the following year—losses to the new settlements did affect growth.[13]

The *cabildo's* arguments notwithstanding, the population had managed to grow during the 1750s. The governor's count during an inspection in 1762 agreed with the presidial commander's muster for the same year that there were 103 *vecinos* capable of militia service.[14] Other sources bring the total number of adult male residents to 125. The increase in civilian households was somewhat offset by the loss of the twenty-two soldiers at the presidio; but nevertheless, by 1762 Béxar's Spanish population had grown to approximately 661 persons.

Crown policy continued to play an important role in shaping Béxar's growth during the late 1760s and into the 1770s. In great measure, the settlement benefited from the failure of the expansion program of the 1750s. Unsuccessful efforts to found a new settlement on the coast at the northern end of Galveston Bay, and the decision to abandon the moribund East Texas missions and Los Adaes presidio, all directly contributed to a population boom at Béxar. The government focused its available resources on Béxar as the most dynamic and developed settlement in the province, attempting to build upon that success.[15]

The Apache mission's failure and the San Sabá presidio's ineffectiveness in the face of attacks by the Apaches' enemies, saw the return to Béxar of some families. The spurt in population growth began with the stationing of a detachment of twenty-one men from San Sabá in 1769.[16] The following year the townspeople petitioned the new governor, Juan María, Barón de Ripperdá, not to permit the troops to depart after their replacements arrived. Instead, they asked that the first detachment be kept in Béxar and that the just-arrived troops be sent to guard the outlying ranches. In this 1770 petition the town council provided the first estimate of Béxar's total population—860 men, women, and children—since Governor Almazán's estimate of two hundred in 1726.[17]

Even as Bexareños clamored for the retention of the San Sabá detachment, the viceregal government was implementing the Marqués de Rubí's recommendations for the province's restructuring. According to Rubí, the East Texas missions had long been moribund and the presidios at Los Adaes and Orcoquisac no longer served a useful purpose after Louisiana's transfer to Spanish rule. Disbanding the two companies and transferring the civilian population of Los Adaes to Béxar would result in savings that could be invested in making Béxar a more viable settlement.[18]

By 1773 Presidio de Béxar's complement of soldiers had been expanded to eighty men, including the best from the disbanded companies of Orcoquisac and Los Adaes. In that same year, the government forced the entire population of Los Adaes to abandon its settlement and relocate at Béxar.[19] Although the transfer was not entirely successful (the majority moved back toward East Texas the following year[20]), approximately sixty Los Adaes *vecinos* decided to remain at Béxar with their families. Many of these Adaesanos settled at the nearby missions, while others became residents of the town, providing a substantial population increase.[21]

The dramatic increase in Béxar's population occasioned by the province's restructuring is reflected in the first house list census for Texas, made in 1779.[22] The presidio counted eighty non-commissioned officers and enlisted men, including retirees and invalids, and 191 dependents. The civilian population stood at 1,203 men, women, and children in 294 households. Although over a third of all household heads were natives of Béxar, and another third were from nearby frontier areas, the ethnic mix of the remainder of the community revealed its ever-wider attraction to settlers from the interior of the viceroyalty, including the capital, and from as far away as Canada, France, and Ireland as well as various parts of Spain.

The last two decades of the eighteenth century were a time of consolidation for the community. By 1781 the garrison had increased to one hundred active men, a strength maintained into the nineteenth century. Even after Governor Domingo Cabello signed peace treaties with the Comanches and other tribes in 1785, allowing many residents to return to their abandoned ranches, drought and epidemic served to restrain the quick growth that had characterized previous decades.[23] During the 1790s the Spanish population of San Antonio de Béxar stabilized at approximately two thousand, about sixteen hundred of whom lived within the limits of the presidio, town, and the by then extinguished Mission Valero.[24] The others lived at the other four missions, which themselves began the process of secularization at this time. The attraction was the availability of land and shelter at the missions, where Spanish civilian labor increasingly replaced that of neophytes (Indians under missionary tutelage).

II

The typical eighteenth-century Béxar household consisted of husband, wife, and children. As in other non-mining areas of the frontier, expansion into Texas was carried out by family groups,[25] as shown by the relatively well balanced nature of the population from a fairly early date. Despite the large disproportion of male to female settlers in the most remote locations, overall male-to-female ratios were not extreme on the frontier, and certainly not in Béxar.[26] In 1790 Texas, where the overall ratio was 125 males per 100 females, Béxar's ratio was 108.5 males per 100 females.

From the early planning stages in 1714–1716, viceregal authorities envisioned a Texas settled by families, where male heads of households would double as soldiers. The missionaries involved in occupying Texas adamantly argued that a purely military escort would prove detrimental to their efforts, and that only soldiers with families could be safely settled among the Indians. Although few women made the initial entry with Alarcón, wives soon began to join their husbands. A missionary who served in Texas at the time later wrote that many of Alarcón's soldiers brought their families to Béxar.[27]

The number of households also increased as a result of numerous marriages during the settlement's first years. Unlike other isolated areas where clergymen were in short supply, Béxar's population had access to missionaries from the founding of the town, and to parish priests after 1731. Also, unlike more settled areas where church fees could be high, some leeway was provided for the poverty of many frontiersmen.[28]

Older soldiers brought not only their wives but also their daughters of marrying age. Cristóbal Carabajal and his wife, Juana Guerra, married off three daughters in 1721–1723, two to Béxar soldiers.[29] All told, eight daughters of Béxar residents can be identified as having married soldiers in the period 1720–1724. Another four marriages involved widowed women and local soldiers. By 1730 there were approximately forty married couples in the settlement, of whom at least twenty-two married locally.[30] The high incidence of marriage among Béxar's adult population in the last decades of the eighteenth century was a pattern that had been established in the settlement's first years.[31]

Frontier conditions do not seem to have delayed young people from finding partners. In 1772–1790 the average age of women at the time of their first marriage was eighteen years old; at slightly over twenty-four years old, men were older. In general, the marriage age of women conformed to colonial averages,[32] and childbearing quickly followed marriage. The early death of a spouse was frequent, but the available evidence indicates that widows and widowers frequently found new partners, even into middle age, and that the waiting period between death of spouse and remarriage was not long. Rosa Guerra first married in 1728; her second husband died in 1750, and she married a third time that same year. Ana María Valdez and Gertrudes de la Garza, like many widows, remarried within two years of their first husbands' deaths. The same situation existed for men: José Pérez Casanova remarried the same year his first wife died, as did Luis Pérez. In remarriage, it was just as likely for single men to marry widows as for widowers to marry single women, reflecting a balanced opportunity for individuals of both sexes to find new partners.

High infant mortality combined with a dangerous environment for the adult population required high birth rates. Florencia Rincón bore José Cantú ten children between 1750 and 1770; seven are recorded as dying in the first year of life and an eighth in the second year. Only the names of two daughters are absent from burial records. Many couples lost half or more of the children born to them. Felipa Maldonado died giving birth to her third son, who also died. Her first son had died three days after birth, her second at ten months. Among the 929 legitimate births recorded at Béxar from 1719 through 1760, there are 268 recorded burials of children ten or younger.[33] Of the 243 burials of children whose ages are indicated, 202 were one year old or less, most dying within days of birth. Another twenty-one children are recorded as dying in their second or third year. Despite the century long incidence of high infant mortality, the single largest population group in 1793 consisted of children below eleven years of age. The 25 percent of the population represented by this group fits well into the northern pattern of age distributions in well-settled and predominantly Spanish areas.[34] It also attests to the vigor of the reproducing population.

As far as the parish records can be trusted, illegitimacy was not substantial in early Béxar. Of the 442 recorded births at San Fernando church between 1733 and 1761, only thirty-one are identified as illegitimate. María Rios, a widow known as "La Vieja," was responsible for five of these births. Between 1749 and 1758 she baptized four sons and a daughter, at least two of whom were of mixed-blood. In all, almost a third of the illegitimate children (nine children) were born to slaves or Indian servants, and half (fifteen children) are clearly identified as mixed-bloods. However, despite the low numbers, no segment of the population was devoid of illegitimate births; Josefa Leal and Leonor Delgado, Canary Islanders, both bore illegitimate children in the 1750s.

The trend toward increasing numbers of illegitimate births seen near the end of the eighteenth century[35] coincides with Béxar's large population increase of the 1770s. The transfer and settlement of a sizable portion of East Texas's population at Béxar in 1773, along with the garrison's steady expansion from 1769 to 1781, swelled the town's population to almost double what it had been in 1770. Secularization of Béxar's missions in 1793–1794 added to the flow of mission Indians into the Spanish community[36] and offered increased opportunities for irregular unions and extramarital sexual contacts resulting in illegitimate births.[37]

III

By the end of the eighteenth century Béxar's settlers were a racially mixed group, representative of northern New Spain's heterogeneous population. While the Spanish colonial *sistema de castas* (caste system) was not entirely inoperative, factors on the frontier restricted its effects. Indian hostilities tended to draw communities together, as did physical isolation. The scarcity of potential mates within one's own caste also weakened ethnic barriers.[38] The state of racial mixing at Béxar at the time of Fray Agustín Morfi's visit in 1778 was such that he described the town council—Béxar's most prominent men—as "a ragged band of men of all colors."[39]

Béxar's early population had consisted of three broad groups: frontiersmen from other parts of northern New Spain; a fluctuating number of mission Indians; and a small group of Canary Islands immigrants. In the course of the century they were joined by a steady stream of settlers both from other parts of Texas and from neighboring provinces. Much of this population claimed *español* status despite, as we shall see, evidence of mixed parentage.[40]

In Texas the caste system became subjective and arbitrary. The few Europeans do not appear to have enjoyed higher status than those individuals in the predominantly creole population, a situation that seems to have been repeated elsewhere.[41] The designation "Indian" included both Texas natives and Hispanicized Indians from other provinces who formed part of Béxar society. Bexareños employed other terms, such as *gentiles*, *enemigos*, and *bárbaros*, as well as tribal names, to designate the surrounding unacculturated Indian populations. The term *negro* appears infrequently, and usually in association with slavery. *Mestizo* (technically the offspring of Spanish–Indian unions), *mulato* (the result of Spanish–black mixing), and *coyote* (Indian–mestizo) were often used interchangeably. The term *lobo* (supposedly the result of Indian–African unions) was rarely employed in the early parish registers, but appears more frequently in late-century reports.

Isleño, while not an ethnic term, carried considerable social significance. Unlike the terms *español* or *europeo*, the term *Isleño* bore certain connotations unique to Béxar's social structure. The royal privileges the Isleños enjoyed, although no different from those granted to original settlers elsewhere, had been granted despite the previous settlement of Béxar by American-born families. The Isleños' early monopolies of town council posts, farmland, and water endowed them with high social status, but their economic fortunes varied substantially from family to family. The disputes that embroiled them with governors, presidial commanders, missionaries, and each other during their first twenty years of residence in Béxar contributed to their separate identity, but the group's small size meant that marriage partners had to be sought among the larger, American-born population. Vicente Alvarez Travieso, who married a daughter of Juan Curbelo before arriving in Béxar, had seven children, all but one of whom married non-Isleños. José Leal and Ana de los Santos married their six daughters and three sons into non-Isleño families. In those cases where Canary Islander offspring married other Isleños, their children in turn married outside the group. Consequently, over the course of three generations, a substantial portion of Béxar's population could and did claim Canary Islander descent, even though no undiluted Isleño stock remained. Even after their separate ethnic identity became lost through mixing, the Isleño label continued to provide prestige to a large portion of the Béxar-born population of later generations.

The Isleños' absorption into the larger Béxar community was part of a broader, ongoing racial amalgamation, much of which took place through the misrepresentation of an individual's true racial background. Priests who maintained the settlement's vital statistics were parties to the circumvention and obfuscation of the boundaries imposed by racial backgrounds.[42] There was little consistency from cleric to cleric, or even among the entries of a single priest, in providing race information in marriage, birth, and death records.

The Francisco de Urrutia and Catarina Valdez family serves as a good example of the vagaries of church records. Their first child (born and died 1744) is not assigned a race, but Francisco is listed as a *mestizo*. In their second child's baptismal entry (1749) there is no indication of race for parents or offspring. A son born in 1754 is listed as a *mestizo*, while his burial record four years later lists his parents as *coyotes*. In the 1760 baptismal register of their daughter, the entire family is listed as *español*, only to fall back to *coyote* status at the baptism of another daughter four years later. Father Pedro Fuentes y Fernández, whose two-decade tenure (1771–1790) was the longest of any San Fernando parish priest, did not employ the term *coyote* until 1777, one third of the way through his stay in Béxar. Between 1777 and 1782, he used *coyote* sparingly. By 1785, however, the term *coyote* is more prevalent in his entries than is the term *mestizo*. Beginning in 1786 and continuing until the end of Father Fuentes's tenure in 1790, the term *coyote* completely displaces the term *mestizo* in the baptismal register.

Some ethnic labels employed by Bexareños carried different meanings from those commonly employed in other parts of the Spanish world. Béxar's surviving records are devoid of such Mexican usages as *castizo* and *morisco*, employed in other areas of the north.[43] The terms *mestizo* and *coyote*, as employed in Béxar, frequently have been misunderstood by scholars.[44] Yet a reexamination of the records available for Béxar in light of more recent works stressing the complexities of socio-racial categorizations in colonial Spanish America reveals that racial distinctions in Béxar were neither as simple nor as rigid as earlier scholars understood them.[45]

Documentation and the observations of contemporaries offer a more fluid view of racial categorization in colonial Béxar. Fray José Francisco López, president of the San Antonio de Béxar missions, reported to the bishop of Nuevo León in 1786 that the Indians of Mission Valero used the Spanish language more often than not because they had "married with mulattos and mestizos, who are called *coyotes* here."[46] Father Fuentes' history of replacing "*mestizo*" with "*coyote*" attests to the popularity of the latter term as the common label for Spanish–Indian mixtures in Béxar. Rather than hiding their "*mestizo*" status, Béxar's population merely explained their social reality differently from other parts of New Spain.[47]

Some families proved to be very successful in transforming their racial identities. Joaquín de Medina and Mariana Rincón, originally listed as mulattos, baptized their first five children as such, the last one in 1762. Beginning in 1763, four children, as well as the parents, were identified as *españoles* in the baptismal and burial registers. José Cantú and Florencia Rincón's first child was listed without race in the burial register (1750), their second child was listed as *español* in the baptismal record (1754), and the priest listed the next two children (1757, 1760) as *mulatos* and the next child (1761) as *mestizo*. From 1763 to 1770, all five children registered were baptized as *españoles*.

Despite the frequency and apparent ease of "passing" (successfully upgrading one's ethnic status as part of improving social status), Béxar's was not an entirely color-blind society, even though many of the local ordinances demonstrate the same ambivalence toward the caste system found in other official records. While most surviving ordinances do not reflect separate penalties for offenders of different races, some reveal a continuing acceptance of colonial proscriptive practices in the frontier setting. In 1751 the penalty for slaughtering cattle outside of designated areas and without permission was twenty-five pesos for *españoles* but two hundred lashes for mixed-bloods. Governor Muñoz's ordinance regulating contact with the Apaches called for a purely monetary fine for *españoles* but added a jail sentence to the fine for mixed-bloods.[48] Such legal discrimination could only have served as an added inducement to "whiten" one's status.

The stain of mixed-blood attached to *mestizos* and the additional stigma of slavery attached to *mulatos* in colonial society[49] often transferred to the frontier, despite the considerable level of miscegenation there. The *mulato* was in a particularly vulnerable position, perhaps because slavery did exist, although on a very small scale, even in such a remote place as Béxar. Use of the term *mulato* as an insult in Béxar society points to the lingering, if somewhat mitigated, importance of racial attitudes on the frontier. While the terms *mulato* and *mestizo* were often used to identify the same individual in official records, surviving legal proceedings indicate that only the former term carried a potentially pejorative connotation. Governor Domingo Cabello, who made an enemy of the prominent Menchaca family, could not help but explain to the commandant general that the Menchacas were in no position to dishonor him, they being:

> no more than poor mulattos from Presidio Rio Grande. Retired Captain Don Luis Antonio [Menchaca's] father is unknown, and [Menchaca] took his last name from his adoptive father, whom [Captain Menchaca's] mother married after his birth.[50]

When José Antonio Villegas delivered Vicente Amador a summons to appear before the town magistrate, Amador called both Villegas and the *alcalde* "mulatto dogs." During an argument over debts owed, soldier Fernando Arocha, a descendant of Canary Islanders, was called a mulato dog by Luis Mariano Menchaca, son of the retired presidial commander whom Governor Cabello had labeled a *mulato*.[51] When Antonia de Armas called the wife of Francisco Rodríguez a *mulata*, that was enough for Rodríguez to declare that, should that be true, he would end the marriage, "for I married her in faith that she was Spanish."[52]

It is no wonder that records often show *mulatos* in the process of changing their identity. For instance, Leonardo Guillén, a servant (*criado*) of Don Luis Antonio Menchaca, is listed as a *mulato* in the 1793 census and as a *mestizo* in the house list of 1796.[53] In the garrison censuses, which begin to appear in the 1780s, the entire company, including families, is listed as español.[54] Yet, in his petition to marry María Rosalia Vargas, Tomás Galván declared himself a *mestizo*, while a fellow soldier who claimed to have known the groom for eleven years testified that Galván was a *mulato*.[55]

Perhaps the most clear-cut and prominent case of racial mobility was that of Pedro Huizar (Guizar). Sometime before 1778 this native of Aguas Calientes arrived at Béxar, where his services as a sculptor were employed at Mission San José. A man of numerous talents, he is reputed to have sculpted the mission church's rose window and the façade. At one point, Huizar was listed as the mission's carpenter. During the 1790s he helped survey mission farmlands at the time of secularization, the La Bahía area for possible irrigation works, and Béxar's presidio for reconstruction. In 1798 he was serving as the appointed justice at Mission San José. First appearing in the 1779 census as a *mulato*, by 1793 Huizar appears as an español. By the time he was listed in the Mission San José census of 1798, Huizar had risen to the honorific of Don.[56]

IV

San Antonio de Béxar was a dynamic and growing population center for most of the eighteenth century. Its people, drawn mostly from neighboring provinces, were well adapted to handle the hostile frontier conditions. Royal and viceregal decision making sometimes adversely affected population growth and at other times fostered it. While troop reductions and transfers to new outposts drained people from the settlement, increased exposure to Indian hostilities resulted in renewed efforts to fortify the strategic outpost. Beginning in the 1750s and increasingly after Louisiana's transfer to Spain, Béxar became the center of Spanish activities in the province, resulting in steady population gains. Restructuring of the presidial system in the 1770s brought a large number of civilians to Béxar, as well as more soldiers. As with any frontier settlement, the constant movement of people through Béxar makes it impossible to determine the amount of natural growth that did take place. It is possible to see, however, that there was considerable natural growth based on those families, descended both from the original Mexican and from Canary Islander stock, who formed the settlement's core population.

In most respects, Béxar's population conformed to the norms of New Spain's late colonial frontier. People were married and often widowed young. High infant mortality kept most families small. However, a considerable number of families had Indian dependents, many of them captured members of the Apache nation. Racial mixing was so thorough and ethnic labels so confused that the term *español* should be considered little more than a social label. Imprecise reporting of race, as in other parts of the empire, reflects the increasing divergence between social reality and superimposed imperial norms. On the frontier, where scarcity and necessity limited choice of partners, adherence to the caste system was of secondary importance. Yet, use of the term *mulato* in a derogatory manner, continued employment of separate and more severe punishments for lawbreakers of mixed race, and the frequency of "passing" all demonstrate that palpable differences continued to exist that made the lighter racial categories preferable.

3

Building a Frontier Town

As of this date the presidio has no structure whatever, as only its
poorly made houses make up the square of a plaza, without any
wall or stockade (which is the reason that the Apaches have en-
tered by night and taken from the plaza the horses tied up there).
Not for lack of abundant and very fine stone, of which there are
substantial deposits nearby. Only timber is lacking, for it is distant
and its cutting and transportation requires an escort because the
whole country is invaded with enemy Indians.

—GOVERNOR TOMÁS FELIPE DE WINTHUISEN, 1744[1]

During the eighteenth century San Antonio de Béxar existed as a proto-
typical frontier community. Military post, civilian settlement, and missionary establishments coexisted, often in great tension with one another,
but in undisputed interdependence. Despite the vast expanses of well-
watered and unsettled lands available in central Texas, the need to remain
close to the settlement for protection produced a sometimes intense competition for local resources, particularly water and farmland. While circumstances and customs fostered compact living, they also bred a
disregard for the formal rules and theoretical principles of Spanish urban
development embodied in the *Laws of the Indies.* Mutual dependence grad-
ually blurred the lines between the community's different entities, so that
by the end of the century the presidio of San Antonio de Béxar, the town
of San Fernando de Béxar, and the secularized mission of San Antonio de
Valero were essentially one. In building their community the people of
Béxar proved themselves to be as loyal subjects of His Catholic Majesty as
they were poor keepers of his laws.

I

Isolated and compact, Béxar's early population existed largely outside the bureaucratic world of paper land titles. Governor Martín de Alarcón's instructions called for granting the first settlers all the privileges and concessions allowed by the law: "the lands, pastures, water, and proportionate woods, with the sole reservation that there be left vacant enough lands for one hundred families who will be introduced in time."[2] At the act of possession in May 1718, the settlement received the name Villa (town) de Béxar.[3] However, there is no evidence Alarcón ever had the founding act recorded or that he made an effort to distribute land individually to the soldier-settlers.

With the exception that no formal paper titles to lots were recorded, the occupation and early use of land closely mirrored the Spanish experience elsewhere in northern New Spain. Despite the Spanish penchant for paperwork, Béxar was not unique in being established so informally. Albuquerque, New Mexico, for instance, was founded similarly. As early as Culiacán's and Durango's settlement in the sixteenth century, occupation had been spearheaded by soldier-colonists who received lots and agricultural land along with livestock, seed, and implements. This process continued with the settlement of Sinaloa, Sonora, and Coahuila, where towns were first established as military posts with small-scale farming and ranching as additional attributes.[4]

The process of building a self-sustaining settlement quickly began in Béxar. *Acequias* (irrigation ditches) were opened for the settlement as well as for Mission Valero. The *acequias* were vitally important to provide water to both agricultural fields and urban homesteads. Lands were cleared and maize and *huertas* (vegetable gardens) planted. When the Marqués de Aguayo determined that the presidio's original location was too exposed, he chose a new site between the river and creek. There the settlers dug a new *acequia* "capable of irrigating the two leagues of fertile land found within the angle formed by the San Pedro and San Antonio, taking the water from the former for the benefit of the presidial troops and settlers that might join them."[5] In 1721 and 1722 the original soldier-settlers, with the assistance of mission Indians, cleared enough land to plant subsistence crops for the garrison.

The fact that San Antonio had been founded as a *villa* was soon forgotten, as the absence of significant numbers of civilian settlers assured the preeminence of the presidio in the community's life. Although the civilian population grew toward the end of the 1720s, as a result of the reduction in the force of the garrison, the simple structure of community life remained. Soldiers with families built their homes near the post, and when they left military service continued to reside in them. Consequently, soldiers, former soldiers, and other settlers lived side by side. As Béxar's permanence seemed assured, improvements such as adobe or stone houses began to replace stick and mud *jacales*, and fruit orchards put in an appearance.[6] Ownership under these simple and familiar circumstances did not rest in paper titles but in acknowledged possession and actual use.

II

The presidial system placed a heavy burden on the Crown. Texas garrisons were especially costly to the royal treasury because the province produced no compensating wealth. Like the missions, presidios were viewed as somewhat temporary institutions. Their purpose was to hold an area until it could protect and sustain itself, at which time the presidio would be moved or disbanded.[7] During the 1720s a number of officials recognized that Texas offered few incentives to civilian settlers and that the Crown should take an active role in fostering growth of the province's population. Colonists required only a one-time expense for transportation and supplies, while soldiers required salaries and administration. By 1727 Brigadier Rivera had already dismantled one Texas presidio and reduced forces at the remaining three, in spite of protests from the missionaries.

Such factors led the government in Madrid to launch an effort to settle four hundred families in Texas.[8] While it was the Crown that set the process in motion by ordering the recruitment of colonists in the Canary Islands, the management of details was left to Mexico City. And just as Madrid did not consult with viceregal officials on the matter, the latter failed to take note of current local conditions at Béxar. Instead, Mexico City authorities turned for advice to the two men in the capital with the most knowledge of Texas—the Marqués de San Miguel de Aguayo, who had moved the presidio to its permanent location in 1721, and Brigadier Pedro de Rivera, the cost-cutting inspector who had visited Texas in 1727.

Although the two men agreed that Béxar was the best site for the new settlement, they disagreed on the specific location. Aguayo recommended a site on the left bank of the river, below Mission Valero, where the new settlers would have access to the mission's *acequia* and be far enough away from the garrison to avoid clashes between the two groups. Rivera, on the other hand, felt the best location would be on a rise west of San Pedro

Creek, where the town could be both within view and within easy access
to the presidio.⁹ In advocating separation of the settlements, both Aguayo
and Rivera recognized the interests of the existing community and the role
it could play in training the new arrivals for life on the frontier.

Captain Juan Antonio Pérez de Almazán, commander and *justicia mayor*
(magistrate) of Béxar, in attempting to carry out the order for settling the
Isleños, used his discretionary powers to correct problems in the viceroy's
instructions. Observing that the proposed town site west of San Pedro
Creek was exposed to attack and could not be irrigated, Almazán decided
on a new center for the settlement—immediately east of the presidio in the
direction of the river and Mission Valero. Here the Isleños could better
enjoy the garrison's protection, as well as running water from the *acequia*
built by the Marqués de Aguayo.¹⁰ The town's official dedication was
delayed for three months while the Isleños performed the more important
task of planting their first crops. On 2 July 1731 Almazán began laying out
the town and its lands, a task that took five days. The town tract included
propios (corporate land) and *ejidos* (commons).¹¹ Claims by the Isleños to
water from the San Antonio River, and protests against these claims by the
missionaries, kept Almazán from formally granting water rights to the new
settlement. This did not, however, prevent the San Pedro *acequia*, which
had to provide water both for agricultural and urban use, from being
operated.

Almazán's efforts to follow the detailed orders for laying out the town
ran into other difficulties. Having moved the town site to the area enclosed
by the two streams, and with Mission Valero on the east bank of the river,
Almazán laid out the town tract in a great triangle.¹² He also had to work
around the presidio, located immediately to the west of the town plaza.
Here, he made no attempt to incorporate the dwellings immediately surrounding the military plaza into the new town. After dedicating land for a
parish church on the west side of the new town plaza, and lots for public
buildings on the east side, he distributed house lots for the Isleño families.
Dissatisfied with the captain's efforts in this regard, a number of families
soon moved the location of their homesteads.¹³

Although the instructions contained provisions for granting land to
additional families, Almazán did not grant lots to the fifteen or so settlers
already at Béxar. Perhaps confused by the Isleños' claims that the other
families mentioned in the order were to be fellow Canary Islanders, the
captain asked for instructions from the viceroy regarding whether or not
military settlers should be granted lots.¹⁴ Through the beginning of 1734
only three lots were granted to other settlers, former soldiers Alberto

López and José Martínez and the French blacksmith Juan Banul. None received water rights.[15]

Stinginess toward the military settlers continued over the next few years. Governor Manuel de Sandoval, who took over the province at the beginning of 1734, was unsuccessful in challenging the Isleños' monopoly over land and water despite his having the viceroy's support. Without water rights, only two of the four individuals to whom the governor issued lots in 1734, Gerónimo Flores and Bernabé de Carabajal, remained residents of the town. Subsequent titles issued by Sandoval have not survived, although there is evidence that one was granted to the soldier Pedro Ocón y Trillo.[16]

Sandoval's successor, Carlos Benites Franquis de Lugo, took a different and more successful tack. Four of the five lot grants made by him, three to military widows and two to retired soldiers, were decreed shortly after his arrival in 1736 and reflect his view of the settlement as a military post. Franquis had the presidial commander, not an Isleño town official, place the grantees in possession of their lots. The fifth grant, to Nicolasa Ximénez, widow of Captain Nicolás Flores, was made the following spring, by which time the town council had reasserted itself and the town constable, Vicente Alvarez Travieso, handled the proceedings.[17] Nuevo León's governor, José Antonio Fernández de Jáuregui, who was in Texas to take the *residencia* (official review) of Franquis' administration, granted Nicolás Benavides a lot through the auspices of the town council. However, when Benavides was informed he would have no water rights until the San Antonio River ditch was built, he declined the grant.[18]

By the time Prudencio Orobio y Basterra took over the province in October 1737, the Isleño-controlled town council was clearly asserting its right to withhold grants of water from the San Pedro ditch. In granting a lot to Domingo Flores de Abrego, a retired soldier, the governor conceded that he could not grant any water for his vegetable garden because the only water available was from San Pedro Spring and the Isleños (that is, the town council) possessed it. All he could do was grant water from the San Antonio River in anticipation of an *acequia's* being dug there.[19]

After Orobio's departure for the official provincial capital of Los Adaes, the town council in Béxar was left to grant lots on its own. For the next fifteen or so years, governors resided mostly in East Texas and left land matters to local authorities. Allowed to function independently, the council was quite willing to issue urban grants to military settlers and more recent arrivals. Despite the council's early insistence that there was insufficient water in the ditch for all residents, lots granted after 1741 did not carry the water restriction, suggesting that improvements to the *acequia* had been made, increasing the available supply under regulated conditions. *Alcalde* Francisco Delgado's 1752 ordinance cited the repeated abuses of garden owners in taking water from the main ditch on days other than those set aside for public use.[20]

The 1740s saw Béxar experience its first growing pains when the boundary of the town's *propios*, those lands granted to the town in its charter for the purpose of raising local revenue for public works, was reached. Already in 1741 Diego Hernández's petition for an eighty-vara[21] lot had to be reduced to fifty varas square because there was no more room. Within the next two years the council made other grants bordering on the *propios*, and toward the end of 1743 advised the governor that there were no more lots to grant because the northernmost ones now touched corporate lands.[22] The solution to Béxar's space problem was simple and to the benefit of the town's coffers. Citing the difficulties of fencing the *propios* for livestock, the resulting loss of income, and the area's suitability for irrigation, the council decided to open nine *propios* lots of eighty varas square. Grantees to these lots would pay an annual rent of one and one-half pesos in perpetuity.[23]

The urban space problem had been exacerbated by the closing to settlement of the relatively unencumbered area east of the town plaza. Having reached a compromise with Mission Valero on a number of outstanding issues in August 1745, the council prohibited settlement between Juan Banul's house and the river, an area known as the Potrero. This action proved to be no small inconvenience to at least one Isleño, José Pérez de Casanova, who had been granted a large lot close to the river in 1744 and was now asked to remove the stone he had placed there to build his house.[24]

Residents eager to establish their independence turned in other directions to establish homesteads. Unoccupied spaces between recognized lots and abandoned homesteads proved attractive to those wishing to stay near the community's center. Already in 1744 Antonio Guerra had asked for a lot abandoned by Rosa Guerra after his first choice was turned down because it lay in the *propios*. Days before the town council made its decision to expand into the *propios*, it granted Luis Antonio Menchaca a vacancy north of the presidio over the objections of adjacent property owners.[25] The demand for even small pieces of land, particularly around the presidio, resulted in numerous small grants being made in the town's center throughout the rest of the century.

The Béxar–Apache peace after 1745, which allowed missionaries and

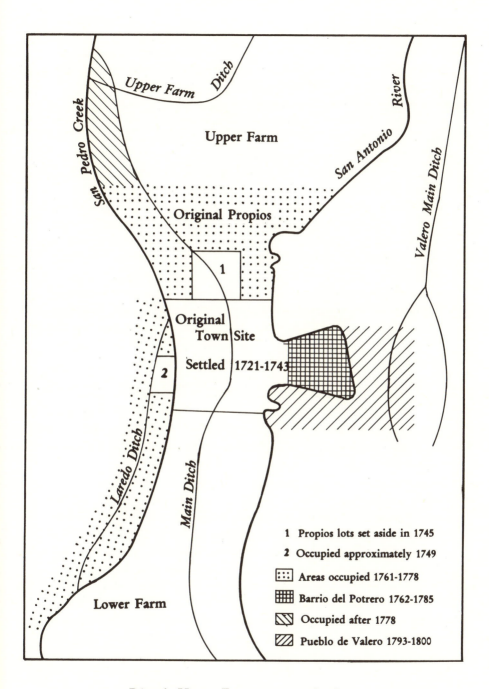

Upper Farm Ditch

San Pedro Creek

San Antonio River

Upper Farm

Valero Main Ditch

Original Propios

1

Original
Town Site

Settled 1721-1743

2

Laredo Ditch

Main Ditch

Lower Farm

1 Propios lots set aside in 1745

2 Occupied approximately 1749

Areas occupied 1761-1778

Barrio del Potrero 1762-1785

Occupied after 1778

Pueblo de Valero 1793-1800

BÉXAR'S URBAN EXPANSION, 1718–1800.
(Cartography by Caroline Castillo Crimm.)

townspeople to move into the countryside and slowed growth in town, contributed to a reduction in the number of urban grants. As population growth resumed after the collapse of missionary efforts in central Texas, the demand for town land once again increased. Members of the 1760 and 1761 town councils, hoping to profit from the situation, issued a number of grants in the *propios* on the basis of Governor Jacinto Barrios y Jáuregui's permission to the council to make urban grants.[26] It was a tactic to which the *cabildo* would repeatedly return.

Governor Angel Martos y Navarrete, who had succeeded Barrios two years before, did not take kindly to the council's usurpation of power. Citing the 1760 and 1761 councils' lack of authority to distribute lots from corporate lands without permission, Martos ordered *Alcaldes* Alberto López and José Padrón to return the fees they had charged for the grants.[27] Moreover, Martos undermined the council's efforts to make the northern lots a source of revenue by ordering the council to give clear title to all the lots already in the *propios*, and to lay out new lots to be granted.[28] Before his departure from Béxar, Governor Martos admonished the council that the first order of business was to see that the town grew, and that if it meant that the *propios* had to be moved to make way for new lots, then new land further on would be found for the public purse.[29]

When the town council began making lot grants under Martos' successor, Governor O'Conor, it did so on lands it designated as *propios*, and once again it imposed yearly rental fees. Juan Leal Alvarez Goraz, the council's first grantee in the new *propios*, was asked to pay a yearly rent of two pesos for his eighty-vara lot despite his Canary Islander descent. In 1770 Juan José Bueno de Roxas and his mother-in-law, Juliana de la Garza, received adjoining eighty-vara lots under the same conditions. The following year two other Garzas, brothers Leonardo and Salvador, received sixty-vara lots in return for the annual fee of two pesos.[30] When Leal and Juliana de la Garza sold their lots to Pedro Huizar in the early 1780s, the parcels still required payment of one peso annually in rent.[31]

The role of San Fernando's town council in land grant matters dramatically decreased after the transfer of the provincial capital to Béxar. With the authorized granting agent present in the form of the governor, the council was reduced to making recommendations upon his request. Often, the council was bypassed and the town *procurador* (attorney) or other local official was consulted on the merits of a petition. Sometimes the governor himself would perform the act of possession for a grantee.[32]

When most of the land up to the boundaries of the original *propios* had been granted by the early 1740s, another area for expansion opened west of town. During the mid-1740s, after peace with the Apaches, the first legal grants were made on the west bank of San Pedro Creek. Diego Ramón, a retired officer from La Bahía, requested a lot bounding on the creek between the lands of Juan Delgado and Juan Cortinas in 1745. Four years later, Sebastián Rincón and his son-in-law, Juan Cantún, asked for lots in the same area, the former's bounding on Jacobo Hernández's.[33] These grants lay directly west of the presidio.

Until the 1760s only a handful of residents made up what came to be known as the Barrio de Laredo, but then occupation of the area began in earnest.[34] Between 1761 and 1778 more than thirty grants were made west of San Pedro Creek. Although some lots were north of the presidio, most were located on either side of the Laredo Road (hence the neighborhood's name) leading south out of town. Besides the road's presence, the neighborhood may have grown in that direction because of the presence of an *acequia*.

The neighborhood's early residents dug at least a rudimentary ditch, for by the early 1770s the grants mention whether or not lots were irrigated.[35] Diego Iríneo Henríquez's sale of land to Juan José Córdova in 1791 describes the western boundary of a twenty-vara parcel as "the ditch that irrigates said lands."[36] The *acequia's* importance in determining the direction of settlement is discernible in the fact that Pedro Miñón's petition for land somewhat north of the other west-bank residents stated that the lot had no irrigation.[37]

The same forces that fostered settlement to the west of San Pedro Creek and led Governor Martos to open the *propios* to settlement also contributed to settlement of the area between the center of town and Mission Valero. The neutral zone created by the town-mission compromise of 1745 endured for seventeen years, but in 1762 Governor Martos granted Silvestre Joaquín de Soto a lot bounding on the river and effectively canceled the agreement. Despite this, settlement was slow in the Potrero, perhaps because irrigation water was not available in the area, and it took over twenty years for the neighborhood to be completely occupied.[38]

The Potrero was already filled, and all vacancies and abandonments in town had been occupied by the time the missions were secularized. For decades the missions had provided somewhat of an outlet for San Fernando's excess population. Many transferees from the abandoned Presidio Los Adaes in East Texas found homes and fields to plant at the missions in the 1770s. The secularization of Mission Valero in 1793, in particular, eased some of the town's land problems during the rest of the century. Although Valero was not fully incorporated into San Fernando, remaining a separate village with its own appointed magistrate until 1809,[39] its lands were made available to townspeople. Mission farmlands continued to provide Béxar's population with opportunities for expansion well into the nineteenth century.

The end of Governor Ripperdá's tenure marked the end of San Fernando's own expansion. The few grants made in the Potrero and around the presidio in the 1780s indicate the absence of any more vacancies or abandonments as well as the legalization of small plots long held without paperwork. Some of these grants were large enough to accommodate only the dwelling that occupied the land. By the late 1770s the process of integration between town and garrison had reached the point that land long held to be within the presidio was fully incorporated into the town.[40] In making her petition before Governor Cabello for a lot of five varas by twenty-two varas, María Luisa Guerrero explained that she had occupied the land for sixteen years under a verbal grant from Captain Luis Antonio Menchaca. She now wished to secure title "so my mother, children and myself will not be placed at jeopardy."[41]

III

While small grants were made for homesites, the purpose of most urban land grants in Béxar was not merely to provide the grantee with a residence. The typical frontier dwelling, whether *jacal*, adobe, or stone house, used only a portion of the land granted. The larger part of a grant was made to provide the recipient with enough land for a corral and a *huerta*.[42] In Béxar lot sizes ranged from twenty-four hundred to sixty-four hundred square varas, depending on the location and on the year of distribution.

Although squatting undoubtedly went on, Béxar's land records suggest that with the passing of the Isleños' monopoly over the town council in the 1740s, grants were available to the poor as well as the wealthy, to both newcomers and well-established families, and to young and old. However, in the early years the council did employ a financial requirement for would-be residents, another manifestation of the Isleños' attempts to exercise complete control over the town. Francisco de Estrada's first petition for a lot was suspended because the corporation believed him unable to afford a stone house; the grant was made only after he paid Mateo Carabajal for the stone.[43] Other early petitioners also stated their intentions to build stone houses.[44] Beginning in the late 1740s, a grantee need only prove his need, indicate his intention to occupy his lot, and pay the appropriate fees.[45] Francisco Luis Charo's petition stressed reliance on his own field work, ending: "I ask it as a poor stranger, who this year was forced to work a piece of land loaned to me at Valero, but I could harvest nothing because the town's cows ate it all."[46] Invariably, need included the presence of a wife and family to support.[47]

Little is known of the amount and distribution of the fees paid for lot grants. When governors issued titles, they received the money, sharing with those local officials who participated in the formalities. Antonio Rodríguez Mederos believed Governor Pedro del Barrio y Espriella to be abusing his position by charging six pesos to confirm titles and twelve pesos to issue new ones. On the other hand, Governor Martos required the magistrates for 1761 to return the fees they had charged when they illegally granted lots that year. In 1771 José del Valle paid nine pesos for the paperwork to a town lot.[48]

Although many grants do not state whether an individual was married or had dependents, only a few grants clearly defined grantees as being single. Juan Francisco Granado, upon reaching his majority in 1761, occupied a lot to which he requested title in 1774. Among the personal merits he cited for receiving the land were his Canary Islands roots, service in the town council, sentry duty at the presidio and royal horse herd, and involvement in building fortifications. Never did he mention having a family or other dependents.[49]

Women were also recipients of land grants. Most petitioned for land as heads of households.[50] The widow Gertrudis Guerra, determined to move her family to Saltillo, sold her house and lot, then found out she still lacked sufficient means to make the move. She therefore requested and received another lot.[51] Gertrudis Sánchez, whose lot was west of San Pedro Creek and exposed to Indian attack, asked for a lot of fourteen varas by six varas near the town plaza in order to construct a house for her eighteen-member family.[52] Among the few women who received land for reasons unconnected to their civil status was Rosalia Flores y Valdez, who based her claim on her father's having given her land adjacent to which she had improved some vacant land. Her request was for clear title to a 3.5 vara-wide excess that she had possessed many years.[53]

Aside from basic need, lot grants were also made to individuals practicing professions. Asencio Guadalupe, a journeyman hatter, requested a sixty-vara lot for house and workshop, as well as corral and garden. Carpenters Luis Antonio Durán and Bartolo Seguín petitioned for land on the basis of their profession.[54] Even the local school teacher in 1746, Cristóbal de los Santos Coy, asked for a lot so he would have a place to teach.[55]

Francisco Guadalupe Calaorra, who requested a lot on the basis of his advanced age and past military service, received the land he requested because he had a canoe and could help travelers ford the river.[56]

Perhaps the most interesting case is that of Juan Antonio de Medina, a nine-year Béxar resident when he requested a lot in 1773. The lieutenant governor, Simón de Arocha, observed that the petitioner was a journeyman weaver, "which is good to have here," but that the land petitioned had already been requested. He suggested splitting the lot in two. The governor, even more interested in Medina's profession, observed that there were enough lots in the town and presidio to go around, and that the weaver should get the land he requested.[57]

Throughout the eighteenth century, Presidio de Béxar and the other garrisons continued to supply settlers from the ranks of their retired veterans.[58] When Lieutenant Diego Ramón retired from the company at La Bahía, he asked for a lot in Béxar.[59] José Feliciano de la Zerda was an active thirty-year veteran when he petitioned for land in 1797.[60] Nicolás de Carabajal, a long-time soldier wishing to retire in order to take over his father's carting business, asked for a lot. His request, deemed conducive to the public good because it would avoid an interruption in the delivery of building stone to the town, was granted.[61]

Small populations in the early years and economic conditions later in the century combined to make the land granting process somewhat flexible. A number of individuals who, for various reasons, alienated their first grant received another. In the early years, Canary Islanders turned a profit by selling their original grants and acquiring new ones. In 1740 Alberto López petitioned the council for a new lot, after having given his first one to his mother-in-law.[62] Juan Banul sold his house and lot in 1737, determined to move away for lack of business. After being convinced by the town's residents of "the reverses to be suffered because there is no other blacksmith but me," he requested and received a new lot.[63] Financial need forced Francisco de Urrutia to sell the lot he had been working for twenty-five years, and he asked for a new one.[64]

Other residents received extensions on their original grants or additional grants. Here, too, the Isleños took early advantage of their position to gain extra land. Among the most enterprising was Juan Curbelo. Along with his lot near the town plaza and two fields in the town's farm, he was granted a field just north of the farm and leased another tract next to his lot in town.[65] A complaint often heard was that the original grant was insufficient and that an extension or separate grant was required.[66]

Combining extra grants with purchases, some individuals amassed considerable amounts of urban property in Béxar. At the time of his death, Vicente Alvarez Travieso, the last member of the original town government, declared as his urban property one lot on the town plaza, another facing the military plaza, another near the presidio, and one on the other side of the creek.[67] Surprisingly, however, Isleños ultimately acquired no more property than did *agregados*. Between February 1783 and December 1784 Pedro Huizar, a late arrival in town, bought three eighty-vara lots in the *propios* and later added land at Valero in payment for his services as surveyor during the distribution of lands vacated by the discontinued missions.[68] María Josefa Flores outlasted three non-Isleño husbands and left four lots to her heirs.[69]

The prestige of having a dwelling on the town's plaza, and the security of a home near the presidio, made the vicinity of the town plazas the most densely populated area in town. Owners of larger lots were quite willing to accommodate buyers for small corners of their parcels. Those families whose allotted tracts were far removed from the town center were at risk for their lives if they built on their lots. Consequently, some chose to devote their outlying lots to agricultural use and resided on smaller properties held through inheritance, purchase, or grant in a more central location.[70]

The price of land varied not only on the basis of its improvements but also on its location. A parcel of land on or near the plazas just large enough for a house usually brought twice or even three times the price of a large lot in the northern part of town or west of San Pedro Creek. In some cases, apparently when a substantial house was included, the price could be much higher. No transactions equaled those performed by Francisco Galán in 1790 and 1800. In the former year he bought a twenty-one by nineteen vara lot on the town plaza from Vicente Flores for 140 pesos. A decade later he sold the same property, now containing a stone house of eight rooms, for four thousand pesos in debts he owed to the Saltillo merchant Francisco José Pereira.

The makings of a good house in other parts of town could also lead to a good price. Antonio Bustillo y Zevallos sold Francisco Amangual a lot of nineteen-varas frontage near the river for four hundred pesos. The price included a roofless stone living-room and one roofed room facing the street, a separate roofless room that served as kitchen, two doors, and a kitchen frame. In 1765 Juan Banul sold a thirty-six hundred square vara lot with a stone house, *jacal*, and other property for 276 pesos. But interest in living near the center of town usually kept land prices to the north and west of the creek depressed. Lots of thirty-six hundred to sixty-four hundred square varas regularly went for between thirty and seventy pesos in both areas.[71]

Analysis of a 1779 water-tax levy[72] offers a general summation of the history of urban land tenure. Reconstruction of the town hall required more funds than the town council had at its disposal, so the *cabildo* determined to assess one peso for each lot of sixty varas square (or its equivalent) that received irrigation water from the *acequia* "as has been the custom." In order to preclude complaints by lot owners west of San Pedro Creek that they did not receive the amount of water through their ditch, for which they were assessed, the main *acequia* was to be tapped to the degree necessary to irrigate those lots.

In all, 127 Bexareños were taxed including six women, proving the ready availability of water to a large proportion of properties. Among proprietors, four owned the equivalent of six lots, one owned the equivalent of four lots, and another four individuals owned lots assessed three pesos in taxes. The absence of a Canary Islander predominance in what could be called premium-land ownership is reflected in their not appearing among the owners of lots assessed taxes of three to six pesos.[73] And, with the exception of Marcos de Castro and possibly Félix Menchaca, none of the large owners had been in Béxar for more than twenty years.

Clearly, land ownership in Béxar was widespread. It was, in fact, a necessary step to becoming a full citizen of the community rather than a mere resident. There were, however, many who did not own real estate or who occupied unused land on the town's fringes. Unfortunately, the verbal agreements and extralegal practices under which these people lived have been lost. For instance, although urban land and dwellings were rented, there are no sources on rent prices or on the number of rental properties.[74] The matter is complicated by use of the word "loan", as in the case of María Ignacia Núñez Morillo, who in her will declared ownership of a lot on which José María Esparza had been living for some years, and which she 'lent' to him because "he had need of it."[75] These people were the laborers, servants, and marginals who formed an indispensable but low-status sector of the community.

IV

Occupation of land involves not only growing crops and grazing animals but also building homes and planting gardens. The two most important observers of eighteenth-century northern New Spain, Nicolás Lafora and

Agustín Morfi, devoted more attention to the size, layout, and buildings of the towns and cities along their routes than they did to the size and layout of farms and *haciendas*. The traditional urban bias of the Spaniards, as evidenced in the elaborate urban planning rules of the *Laws of the Indies*, meant that all towns were judged on how close they came to the Iberian ideal of a city.

Béxar's early construction was of the most primitive kind, reflecting the uncertainty of success and the scarcity of labor common to frontier settlements. Most buildings—simple structures composed of upright wooden poles plastered with mud or clay and called *jacales*—had the principal merit of being easy to build and abandon. A significant drawback to the thatch-roofed *jacales* was, however, the ease with which they caught fire. Late in 1721, for instance, sixteen soldiers' *jacales* and a similarly built granary burned, affording the Marqués de Aguayo an opportunity to move the settlement to a more favorable location.[76] After 1722 *jacales* and adobe buildings began to give way to some stone structures, though most construction remained primitive.[77]

Béxar's poor appearance continued to be noticed throughout the century. Former Governor Tomás Felipe de Winthuisen reported to the viceroy in 1744 that a presidio, as such, did not exist "for only its poorly formed houses make up a square plaza, without any wall or stockade."[78] During his 1778 visit to Béxar, Fray Morfi found a considerable number of stone houses but little to be impressed about.

> The town consists of fifty-nine houses of stone and mud and seventy-nine of wood, but all poorly built, without any preconceived plan, so that the whole resembles more a poor village than a villa, capital of so pleasing a province.[79]

Despite these and other disparaging comments, Béxar's growth did follow certain logical paths. Naturally, the two streams formed the margins within which the town developed. The main *acequia*, which ran parallel to the river and San Pedro Creek through the center of town, lent its name to one of the three streets that began at the plazas and ran northward to the upper agricultural lands. To the west of Calle de la Acequia ran the early Calle del Norte, which by the late eighteenth century was known by its modern name, Calle de las Flores. Between the river and Calle de la Acequia there emerged a Calle Real, which by the end of the century was known as Calle de la Soledad. Most formal lots fronted on one of the water courses or one of these streets, the owners leaving alleys between adjoining grants and along the San Antonio River and San Pedro Creek. Naturally, the windings of all three water courses affected the shape of lots, adding to the town's disorganized look.

If Béxar did not make a positive impression on observers, neither did much older and larger cities in the viceroyalty's interior. The best Lafora could say of Querétaro, a city of fourteen thousand in 1767, was that "the houses are, most of them, of adobe, protruding among which are ten religious convents, three for nuns, and other sundry churches whose considerable heights contrast even more with the lowness of the rest of the buildings."[80] Fray Morfi, who did not like Zacatecas's location and layout, had little better to say about its homes.

> The private houses, although they all have large and luxurious gardens, are generally low with very few exceptions. That of the Count of Suchil . . . and that of the canon accountant are the only ones of stone and mortar in the whole city. The others, including the convents, are of adobes, which in my opinion, contributes mightily—if it is not the principal cause—to the plague of scorpions that is suffered here; so malignant that every year it costs some lives, especially of children.[81]

Whether jacales or made of stone, Béxar homes were generally rectangular.[82] Typically, a dwelling was five varas (14 feet) wide by seven to fifteen varas (19 to 42 feet) long and divided into two or three rooms. Kitchens, usually *jacal* structures, were built separately to reduce the risk of fire. Many homes appear to have had an additional freestanding room that probably served as quarters for servants or other dependents.[83] In this respect, as in so many others, Béxar resembled the towns of New Spain's interior.

Most inhabitants planted vegetable gardens, orchards, and even sugarcane and maize behind their homes.[84] The presence of such gardens, even in the more central areas of town, is not surprising, for such was the case even in large cities such as Durango.[85] The importance of these urban farms is evident in Governor Cabello's description of vandalism committed by unknown Indians.

> I was informed that the [Indians] had been in most of the gardens facing west [perhaps in Laredo neighborhood] where they

destroyed untold watermelons, melons, squash and maize in such a
way that many [garden] owners have left them without being able
to enjoy the least benefit from the efforts of their work.[86]

Failure to plant on a lot, not just build on it, was considered grounds for
canceling a grant.[87]

Toward the end of the century a few residents could afford more elaborate dwellings. Clearly-defined living rooms and bedrooms began to appear, along with porticos.[88] Father Pedro Fuentes, who served as parish
priest during the 1770s and 1780s, built what was probably the only two-
story house in town. The project was so extraordinary that he requested
permission from his neighbors to proceed, "not wishing to break the law
or cause any harm." He argued that such houses were found in all cities
and towns, and that it would add "to the beauty, spaciousness and defense
of the town."[89]

The most impressive home in eighteenth-century Béxar was that of
Fernando de Veramendi. A merchant and native of Pamplona, Spain,
Veramendi first established himself in Texas at Presidio La Bahía around
1770.[90] Business brought him to Béxar on occasion, and there he married
a Canary Islander daughter in 1776. Once established in Béxar, Veramendi's business thrived. He opened a store, acted as moneylender, and
bought extensive tracts of agricultural land. His success allowed him to
build an opulent house that came to be known as the Veramendi Palace
around the time of the Texas War of Independence.[91] It included a hall
with doors on the street, a patio, a living room, and a bedroom. The
enclosed patio separated the main house from the large kitchen with its
own door that opened on the river. At a time when most stone houses were
valued at between 200 and 500 pesos,[92] the Veramendi home was built at
a cost of 1,880 pesos.

v

Béxar's development from 1718 to 1800 may be properly divided into
six parts. The first period, 1718–1731, was marked by house-building close
to the presidio and by the communal working of fields, including labor by
the military population. With the arrival of the Canary Islanders in 1731,
a second period began that lasted until the mid-1740s. These years were
marked by the formal distribution of lots and farming fields, and by the
strict control of land and water resources by the preeminent Isleños. The

truce reached with the Apaches in the latter 1740s initiated a third period which allowed expansion into the countryside and attempts at new settlements; population growth in Béxar slowed and so did land distribution. This third phase lasted until the 1760s, when Indian hostilities forced the population to return to the urban nucleus. By this time, the Isleños' monopoly over urban land and water had lapsed, allowing for a wider latitude in grants. The fourth period, an expansion phase that began with Governor Martos's opening of the *propios* to settlement, lasted through the mid-1780s, when the town began to run out of close-in land. The resulting lull in land grants, constituting a fifth period, was reversed after 1793, when the secularization of Mission Valero allowed growth in that direction. Thus, urban land occupation mirrored Béxar's population growth throughout the century.

Despite the Indian menace and small population, Béxar's development as an urban entity duplicated many of the features found in New Spain's older cities and towns. The central part of town was bordered by small agricultural parcels which provided subsistence for part of the population and probably also contributed to the town's produce market. Even in the areas closer to the center, the garden and corral were standard. Although criticized, Béxar's low and simple houses were little different from those to be found elsewhere in northern New Spain. And, despite its economic backwardness, Béxar enjoyed an incipient real-estate market which allowed for some concentration of ownership and rental of urban land.

ILLVSTRATIONS

This map indicates the Spaniards' lack of knowledge of northeastern New Spain. The map shows the mythical Gran Quivira at the top center and locates Santa Fe, New Mexico, in close proximity to Gran Quivira and to the newly occupied Texas. (Original in the Archivo General de Indias, Seville, Spain. Courtesy, Archives Division, Texas State Library.)

JUAN DE OLIVÁN REBOLLEDO'S

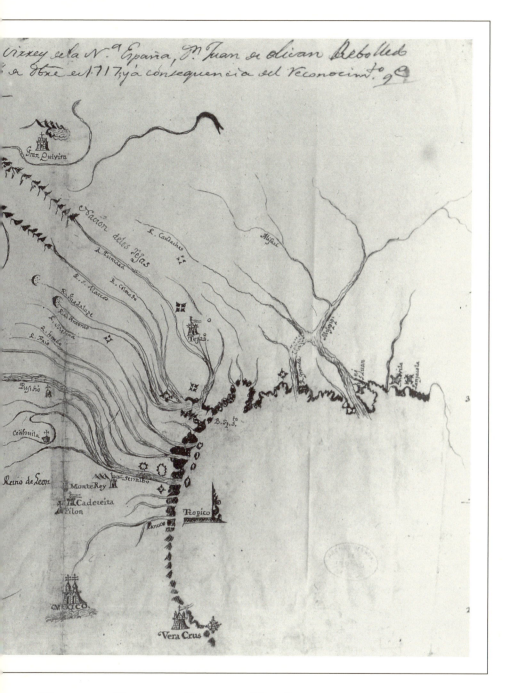

1717 Map of the Northeast Corner of New Spain.

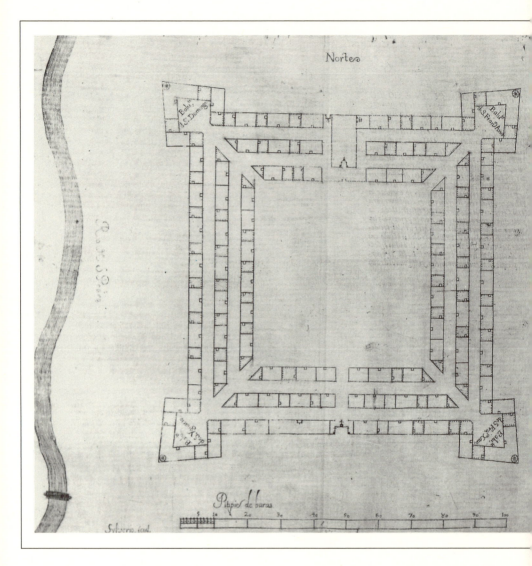

THE MARQUÉS DE SAN MIGUEL DE AGUAYO'S 1722 PLAN FOR PRESIDIO

This plan was one of four the marqués prepared for Texas garrisons. With the exception of the one at Los Adaes, which was constructed of wood, his grandiose plans were never executed. Note the abundance of wildlife along the banks of the San Antonio River, a feature often commented upon by early travelers through the region. (Original in the Archivo General de Indias, Seville, Spain. Courtesy, Archives Division, Texas State Library.)

SAN ANTONIO DE BÉXAR.

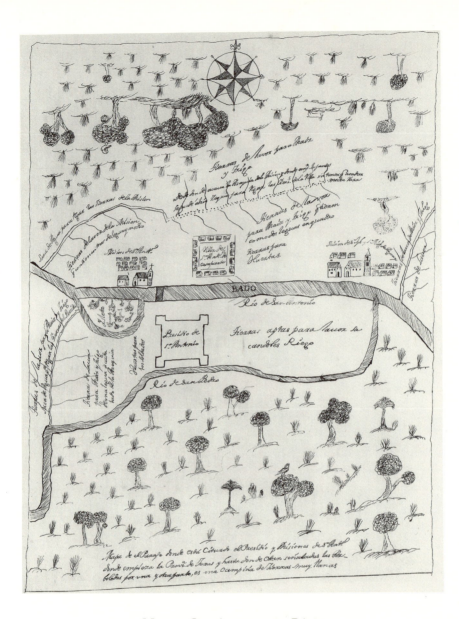

MAP OF SAN ANTONIO DE BÉXAR
DRAWN BY THE MARQUÉS DE SAN MIGUEL DE AGUAYO IN 1730.

In 1730, from memory, the marqués prepared the above map for Viceroy Casafuerte. The map incorporates a projected new settlement for Canary Island colonists, here called Villa de San Antonio de Casafuerte. The map contains errors: The bend in the San Antonio River goes in the wrong direction; the presidio's irrigation ditch is misplaced; and Mission San José is on the wrong side of the river. (Original in Provincias Internas, Vol. 236, Archivo General y Público de Mexico. Courtesy, The Institute of Texan Cultures, San Antonio.)

54

LIBR[O]

EN QVE

SE ASSIENTAN LOS

Bautismos

De los Indios de esta Mission des Ant.

DE

O TLCRO

sita a la Rivera del Rio de S. Antonio

De la

Governacion de esta Provincia de los

Texas.

Nuevas Philippinas, pertene-

ciente al Colegio Apostolico de propagan-

da Fide

MISSION SAN ANTONIO DE VALERO'S
BAPTISMAL REGISTER.

In this document were recorded the baptisms of Indian converts from 1703 (when the mission was called San Francisco Solano and was located on the Rio Grande) to 1793. Between 1718 and 1731, children born to the presidio's military and civilian families were also recorded in this register. (Original in the Archives of the Archdiocese of San Antonio, Texas. Courtesy Catholic Archives of Texas.)

Urrutia, a member of the Marqués de Rubí's inspection tour of Spanish frontier presidios, recorded the sparse urban landscape of the town and presidio in this map. Despite his detailed rendition of the settlement, Urrutia misidentified San Pedro Creek as an irrigation ditch. (Original in the British Museum Library. Courtesy, Museum of New Mexico.)

PLANO

De la Villa, y Presidio de S. Antonio de Vejar situado en la Provincia de Tejas en 20 grad. y 52 minutos de latitud bor, y 276 y 5 de long contados desde el Meridiano d'Tnerife

Explicacion

A   Casa del Presidio
B   Casa del Capitan
C   Cuerpo de Guardia
D   Plaza de la Villa
E   Casas Reales
F   Iglesia
G   Mission de san Joseph

NOTA

Todas estas obras son De Adoves

Escala de Doscientas Toesas

Joseph de Urrutia

JOSE DE URRUTIA'S

Text visible within the map:

Acequia Madre

ANTONIO DE VEIAR

para regadio

para regadio

Camino Para el Bofque

G

E

D

F

A
C
B

1767 MAP OF SAN ANTONIO DE BEXAR.

A JACAL.

This photograph purportedly shows a jacal *in late-nineteenth-century San Antonio, Texas. Note the adobe-brick-stone chimney. (Courtesy, San Antonio Conservation Society.)*

AN ADOBE HOUSE.

This early-twentieth-century postcard purports to picture an adobe (mud) house in San Antonio, Texas. Note the absence of windows and the use of stones in the foundation. (Courtesy, San Antonio Conservation Society.)

THE "VERAMENDI PALACE."

This well-known San Antonio establishment served as a home and store, a saloon, and an early-twentieth-century tourist trap before it was demolished. The structure was occasionally remodeled, but its late-eighteenth-century pillar-flanked main doors attest to the wealth of its original occupants. (Courtesy, Institute of Texas Cultures.)

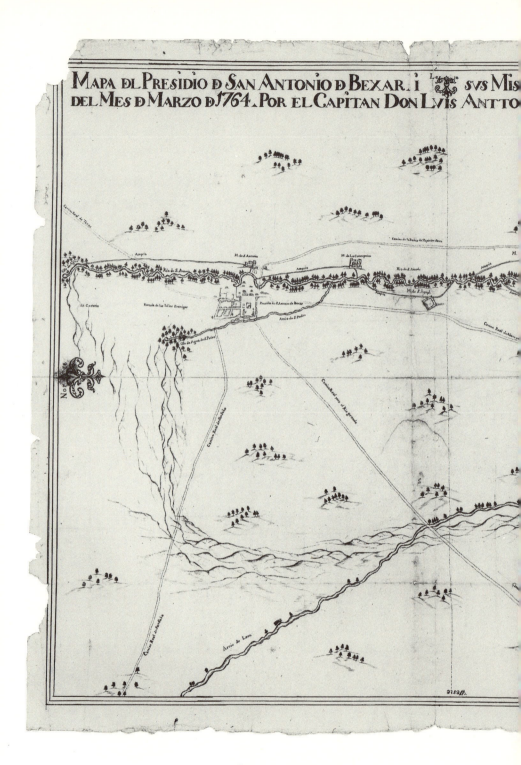

LUIS ANTONIO MENCHACA'S MAP OF SAN ANTONI

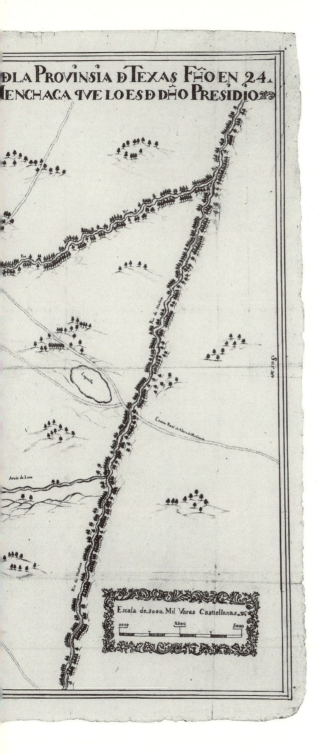

DLA PROVINSIA D TEXAS FÑO EN 24.
ENCHACA QVE LO ES D DÑO PRESIDIO

Luis Antonio Menchaca, presidio commander, drew this map in 1764. His rendition clearly indicates the importance of irrigation water to the settlement complex. However, while Menchaca carefully delineated all of the missions' acequias, he neglected to indicate the town's own irrigation ditch. (Courtesy, John Carter Brown Library, Brown University.)

DE BÉXAR.

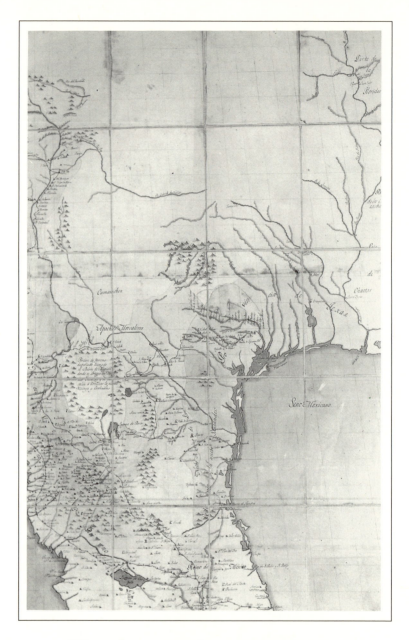

"Carta ó mapa geográfico de una gran parte
del Reino de Nueva España . . . ."

*This map was prepared in 1777 for Viceroy Antonio María Bucareli in order
to carry out the division of New Spain and the Comandancia General de las
Provincias Internas. Of particular interest is the considerable detail of the
province of Texas. (Original in the Archivo General de Indias, Seville, Spain.
Courtesy, Archives Division, Texas State Library.)*

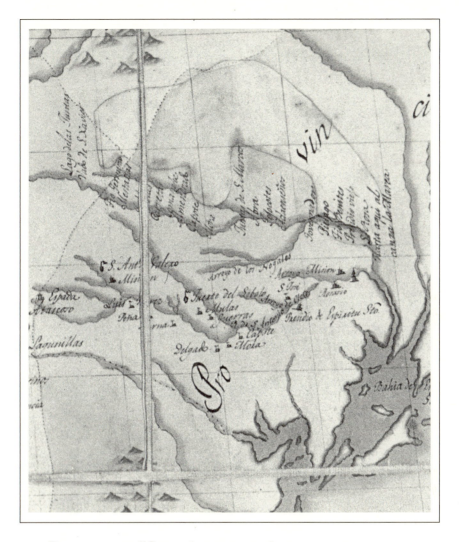

The inclusion of the names of numerous ranches and the military post on
Cibolo Creek is unique to eighteenth-century maps of the Texas region.
(Original in the Archivo General de Indias, Seville, Spain. Courtesy, Archives
Division, Texas State Library.)

llevamos pedido que en ello recivieremos justicia y juramos
en forma &
Otro sí Suplicamos nos admita este en el presente papel por
no haverlo de ningun Cello en esta Prov.ª

Joph Phelix menchaca   Bar.tte Albare[?]
Jasinto Delgado   macielo[?]
Juachin
        menchaca franco Flores de Abre[?]

        Joo Jimenez   Marcos de casno

Joph Antto curbelo   A.tu.º de Juachin de
                                        la gansa
A Ruego de Joph de rosa   Joph Antto curbelo
Joph Antto curbelo   A Rug de Joh perez
    Joph Martin   Casanova
Zirigaza[?]   Manuel delgado   Joph Antto curbelo
Miguel de Gortari   Jul Andres trabieso
Ignasio Coll.illo   Juachin lial

Sebastian mongaras   Atu gnasio
Leando de la garsa   alexini
A Ruego de carlos
    martines
Joph Antto curbelo   Joph Juachin flores
                                        A ru.º Joph plasido ernan
franc.º xavier Rodriguez   Bz Joph Juachin flores
Joseph macario Sambrano   En El R.do Pres.

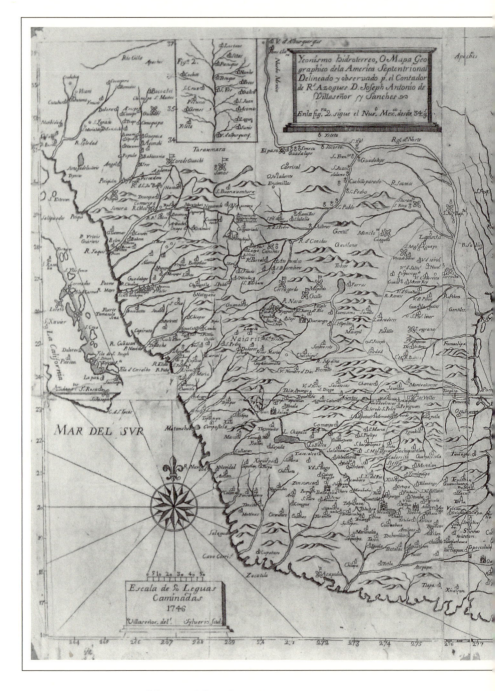

MAP OF NEW SPAIN IN 1746.

66

Reflected in this map is the Spanish worry over the proximity of French settlements in the Mississippi Valley to the frontier colonies in northern New Spain. (Original in the Archivo General de Indias, Seville, Spain. Courtesy, Archives Division, Texas State Library.)

A CARRETA.

These rough-hewn, solid-wheel carts were the mainstay of local transportation in San Antonio during the colonial period. No San Antonio drawing or photograph of this type of cart has been found. However, this photograph, taken in northern Mexico during the 1880s, well illustrates its home-spun characteristics. Although slow footed, oxen were plentiful, hardy, and useful in farming. (From the Calleros Estate. Courtesy, Institute of Texas Cultures, San Antonio.)

THE SPANISH GOVERNOR'S PALACE IN SAN ANTONIO, TEXAS.
This structure was the longtime residence of presidio commanders and other local prominent families. It also served as a general store during the colonial period, throughout the nineteenth century, and well into the twentieth century, before its reconstruction in the 1930s. (From the San Antonio Light Collection. Courtesy, The Institute of Texan Culture, San Antonio.)

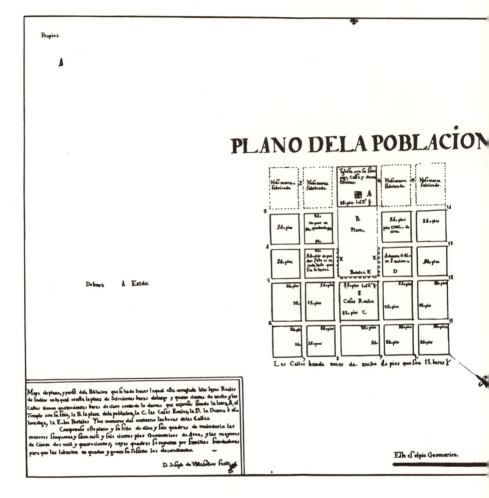

ROYAL PLAN FOR SAN FERNANDO, 1730.

Spanish royal officials tried to incorporate order and civilization in their plans for new settlements. This optimistic design for San Fernando includes two-story dwellings, a public granary, a customs house, and other public buildings. Alas, visitors to Béxar describe a settlement with tortuous streets, poorly constructed and run-down buildings, and an almost complete lack of form. (Original in Provincias Internas, Vol. 236, Archivo General y Público de Mexico. Courtesy, The Institute of Texan Cultures, San Antonio.)

THE COAT-OF-ARMS OVER THE DOOR
OF THE "GOVERNOR'S PALACE" IN SAN ANTONIO, TEXAS.

Placed over the entrance to the presidio commander's house in 1742, this keystone reminded all visitors that the Crown's reach was indeed long. (Courtesy, San Antonio Conservation Society.)

THE SAN FERNANDO CHURCH IN SAN ANTONIO, TEXAS.

As in other colonial settlements, much of San Antonio's public life focussed on the church. This mid-nineteenth-century photograph shows the original structure of the San Fernando church before the addition of a French Gothic nave in the 1870s. (From the San Antonio Light Collection. Courtesy, The Institute of Texan Cultures, San Antonio.)

4

Wealth of the Land

Béxar has the best conveniences for all manner of crops owing to the fertility of the soil and availability of irrigation, these natural benefits being fruitless however because of the indolence and poverty of its inhabitants . . .

—GOVERNOR DOMINGO CABELLO, 1779[1]

San Antonio de Béxar was dependent on subsistence agriculture. Many families had the opportunity to grow at least some of their food within the confines of the urban lots which most often also included their homes. A smaller number of families were more fortunate in having access to irrigated farmland, and an even fewer number of families acquired grazing land in the form of open-range ranches. The two latter types of landholding permitted small commercial agricultural and ranching sectors to establish themselves over the course of the century. In taking possession of the rural landscape, just as in organizing the urban landscape, the people of Béxar adapted to circumstances that tended to limit growth and opportunity but provided enough to hope for a better day.

I

Land defined as strictly agricultural was distributed in Béxar on three different occasions in the eighteenth century. As in other parts of the frontier, farmland lay adjacent to the town. Béxar's fields were organized in blocks called *labores*, each one containing a number of *suertes*, sections of land assigned by the drawing of lots among the recipients. The need for irrigation works, as well as the fear of Indian attack, made the compact

75

arrangement of farmland practical although sometimes inconvenient for
individuals. As throughout much of New Spain, at Béxar farmland and
water went hand-in-hand, the value of the former determined by the
availability of the latter.[2]

During the 1720s irrigated farmland was maintained communally. The
soldiers dug *acequia*s and cleared and planted fields south of the presidio
with the assistance of a small number of Indians. Until presidial regulations were issued in 1729, the farm work conducted at San Antonio was
paid for by the governor, who supplied oxen, plows, and seed to the
military settlers. The object of the presidio's farm was to make the garrison as self-sufficient as possible, because the cost of provisions came out of
the soldiers' pay and freight charges for imported products were high.[3] It
was this irrigated land, lying between the San Antonio River and San
Pedro Creek, that Captain Juan Antonio Pérez de Almazán used to supply
the Canary Islanders with suitable farms upon their arrival.

Faced with the advent of the growing season, recent Apache attacks, and
limited labor resources, Captain Almazán had no choice but to hammer
out the best compromise possible on where and how to settle the Isleños.
The viceroy's instructions called for the new families to make use of both
river and creek water. No effort, however, had yet been made to irrigate
land west of San Pedro Creek, the site designated in the orders for the site
of the *villa* and farmlands, and construction of an *acequia* there with the
planting season beginning was out of the question. Because the soldiers
who had been working the irrigated fields south of the presidio did not
own the land individually, Almazán dispossessed them and informally distributed the lands among the new arrivals on 12 March 1731.[4]

By the time Captain Almazán formally apportioned the land to the
Isleños in July, they had already planted twenty-two *fanegas*[5] (approximately two hundred acres) in maize, as well as smaller plots in beans,
cotton, pepper, watermelons, melons, and squash. Almazán found an additional 10 1/2 *caballerías* (approximately eleven hundred acres) suitable for
irrigation below the presidio, between the river and creek. In order to
distribute the land equitably, he gave each family a portion of the cleared
land and provided for a future distribution of the uncleared balance. A
subsequent distribution was needed because the strips of productive land
distributed, while of a uniform width of 105 varas, were of uneven length.[6]
Irrigation water from the San Pedro *acequia* was also partitioned, allowing
one day of use in twenty for each family, and leaving four days of water
available for sale by the town as part of its *propios*.[7]

As in other parts of the north, the vague descriptions of water rights in

San Fernando's founding documents created one of the earliest points of contention. Having received outright possession of San Pedro Creek's water and some rights to the river's flow, the Isleños attempted to circumscribe the nearby missions' water rights. They were also in a position to ward off efforts by the military settlers to gain farmland. Both Captain Almazán and Governor Bustillo had recognized that the San Pedro *acequia* did not carry enough water to meet the agricultural needs of all the residents, and in 1733 Governor Bustillo received permission from the viceroy to grant the town another water source on the river. From then on, the majority of Isleños took the position that new residents desiring lands of any kind would have to wait to receive their water from the *acequia* to be constructed from the river.[8]

The strain of holding land without specified boundaries occasioned discord among the Isleños, who sought to remedy the situation early in 1734 by petitioning Governor Manuel de Sandoval for the balance of their farmland. As the governor explained:

On the third day of being at this presidio the *vecinos* of the town of San Fernando made clear to me the impossibility of their making plantings this year because of the dissension and controversy among them, for each desires the lands of others.[9]

Governor Sandoval apportioned to each of the sixteen families a second *suerte* in January 1734. The new partition included no additional water rights, and so the twenty-four hours of water each family received was spread more thinly. Each grantee received over eleven *fanegas* of land, that is, almost one *caballería* (105.75 acres). The two *suertes* taken together were, therefore, approximately the size of the typical farmland grant in other parts of New Spain. The distribution pattern employed in Béxar is also found in other frontier Spanish settlements and missions. It is not unlikely that the Spanish model for Indian mission towns—a core homesite area surrounded by well organized agricultural fields bounding on *acequias*—served as a model for Spanish settlements along the frontier.[10]

Distribution of a second *suerte* to each Canary Island family did not reduce frictions, however. Soon after the Isleños' arrival, the presidio's residents, now relegated to the status of *agregados* (new settlers), began a drive to assert their rights. As time elapsed some military settlers lost interest in remaining at Béxar and moved away. However, Governor Sandoval's arrival gave those who remained a new opportunity to claim land

and *vecino* status. For their part, most Isleños sought to prevent the acquisition of any rights by other residents. Arguing against new land grants on the basis of limited water supplies, the Isleños declared that San Pedro Spring's flow was insufficient to accommodate more families. An inspection of the town's only active water source convinced Sandoval to the contrary, and he proceeded with the distribution of town lots and *suertes* to military settlers.[11]

When Governor Sandoval finally distributed lands and water to the six *agregados* who had pledged to remedy the water shortage with repairs to the *saca de agua* (weir or dam designed to divert part of a river's flow into an irrigation canal) on the San Pedro, the Isleños challenged the possession on a number of counts. They argued that the San Pedro did not produce enough water for themselves, let alone for *agregados*; that not everyone in the town should be a farmer, otherwise there would be no one to buy the grain; that grants to *agregados* should not be on the same terms as those made to the Isleños as *primeros pobladores* (original settlers); and that eleven Isleño youths were about to reach their majority and there was not enough land even for them. Nevertheless, in January 1736, the viceroy recognized Governor Sandoval's right to make the grants and instructed the Isleños to build additional waterworks on the San Pedro if the weir did not provide enough water for all. Governor Sandoval so ordered the Isleños, even though the other *vecinos* were not making use of the San Pedro *acequia*.[12] No subsequent record exists of any of the *agregados* holding on to the *suerte* grants made by Sandoval, indicating that the Isleños were successful in fending off the first challenge to their control of the town, perhaps through their recognized control of all available irrigation water.

The Canary Islanders' ambition to control the area's economic and political life soon became apparent with regard to the missions as well. Matters were complicated by the presence of the five missions strung along the San Antonio River, three of which had only recently been relocated from East Texas and had no clear titles to lands and water. Recognizing the conflicts emerging within the civilian community, the friars in charge of the new missions pressed Captain Almazán for titles to their lands and for suspension of the distribution to others of water rights from the river. The Isleños interpreted this act of self-preservation as arising from economic interests, and argued that the missionaries did not want the town to enjoy a surplus because the missions produced enough maize to satisfy the presidio's demand at a price below the official rate of three pesos per *fanega* (in Mexico, 2.58 bushels). The Isleños argued successfully that they were entitled to a share of the water. In his decree of May 1733 the viceroy accepted the argument and reiterated that all the waters available be distributed equitably among missions, presidio, Isleños, and other *vecinos*.[13]

Later that year the final distribution of water to the town took place. Governor Bustillo granted the town permission to establish a *saca de agua* at any point on the San Antonio River from the town site to the river's source. He restricted the volume of water that the town could take from the river to no more than what it was taking from San Pedro Creek. On 27 October 1733 Mateo Pérez, acting commander and *justicia mayor*, placed the Isleños in possession of a *saca de agua* site at the "Paso de Texas."[14] The *acequia* would not be built for more than forty years, however.

Until the mid-1770s the *suertes* south of town, known as the *labor de los isleños* (Isleños' farm), and later as the *labor de abajo* (lower farm), constituted the only irrigated farmland in Béxar outside of the missions. This farmland was associated with the Isleños, even though ownership of some parcels soon passed into the hands of military settlers. Between 1739 and 1741 four Isleños sold both of the *suertes* they had each been awarded. Another, José Cabrera, sold one of his *suertes* to Antonio Rodríguez Mederos, an Isleño who had sold his farmland to a military settler. In November 1741 Juan Leal Alvarez, who was moving his family to Santa Rosa, Coahuila, sold his farmland, a lot with a stone house, another large lot in the town, and all his water and pasture rights to Toribio de Urrutia, the new presidial commander.[15]

Most land in the lower farm, however, remained in the hands of the families to whom it was originally granted until, with the deaths of the original owners, the subdivision process began among the heirs. Juan Leal Goraz died intestate in 1743, and the executors divided his land and water among six heirs, each receiving four hours of water and the corresponding land. Vicente Alvarez Travieso's nine heirs each received two hours and forty minutes of water with the corresponding land. Jacinto Delgado was the heir to four hours of water and accompanying land, which he divided evenly between his two children.[16]

Yet some enterprising individuals found ways to preserve intact large parcels, sometimes entire *suertes*. Ignacia de Castro, one of six heirs to her parents' estate, complained to Governor Ripperdá that her brother Marcos, who was in possession of their father's two *suertes*, had not properly paid her for her share. It took three years for the governor to order Marcos to return Ignacia's share to her.[17] When Juan Curbelo died, his son José purchased the two *suertes* and one day of water in the estate, the heirs sharing the proceeds rather than the land.[18]

II

Efforts to break the irrigated farmland monopoly held by the lower
farm's owners spanned almost a half-century. Between the formal distribution of *suertes* in 1734 and the opening up of the upper farm in 1777–78,
the *agregados* made petitions to governors and viceroys for their own farmland. Occasionally, an Isleño found it politically expedient to support such
efforts. In 1734 Juan Leal Goraz, nominal head of the Canary Islanders
and at odds with a faction led by Juan Curbelo, disassociated himself from
Isleño efforts to contest the possession given to *agregados* by Governor
Sandoval.[19] Eleven years later, Antonio Rodríguez Mederos, who had
originally opposed the grants, came out in favor of the *agregados* in the
course of his own political intrigues.[20]

Forty-nine families made up Béxar's non-Isleño population in 1745. Of
these, only four had access to agricultural land, all of it purchased from
Isleños. Conditions were so bad that the *agregados* banded together to
petition the viceroy for access to land and water. Despite a favorable
response, the governor, Francisco García Larios, never executed the order
to distribute agricultural land to the *agregados*.[21] They renewed their effort
to win access to agricultural land during Governor Angel Martos y Navarrete's inspection of Béxar in 1762 by bringing to his attention the
existence of previous unexecuted orders. Navarrete ordered the river inspected for a suitable weir site. The inspection by one of the *agregados*
disclosed a site on the San Antonio River about 2 1/2 miles above the town
where a weir could be built to divert more than enough water for the
whole town. The governor recommended the three thousand peso project
to the viceroy and, meanwhile, opened the *propios* to individuals wishing
town lots.[22] Although a number of town lots were distributed, the opening
of new agricultural land was once again delayed, for there was no money
for the project forthcoming from the viceroy.

Navarrete's report on his actions to the viceroy denounces the opposition of some Isleños. Opening of new farmland has "always been opposed
by . . . [Vicente Alvarez] Travieso and the rest of the Isleño families, even
though they do not work the two *suertes* of land that were assigned to them
[when] they came to settle."[23] Perhaps income from sharecropping or
other rental arrangements helped stiffen Isleño opposition to new farmland being opened.

What the lower farm owners could not monopolize was Béxar's growth
in the late 1760s, which created favorable conditions for agricultural expansion. Reinforcement of Béxar with soldiers and civilian settlers from

abandoned presidios created opportunities for Béxar's population. As the strains on existing agricultural land increased, many, including Isleños, stood to gain from opening new irrigated farmland.

The process began in 1776. Governor Ripperdá first investigated town and mission rights to San Antonio River water, issuing orders for the town council and missions to present any papers they had regarding distribution of the river's water. The town council produced two documents: a March 1733 viceregal decree ordering that missions and town share the available water flow, and Mateo Pérez's grant of possession to the town of a weir site at Paso de Texas. The missions could produce no document counter-manding the action, but asserted that the diversion of water for the town should not prejudice mission Indian rights. Governor Ripperdá, reviewing the evidence presented, cited "the clear usefulness that will result from it [the weir] to the citizenry" in ordering those who wished to participate to present themselves.[24]

The invitation was not an entirely open one. Individuals wishing to receive grants would have to share expenses, both the cost of opening the 1.75-mile-long *acequia* and of clearing the land, by contributing the labor of one peon for the duration of the work. Consequently, only the more affluent families, some of whom were descendants of Canary Islanders and others of whom were recent arrivals, could afford to participate. Among the Isleño descendents were Manuel and Jacinto Delgado, Joaquín Leal, and Simón and Manuel de Arocha. The new arrivals included José Macario Zambrano, José Antonio Bustillo y Zevallos, parish priest Pedro Fuentes, and his father and brother-in-law. Among the older military settler families, members of the Flores and Menchaca families obtained three grants each.[25] Another consequence of Ripperdá's actions was that the upper *acequia* became a jointly owned project of the grantees, a pattern seen elsewhere in New Spain but not, usually, where a formal town existed.[26]

In recognition of local prerogatives, Governor Ripperdá allowed the *parcioneros* (participants) to elect the project's director, who would receive an extra day of water and corresponding land for his efforts. Toribio Fuentes, the priest's father, was the first director. When he asked to be relieved in July 1776, he nevertheless requested continuation of his extra day of water and land. Ripperdá allowed his requests but stipulated that Fuentes must provide two laborers until the project was completed. Pedro Anglín, who was elected to take over the project, did not have an interest in the farm. He was compensated at the rate of one peso per day, his salary paid through a reduction of the work force from twenty-six to twenty-two laborers.[27]

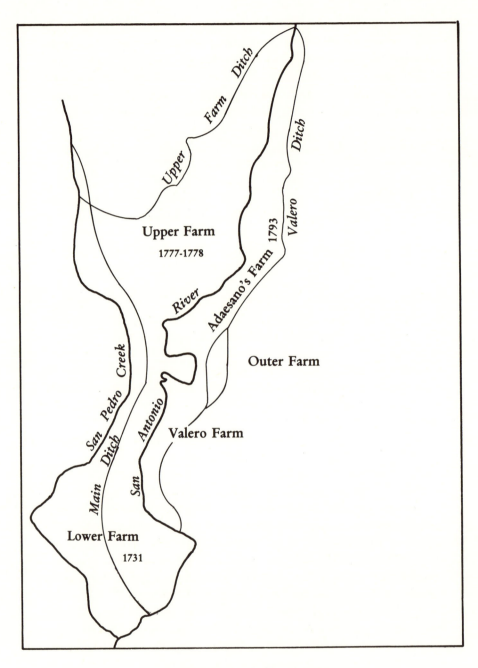

Béxar's Irrigated Farmlands.
(Cartography by Caroline Castillo Crimm.)

Work on the *acequia* had progressed far enough by the end of April 1777 that some of the land nearest the river could be distributed. Following the precedent set in the distribution to the Isleños, therefore, each grantee received two tracts of land, one in the upper part of the farm in April 1777, and one in the lower part the following March. The grants included one day of water in twenty-six. Most *suertes* were long and narrow, stretching between the river and the *acequia*. The farm received the name Our Lady of Sorrows (Nuestra Señora de los Dolores).[28]

An equitable distribution of the land was only possible through the drawing of lots. For the first distribution, twenty-six names were placed in one pot and twenty-six numbers in another. Two young boys pulled names and numbers from the pots. While the same procedure was followed in the second distribution, not all the grantees participated. Francisco Xavier Rodríguez asked for a separate parcel where the new *acequia* crossed the town *acequia* and entered San Pedro Creek. Although this land amounted to 1/2 *suertes*, the other grantees agreed to his request because he offered to clear the parcel himself. The Fuentes clan asked for a similar favor. Wishing to keep their four parcels[29] together, they offered to clear the land at their own cost and take some land that could not be fully irrigated.[30]

As was the case for the Isleños' farm, some land in the upper farm passed quickly out of the grantees' hands. Governor Ripperdá's verbal stipulation that *suertes* could not be sold for a specified number of years was quickly circumvented in at least one case. Manuel de Arocha, one of the grantees, ran out of money during the weir's construction and secretly transferred his allotment to his brother, Simón (also a grantee). Manuel would remain the recognized owner so long as Simón paid the *acequia* contribution on the land.[31] Another arrangement occurred between Félix Menchaca and his brother Joaquín. Félix appeared before Governor Ripperdá offering to pay his brother's share of construction costs until Joaquín could afford to pay again. This arrangement allowed Joaquín to retain full interest in his grant.[32]

Other sales of *suertes* took place soon after the time limit's expiration. In March 1782, Juan José Montes de Oca exchanged his two *suertes* and day of water for Joaquín Flores' sixteen hours of water and land in the lower farm.[33] Flores was himself a grantee in the upper farm. That same year, Fernando de Veramendi, Béxar's wealthiest *vecino*, purchased Clemente Delgado's and Joaquín Menchaca's land and water.[34]

Other sales contributed to a concentration of land and water in a small number of hands. Juan José Flores's heirs sold their inheritance to Pedro

Flores in 1788, and José María Veramendi sold his inheritance of one *suerte* and eight hours of water in 1800.[35] Pedro Flores thus amassed five *suertes* of land, three of which were contiguous, and fifty-six hours of irrigation water. Macario Zambrano, himself a grantee, bought out Mariano de la Garza, one of whose *suertes* adjoined Zambrano.[36] By 1800, seven families controlled half the *suertes*.[37]

III

Distribution of agricultural tracts north of town did not solve Béxar's land-related problems. The *suerte* recipients in the upper farm did not represent all land-seeking residents. Since 1773, when the Crown had abandoned the East Texas presidio of Los Adaes and moved the population to San Antonio, a large group of the transferees had sought their own homesteads and fields. In their attempts to find a solution to the Adaesano problem, the authorities turned to the underutilized lands of Mission Valero.

By the late 1770s Mission Valero's decline as an evangelizing center made it vulnerable to absorption by the town—a goal that Bexareños had held for many years. For instance, in the early 1740s the town council and missions undertook a series of suits in the viceregal courts, each side asking that the other be removed to another place in order to stop damages. The Isleño-controlled town council at that time suggested the missions be moved or reduced to two in order to stop destruction of town crops by mission animals.[38] The real reason for the council's complaints, Fray Mariano Francisco de los Dolores wrote in 1758, was that since their arrival, the Isleños had sought to reduce the missions "in order to benefit from the buildings, *acequias*, farms and other works of the Indians."[39] The dispute over boundaries continued into the 1760s and 1770s, with the town continuing to argue that the missions' territorial claims unduly restricted its growth.[40]

The Adaesanos' arrival in 1773 tilted the town-missions struggle in the former's favor. Although a large number of the East Texans returned to their home region the following year, more than sixty families remained in Béxar. With the town unable to give them land and water, those Adaesanos not in the military turned to sharecropping and day labor at the missions or with the town's better-off *vecinos*. Commandant General Teodoro de Croix's inspection visit in January 1778 afforded the Adaesanos an opportunity to ask for help. The Commandant's chief counsel suggested a new settlement for the group, Béxar being large enough to defend itself. Governor Ripperdá, on the other hand, recommended that Béxar's Adaesanos join their fellow East Texans at the new settlement of Bucareli.[41]

When the town council was asked for its opinion on the matter, it offered two possible solutions: a new settlement on the San Marcos or Guadalupe River, or the secularization and distribution of Mission Valero lands. The council made a very strong case for the latter solution. The members pointed out that San Antonio de Valero had "the principal irrigation works from the spring of the San Antonio River, with much more irrigated land than any of the other missions, or even this town."[42] Great savings could be accomplished, they argued, by distributing the land among the few remaining Indians and the Adaesanos.

It took Croix more than a year to agree to the secularization. In June 1779 he issued an order for Mission Valero's secularization and the distribution of land, buildings, livestock, and crops among the Indian residents, Adaesanos, and other worthy *agregados*. Governor Cabello did not carry out this order, just as he did not carry out a second order for secularization and distribution in 1781.[43] As in other cases of *obedezco pero no cumplo* (I obey but do not comply), the true reasons for the governor's inaction went undocumented.[44]

During the following decade the question of Mission Valero's secularization receded to the background. While the Adaesanos maintained themselves as renters and servants, Valero continued to decline, as did other Béxar missions, so that by the early 1790s the Franciscan College of Zacatecas was ready to reduce its commitments at Béxar. The possibility of opening new mission fields for the Karankawa and other Indian groups spelled the end of Mission Valero.

Fray Manuel Silva, commissary and prefect of the College of Zacatecas, proposed staffing new Texas missions by closing Valero entirely and consolidating the other four San Antonio missions into two. He and the acting governor, the Conde de Sierragorda, agreed that Valero's lands and buildings should be distributed among the mission's Indian residents, the Adaesanos, and the mission's Spanish residents. The Adaesanos and other Spanish residents living at Valero had formed a small settlement below the mission, and distribution of the mission's lands would not only meet their needs and those of Béxar's other Adaesanos, it would leave room for future residents as well.[45]

Secularization took place in January 1793 under the direction of Governor Muñoz. Pedro Huizar surveyed the land to be distributed. Valero had three farms—the *labor de arriba* or upper farm, the *labor de abajo* or lower farm, and the *labor de afuera* or outer farm. The first two ran north and south of the bend in the river where the town and mission met. The outer farm was located due east of the mission.[46] Despite the mission's more than seventy-five years of existence—during which there were periods of prosperity, and throughout much of which its friars had willingly rented land to Spanish residents—some of the irrigable fields still had not been cleared at the time they were distributed.[47]

At the time of distribution there were four distinct groups receiving land. The fifteen mission Indians, who got first choice, took the lower farm. The upper farm went to forty-five Adaesanos. Nine other Spanish residents of the mission received *suertes* in the outer farm. These last were joined by two townsmen. The available evidence suggests that the *suertes* varied greatly in size, from seven to twenty-one acres, with the Adaesanos receiving the largest parcels.[48]

At least one lesson had been learned from the two previous distributions of irrigated land. At Valero, enough land was held in reserve to meet future demands from population growth or new residents. Consequently, the tracts were smaller and only one *suerte* was granted to each individual. Moreover, each grantee received only a half day of water,[49] which allowed for the wider distribution of water rights. Among the earliest additional grantees were Vicente Amador, who in April 1793 asked for and received a tract on the north end of the Indians' farm, and Francisco Villegas, who received one below the farm, just above Mission Concepción's lands.[50] Four years later Governor Muñoz granted six new *suertes* at Valero and regranted one that had been abandoned.[51] He also granted an oversize lot to José Montoya, at the time the settlement's only interpreter of the Comanche language.[52]

IV

During the Isleños', or lower farm's, first two decades of existence, agricultural land and irrigation water acquired a market value that they retained throughout the rest of the century. At the time of the original 1739 Crown grant, each Isleño family's two *suertes* and twenty-four hours of water was valued at approximately two hundred pesos. Two years later, the price had risen to approximately three hundred pesos. Even after farmland began to be subdivided through inheritance, it continued to be appraised on the basis of the original grant of two *suertes* and one day of water, and its value remained unchanged. Three hundred pesos was still the price in 1774 and in the last year of the century.[53] As new land north of town and then at the missions came into production, the value of agricultural land in the lower farm stagnated.

Land in the upper farm was worth considerably less, probably as a result of most of the *suertes'* considerable distance from the town's center. Two *suertes* with a full day of water usually brought in no more than 150 to 160 pesos. In one instance, the sale price for the package was two hundred pesos, and one appraisal, made upon the confiscated *suertes* of José Félix Menchaca, valued the land and water at three hundred pesos. This latter valuation was extremely unrealistic, as the governor was forced to point out when no one stepped forward to buy the land.[54] While demand for farmland had increased, its availability in the new farm and later at the missions, combined with the limited means of most residents, kept prices in check.

Because water was the single most important ingredient in farm operations, the Canary Islanders fought tenaciously to protect their grant from the San Pedro *acequia* and the twenty-day water cycle. Except for a small *acequia* that was dug for the benefit of landowners west of San Pedro Creek, all the *agua de propios* (town's water) came from the main *acequia* once every five days.[55] When the upper farm *acequia* was built, its water was reserved strictly for the fields. There is no evidence of how much water from the Valero *acequia* system was reserved for residential use.

Because water was a valuable commodity, the practice of selling water rights in time allotments developed in Béxar, as it did throughout the north.[56] While the most common practice was for owners to sell land and water together, separate sales of either element were not unknown. The municipal government sold *propios* water and individuals sold their water allotments, which acquired an appraised value independent of land—one hundred pesos for twenty-four hours in the 1770s. Ana Santos, who owned three *suertes* and 1.5 days of water in the lower farm, sold her daughter a piece of land in one *suerte* without any water rights. At the end of the century, Antonia de Armas, who owned three hours of water and the corresponding land, sold Francisco Amangual the water and José Antonio Bustillos the land.[57]

Land tenure in San Antonio was based on a series of well-established practices. Despite individual ownership of parcels, a farm's maintenance was a shared responsibility. All owners were expected to participate in or help defray upkeep of the *acequia*s and fences along the farms' perimeters. Homeowners bounding on the farms also had to maintain fences. Moreover, residents and soldiers with no interest in the farmland were compelled to make sure their animals did not get into crops or damage *acequias*.[58] To prevent damage to crops and *acequias* by domestic animals in the mid-1740s, the *cabildo* hired Antonio Ximénez to watch the fields. His performance earned him the job permanently, and each farmer was required to contribute toward his salary.[59]

Penalties for non-compliance with fencing, cleaning, and animal control were heavy and increased toward the end of the century when the governor became the enforcement officer. Soon after the lower farm was organized, *Alcalde* Juan Leal Goraz ordered the owners to build a fence, fining non-participants four pesos. He ordered that all livestock be watched during the day and confined at night, the penalty for animals getting into the fields being one-quarter peso per head plus the damage done. Leal also ordered that all *acequias* be placed in working order under penalty of a four-peso fine. *Alcalde* Alberto López's 1756 ordinance established a six-peso fine against individuals who allowed their animals to be loose within the lower farm, and the same amount for those who did not keep their stretch of fence in repair. Governor Ripperdá's order of 1773 provided a penalty of fifteen pesos and eight days in jail for failure to help clean the *acequia* or to put up a proper fence. At the request of most *suerte* owners in the upper farm, who complained that a few were not adhering to a 1781 agreement on cleaning the *acequia*, Governor Cabello ordered that all do their part or face a fifteen-peso penalty. This 1784 order also imposed forfeiture of the land for those who did not cultivate their *suertes* in any two consecutive years, no matter the excuse.[60]

The reiteration of these regulations suggests that lack of cooperation was a chronic problem throughout the century. Before the fences were put up on the lower farm, Isleños Juan Leal Goraz, Juan Curbelo, and others had spent time in jail over encroachments and failure to fence. In October 1737 Governor José Antonio Fernández de Jáuregui received a complaint from the town council that damage to crops from mission and presidial animals totaled four hundred *fanegas* lost, despite which the aggrieved Isleño farmers had killed no animals. Upon further inquiry, however, the governor discovered that the Isleños had, in fact, killed four offending animals that year and that only fifteen to twenty *fanegas* had been lost during Fernández's governorship. In response, Fernández admonished the council to be more careful and to make more mature deliberations before submitting complaints.[61] Thirty years later, Vicente Amador showed even less good judgement when he attacked José Antonio Villegas, appointed by Alcalde Jacinto Delgado to confiscate Amador's mare, which had done damage to some crops. Amador's wife accused the *alcalde* of confiscating the animal in order to make money to support his paramours. After spending two months in sanctuary at Mission Valero, Amador presented himself before the *alcalde*, who absolved him but made him pay court costs.[62]

Disputes over water use and abuse were commonplace, although usually settled between the parties.[63] Juan José Montes de Oca, one of the grantees in the upper farm, received a parcel that could only be irrigated by bringing the *acequia* water through Toribio Fuentes' tract. In the summer of 1781, Montes de Oca complained that he had lost all his crops because Fuentes refused him access to the *acequia*. Governor Cabello passed the matter to an *alcalde* who had the area inspected. The *alcalde's* decision, that there was no other way for Montes de Oca to get water than for Fuentes to give him a right-of-way, was met by the latter's warning that Montes would have to pay any damages arising from the work.[64] Santiago Seguín beat *Alcalde* Manuel Berbán senseless because the latter stopped Seguín from irrigating his beans with water he had inherited from his aunt. Adding insult to injury, Seguín claimed that while he was prevented from lawfully irrigating, Berbán had illegally taken a large amount of water for himself while the *acequia* was broken.[65]

V

By the time the Canary Islanders arrived in Béxar, cleared land and irrigation water were available and the Isleños could rapidly set about planting maize and garden crops. Instead of the communal subsistence agriculture of the 1720s, the Isleños quickly organized their farming operations along market lines. During the 1720s at least one missionary had been interested in eliminating competition by having the viceroy close down the soldiers' farm.[66] Now the Isleños tried to make use of their favored status to eliminate the missions as competition to the one commercial market in the province, the military establishment.

In their first year in Béxar, the Isleños attempted a price-fixing scheme with some of the missionaries, by which they agreed not to sell maize for a price below three pesos the *fanega*. Although the scheme did not work because Captain Pérez de Almazán found enough supplies at another mission, the stage was set for further attempts at fixing prices. In late 1732 the Isleños filed a grievance with the viceroy accusing the missions of denying them access to river water and preventing them from selling their produce to the presidio. The result of the complaint was a viceregal order of May 1733 wherein Texas's presidial commanders were ordered to buy the townspeople's maize and to favor them in the purchase of vegetables. This decision was reiterated in January 1736 after the Isleños complained that Captain Almazán's successor, José de Urrutia, was not complying with the previous order. In the late 1730s there were charges and counter-charges by Isleños and missionaries concerning the supply of maize to the presidio and the townspeople's desires to use mission Indians as farm labor. Although the Isleños won a decision in 1741, four years later the viceroy accepted the missionaries' appeal.[67]

While the garrison acquired its maize supply wherever the cheapest price was to be found, especially in times of scarcity, it does seem that townspeople were favored suppliers. In the early years, this would have meant the Isleños had the advantage, but in the course of the century other *vecinos* became prominent suppliers. On occasion, a dissatisfied *vecino* would fall back on the viceregal orders in an attempt to extract a favorable price. In 1791 Macario Zambrano went directly to the commandant general complaining about Governor Muñoz and the company paymaster, Francisco Amangual. Zambrano argued that he should have been pre-ferred in the military's purchase of maize since he owed a debt to the paymaster. Amangual countered that, at the time he requested maize prices from all farmers, Zambrano's asking price was higher, so to round out the company's needs he took two hundred *fanegas* from Espada Mission. The case was settled the following year by Zambrano's widow, who agreed that the debt would be paid in maize at a rate even lower than the two and a half pesos per *fanega* Zambrano had offered to accept.[68]

San Antonio's farmers also benefited from conditions at La Bahía. The coastal plain in which the presidio of Nuestra Señora de Loreto de la Bahía del Espíritu Santo was located, did not lend itself to the gravity-flow irrigation technology available to northern settlers. As Captain Juan Cortés explained in 1794, more than seventy years after that presidio's founding, "In this presidio there is no other industry than dry farming maize."[69] Often the results were not good. La Bahía's population was, therefore, dependent on maize supplies from Béxar to meet local needs.[70] On occasion, Béxar also exported maize as far as the lower Rio Grande Valley and Coahuila.[71]

Despite the commercial aspects of Béxar agriculture, the population had a reputation for laziness. As early as 1740, Captain Urrutia commented that the surplus produced was slight and the income barely enough to make ends meet for the families involved.[72] Ten years later Fray Mariano Francisco de los Dolores also mentioned the townspeople's lack of indus-try. Citing the poverty of the Isleños, some of whom had sold their lands and did not even have a house to live in, he also noted that "few of them are fond of working the land."[73]

Beginning in the 1760s, governors focused on the limited land in use and the absence of wheat culture as also being symptomatic of the tendency toward sloth. Governor Navarrete complained that the Isleños obstructed distribution of land to others even though they did not sow all the land granted to them. In 1779 Governor Cabello complained that because of a bumper crop many farmers had shown little interest in planting a new crop for the coming year. His concern proved valid when, at the end of March, a great storm ruined most of the previous year's maize, which had been improperly stored because the farmers had no granaries of their own.[74] Governor Martínez, citing an abundant wheat crop in Coahuila from which San Antonio could be supplied, noted that wheat was not grown in Béxar, "not because it will not grow here, but because these inhabitants do not have the strength for it."[75] Governor Muñoz blamed the small extent of agriculture on the Bexareños' "laziness," a result of concentrating their efforts on running wild livestock.[76]

These critiques were certainly unfair in some respects. Maize's advantage over wheat in a situation such as Béxar's was significant, and frontiersmen gravitated to it. With limited water supplies, a limited labor pool, and little possibility for export, the low yield and the greater amount of attention wheat required did not make it an economically rational crop on which to spend time. Maize, on the other hand, could be planted and cared for much more easily, had a higher yield, and could be eaten before ripe. The practice of planting *maíz temprano* (early maize) gave the town two seasonal opportunities to provide food for itself.

Failed attempts to grow wheat at Béxar attest to the difficulties. In late 1778 Miguel Ocariz and Francisco Xavier Rodríguez planted approximately six fanegas of wheat between them. When Governor Cabello inspected the field in February of the following year, he described it as "very handsome," although he lamented that there was no mill at which to grind the flour. Unfortunately, the same end-of-March storm that ruined the town's harvested maize also ruined the entire wheat crop. Despite the setback, Rodríguez must have made other, more successful efforts, for in 1784 he requested an export license for a herd of cattle the proceeds from which he intended to use to build a flour mill. Yet the success, if there was any, was short-lived, for in 1790 Governor Martínez makes it clear in a letter to the viceroy that wheat was not grown by townspeople.[77]

Other circumstances contributed to the lack of intensive agricultural production. With the missions producing at surplus levels, and the two

San Antonio River presidios forming the only sure markets, Béxar's farmers probably considered it futile to attempt 100 percent of their production
capacity. The availability of open pasture land made cultivation of fodder
crops unnecessary. Irrigation water was limited, and concentrating its use
made it more effective. Since land and water were granted together and
often sold together, a portion of the land could be allowed to lie fallow
while the water was concentrated on the land used for crops. The proper
application of irrigation water was crucial to producing a good crop under
Béxar's climatic conditions. In exceptionally dry years not even irrigation
helped the sugarcane, pepper, and bean crops.[78]

In normal years, the agricultural cycle provided the people of Béxar an
opportunity to participate in the fair at Saltillo, between harvests of the
early and late maize, and to conduct ranching operations between the late
harvest and the spring plantings. From the evidence available for the entire
century, the annual cycle began in late January or early February with the
mending of farm fences and irrigation works. Irrigation water was used to
prepare the ground for sowing. March was devoted to planting sugarcane,
peppers, beans, and early maize, which apparently was grown without
irrigation. March and April were also the months for starting vegetable
gardens. May and early June were devoted to planting late maize and
beans. The first harvest of the early maize, beans, and peppers usually
came in at the end of June or in early July. The rest of the summer and fall
were taken up with harvesting vegetables as they ripened. The annual fair
at Saltillo in September was ideally timed for Bexareños to collect their
cattle in the summer and make the long trip there and back before the late
crops—potatoes, cotton, beans, and maize—required attention. Late
beans were harvested in November, and the maize crop came in at the end
of December and in January. Livestock was branded during the period
between the late maize harvest and the spring planting.[79]

VI

Until very late in the century there is little knowledge of agricultural
prices other than for maize. There is, therefore, little basis for determining
fluctuations in prices and availability for such basic crops as beans, peppers, and squash. Adding to the difficulty is the official price, which, it is
clear, did not reflect actual cost. The 1729 schedule, having been set when
most produce had to be imported, created the possibility of inflated profits
for the commanders. When Rubí made his inspection in 1767, he noted

that the Regulation of 1729 was generally followed, although some prices had been lowered.[80] In effect, there is little reason to doubt that bean, pepper, and sugarcane prices followed the fluctuations in maize prices.

Unfortunately, no estimates can be made about the number of farmers, the area under cultivation, nor the yields. Although the location of the town's farms is known, as well as the fact that some ranchers grew crops during those times when they occupied their ranches, records on the total amount of land under cultivation at any one time are not available. The few mentions in extant records of the amounts of maize harvested and sold are general references, with no indication as to the number of farmers participating nor the amount of land under cultivation. For instance, in 1794 Joaquín Flores offered five hundred *fanegas* of maize at two pesos.[81]

Years of exceptional abundance were rare, as were years of complete disaster. The absence of a public granary or large storage facilities on the part of farmers attests to their custom of limiting output.[82] Only the missions, with their unpaid labor forces and unique demands, bothered with agricultural storage. Limited demand, more-than-adequate availability of farmland, and subsistence horticulture by most townspeople combined to keep prices stable throughout the year. After unexpectedly small harvests or crop destruction by natural disasters, the people of Béxar imported what food they needed from Coahuila, which provided Texas with wheat throughout the century.[83]

The worst of the lean times coincided with the widespread agricultural crisis of 1785–86, although in Texas the climatic disruptions lasted until 1790.[84] The drought may be said to have begun in October 1785, although no rainfall was reported after June. Attempts at irrigation proved fruitless; most crops were lost, and according to Governor Cabello, the fall maize harvest was one-tenth what it should have been. Having received word that the viceroy might tour the province, Cabello advised that he should bring his own maize for Béxar had barely enough to meet its own needs until June's harvest of early maize. The drought continued into March and Cabello found it necessary to comply with the viceroy's order that tithe maize (that part of the crop annually paid by farmers to the Church) be made available to the poor at reduced prices. Prayers and penitential processions were held to "placate the Lord's ire," but just when the crops were sprouting in early April, a severe frost destroyed everything and damaged all the fruit trees. By this time, the cattle that were not dead were extremely thin, and their slaughter for meat did not prevent shortages of tallow for candles and cooking fat. Conditions grew so severe that many sought nourishment in *raises de lampaso* (burdock roots) and wild sweet *potatoes (camotitos del monte)*.[85] Despite the reverses, new crops were sown and new prayers offered, this time successfully. It rained throughout the month of June and there was evidence of an abundant crop.[86]

Indications are that the summer harvest of 1786 was only a respite from continued climatic disruptions. In June 1787, Governor Martínez Pacheco reported that the province had experienced another drought accompanied by a severe winter, although the early maize showed promise. The years 1788–90 were much worse. In January 1789 Martínez prohibited maize exports from Béxar, including any to La Bahía. He also attempted to establish price controls and eliminate speculation by limiting the whole-sale price of maize to two and a half pesos per *fanega*, and the resale price to two pesos. The commandant general overturned the price control mea-sure—"farmers are free to sell at the price they choose"—and ordered Martínez to share the available maize supply with La Bahía. By the time the crisis was over in the summer of 1791, some farmers had paid as much as twelve pesos the *fanega* for seed maize.[87]

While such agricultural crises quickly strained the resources of even subsistence communities such as San Antonio, maize prices suggest that recovery was just as rapid. Not unexpectedly, the Canary Islanders' arrival put a strain on available supplies and drove the price up to six pesos per *fanega* in 1731. After the Isleños began their own farm operations, the price dropped to three pesos in 1733, and one and a half to two pesos the following year. The bumper crop of January 1779 brought the price of maize down to as low as a half peso per *fanega* which, according to Gov-ernor Cabello, placed a severe financial strain on farmers who could not raise enough funds from the crop to meet their obligations. Following the extremely high price of five pesos per *fanega* in 1790, the price dropped to two pesos the following year.

The bench-mark price for maize in Béxar may be said to have been the three pesos per *fanega* required by the Regulation of 1729 as the selling price to soldiers. While it is impossible to tell how well this price was adhered to, some evidence points to excessively high prices at times. In 1735 the commander of La Bahía accused Béxar's Captain José Urrutia of price gouging in charging the La Bahía detachment stationed at San An-tonio three pesos per *fanega* when Urrutia had purchased it at two pesos. When Rubí inspected San Antonio in 1767, he found that Captain Men-chaca had lowered the distribution price to two and a half pesos.[88] On the other hand, supply could reach such a critical state that the soldiers did not receive their maize ration. During the crisis of 1789–90, the paymaster was forced to pay out the complement's maize ration in money.

Table 4.1: Maize Prices in Béxar, 1724–1799

Pesos per		Pesos per	
Year	Fanega	Year	Fanega
1724	3	1785	4½
1729	3*	1787	2½
1731	6	1788	2 to 2½
1733	3	1789	4½ to 5
1734	1½ to 2	1790	5
1735	2 to 3	1791	2 to 2–¾
1738	2	1792	2
1752	⅝	1793	1½
1768	2½	1794	1½ to 1–⅞
1771	3	1795	1–⅝ to 2
1773	1	1796	2
1774	1½	1797	2
1779	½ to 1	1798	2
1782	3	1799	2½

*Official price set by Regulation of 1729.

The maize rations that should have been distributed to the troops this month and last, was given to them in cash *(reales)* so that they might do business among the mission Indians [buying] from the rations the father ministers give them weekly.[89]

In general, maize prices in Béxar may be said to have moderately declined in the course of the century. Although maize prices throughout the century were higher in Béxar than in major urban centers, perhaps owing to the province's presidios being the only significant markets, the difference seems to have narrowed toward the end of the century.[90] The trend also reflects the quick improvement in the primitive frontier conditions in regard to agriculture as production expanded and the area became self-sufficient. The maize glut of 1779, when prices dropped as low as a half peso per *fanega*, came immediately after the upper farm was opened and soon corrected itself. In all, it appears that capacity was more than enough to meet the needs of Béxar's growing population and to take over the commercial production of the missions as these were secularized.

The essentially agricultural nature of the local economy is clearly revealed by the occupational listings in the late century censuses. The houselist of 1793 lists eighty-eight *labradores* (farmers), including those at the newly opened farm at Valero. Yet there is only one rural property owner listed, Tomás Travieso, and he is described as an *hacendero* (hacienda owner). In other words, even those individuals with considerable livestock interests (to be discussed in Chapter 5) were still primarily considered farmers.[91]

VII

Agricultural land was subject to some of the same forces that influenced the urban landscape's growth—Indians, neighboring missions, the Canary Islanders' initial monopoly over local government, and restricted economic opportunity. The Canary Islanders' early rights and privileges served to restrict access to irrigation water and agricultural land until the weight of kinship and economic bonds with the *agregado* population brought about a change in the attitudes of the leading families. New farmland was opened only when it became economically rational with the expansion of the presidial market, growth of Béxar's civilian population, and decline of the missions. The concentration of agricultural land in the town's immediate vicinity and the parcels' arrangement to take advantage of a common *acequia* made the most of the scarce water and labor resources.

Agricultural production, while limited, was large enough to occasion disputes between Crown officials and local interests. The Isleños' insistence on preferential treatment in the sale of their crops to Texas garrisons was later extended to other agriculturalists, once the Isleño monopoly over farmland receded. Complaints against governors, presidial commanders, and paymasters over crop sales were aimed at reducing the missions' participation in the agricultural economy. At the same time, because markets for agricultural goods were limited, production was often limited, thereby creating an image of laziness for Béxar's farmers.

5

A Ranching Frontier

These people have no other industry, minerals or commerce than
a small amount of agriculture, which is reduced to the cultivation
of maize, and very little beans, peppers, and fruits; not for lack of
water or fields, but because of their laziness and their having
given all their attention to the capture of wild livestock of both
species from the time these settlements were created.

—GOVERNOR MANUEL MUÑOZ, 1794[1]

San Antonio de Béxar's farmland tenure system relied on cooperation within a legal framework of clearly defined boundaries for each land owner. The people of Béxar did not take the land tenure rules and practices of the town and farms into the countryside, although cooperation did emerge as an essential ingredient for the slight economic success Béxar's ranches enjoyed. For the most part, rural land away from town was held in an informal and distinctive manner. And, just as ranching properties were rudimentary, so was ranching as an economic activity. As such, although the ranches contributed significantly to the local economy, they did not raise Béxar, nor Texas in general, from its economically marginal position within the overall colonial economy.

I

Texas ranches were not like the *haciendas* of northern New Spain. The enormous, predominantly livestock-raising concerns, with their village compounds, company stores, and permanent labor forces, did not exist in

colonial Texas.² The "men rich and powerful," those miners and captains
who founded the great estates of Nueva Vizcaya, Coahuila, and Nuevo
León, were not to be found in Texas, where settlement had only a strategic
purpose. Although there were men interested in organizing such vast
landholdings in Texas, circumstances played against them.

Many of the same conditions that had elsewhere led to the development
of the *hacienda* were present in Texas. By European standards the north
was empty, containing only a few roaming bands of warlike and nomadic
Indians. There were no sedentary peoples with claims on the soil and no
Crown officials to interfere in the plans of the adventurous. The colonization laws of 1573, which richly rewarded those willing to "pacify" and
settle new provinces at their own cost, served as an added inducement.
Only rich miners and powerful captains interested in supplying the expanding mining economy with agricultural products took the opportunity
offered, however.³

In Béxar, the absence of the wealthy and powerful miner and captain
made all the difference. There were men in Béxar who aspired to the status
of great estate owners, but geography, demography, and economic conditions conspired against them throughout the eighteenth century. The
limited resources the Crown was willing to invest in Texas were insufficient to raise the province out of its marginal existence. The nonsedentary
Indians, who faced private armies in many other provinces, faced only an
overextended Crown garrison at Béxar, plus a few residents and mission
Indians. The same geographical remoteness that prevented Crown officials from playing too large a role in local matters also contributed to
keeping population away and made the cost of conducting business almost
prohibitive. Even Béxar's most prosperous and best established *vecinos* had
few resources to devote to buying clear titles to their ranches from the
Crown, much less establishing great *haciendas.*

Apart from the mission ranches, which had established themselves earlier and had access to more substantial labor resources than civilians,
eighteenth-century Texas ranches appear to have been very crude affairs.
But even the more elaborate mission operations should not be equated
with *hacienda* compounds. The compound of Rancho Las Cabras, which
belonged to Mission San Francisco de la Espada and was constructed in
the 1750s and 1760s, consisted of a chapel and *jacales* surrounded by a
rough wall.⁴ In a general assessment of the San Antonio River valley
ranches, Fray Agustín Morfi attests to the lack of progress during the
province's first sixty years of existence.

The ranches are of such little consideration and so miserable, that all the way to Santa Cruz and the Arroyo of the Civolo along the banks of the San Antonio river, that I would not mention them if I could disregard the one man who inhabits this very fertile region of this unfortunate province. The ranch called Chayopa contains only eight persons; Pataguilla, 3; Cabras, 26; San Francisco, 17; Mora, 26; Las Mulas, 5; and in all they maintain 85 souls, who live in such dread and imminent risk of loss of life, even within their miserable huts, that not a single one of these ranches deserves the name of "establishment."[5]

Indeed, the very term used for these properties attests to limited development. Typically, a *rancho* meant a small freehold farm, a rural house or small collection of houses, or a marginal portion of a hacienda rented to an independent livestock raiser. The use of the word in colonial Texas testifies to the limited development of the rural estates. Despite its size of fifteen *sitios* (sixty-five thousand acres), the grant to Luis Menchaca was called a *rancho* in legal proceedings of 1759. In his notes to the 1779 census of Béxar, Governor Cabello refers only to *ranchos*, as did the 1791 cabildo in its report on "*ciudades, villas, lugares*, haciendas, y ranchos" within its jurisdiction.[6]

Combatting the hardships, Béxar's ranchers continued to struggle throughout the colonial period to make their ranches prosperous. As Morfi observed, "They only aspire to independence . . . and they call themselves proprietors of extensive possessions from none of which they receive any benefit; this is their character, this is their passion; and in order to indulge it, they·disregard all danger."[7]

II

Although cattle ownership was widespread in Béxar, the possibility of acquiring pastures was limited to those few families with enough livestock to justify a need for separate ranch land. Just how much livestock was needed for a successful petition for ranch land is not clear. Most of the petitions state that the applicant had been keeping his animals on someone else's ranch. Even when an individual was successful in having a rural tract granted to him, circumstances such as hostile Indians could delay occupation.[8] In sum, there were three principal reasons for the tenuousness with which rural land was held and that deterred most from getting valid titles—Indian hostilities, the land claims made by the Béxar and La Bahía missions, and the expense and uncertainty of going before the royal *juez privativo* (property judge) of the competent *audiencia* (high court).

Perhaps the single most destabilizing influence on ranch holdings was the hostility of Apaches, Comanches, and Norteños. Although one large grant was made in 1736 to Francisco Hernández,[9] other claims to rural lands were not made until fifteen years later, coinciding with the Apache peace ratified at San Antonio in 1749. While the peace did not preclude occasional livestock theft and the murder of a shepherd or ranch hand, the period's relative tranquility brought a number of families into the countryside between 1751 and 1768.[10]

By the latter year, however, a marked increase in depredations led to ranches being abandoned. In 1770 Martín de la Peña claimed that he was the only rancher, including the missions, not to abandon his property as a result of the hostilities. Governor Ripperdá built the fort on Cíbolo Creek to protect the ranches, but the effort proved largely unsuccessful. In 1778 Indian hostilities still prevented Felipe de Luna from settling a two-*sitio* (approximately nine thousand acres) ranch that had been granted to him five years earlier by Governor Ripperdá. According to Bexareños themselves, it was not until peace with the Norteños and Comanches was achieved in 1785, that use of the ranches resumed.[11]

The slow return to the ranches was once again halted by Apache hostilities in 1789–90. In the latter year Governor Muñoz reported that a total of twenty-five men had been killed, including three ranchers and six others on five different ranches. The following year the *cabildo* reported that only two ranches had been resettled, while another nine had chattels but no residents. Three ranches remained entirely abandoned.

Over the next few years, however, as the countryside began to enjoy a substantial peace, more of the ranches were reoccupied,[12] even though the town council as late as 1801 was still bemoaning the impact of hostile Indians on landholdings in Texas. The *cabildo* claimed that while there were many good fields east and north of Béxar, the barbarous Indians that inhabited these areas had prevented the land from becoming available for settlement and use. Consequently, the rural land had little value.

Since this province was founded we do not know of any sale other than the eighteen sitios for one hundred pesos made to the late Captain Don Luis Antonio Menchaca. . . . The other ranch possessions have been made gratuitously to some of the more meritorious *vecinos* of the place; some of these lands to this day remain settled and others entirely abandoned without the legitimate owners making any petitions regarding them, with neither they nor anyone else attempting new possessions. From all of which can be determined the little or no value that may be assigned to these lands.[13]

Besides hostile Indians, settlers had to contend with the land claims made by the Béxar and La Bahía missions. The settlers' relatively insignificant number of livestock, combined with chronic Apache depredations, resulted in the missions having organized their ranches first, and by the time townspeople began to infiltrate into the countryside, they found themselves having to challenge the missions for ranch lands.[14] In 1756 the town council complained that, despite the governor's grant of a ranch for thirty people to Vicente Alvarez Travieso and Francisco José de Arocha along the Guadalupe River, the missions had placed herds and flocks on the site to block the grant.[15] In 1765 *Alcalde* Bernabé Carabajal painted a very clear, if exaggerated, picture of the ranch situation in Texas to the land judge in Mexico City.

Sir, Your Lordship must believe that [the reason] some of [Béxar's] *vecinos* have not appeared in that court to get titles for grants to lands and waters is that (meaning no disrespect to the Reverend Fathers) the Missions have generally monopolized the lands and the Isleño families, with their honors and merits that they say they have, want to take control of the little land that—more by force than by desire—the Reverend Fathers leave [available.] Otherwise, this so distant Province could be no less populous than that of Saltillo, because its land is pleasingly fertile, with abundant places to take water, and fields and plains sufficient to receive and maintain large populations; but as these waters and lands are only diverted in order for the missions to make ranches *[estancias]*, the nonholding *vecinos* do not benefit nor does His Majesty in that his dominions are not settled.[16]

The missions, in turn, complained about the Spanish settlers. Fray Mariano Francisco de los Dolores, as early as 1758, complained of the civilian ranches being located next to mission lands: "There having been approximately five thousand beeves at missions Espada and Capistrano before the ranches were formed, after their coming into existence there may be

1,500." To the missions' way of thinking, there were enough lands to the southwest and north to meet Béxar's needs.[17]

In truth, the missions were in little better position to argue about legal rights to ranch land than was Béxar's citizenry. With the exception of La Bahía's Mission Espíritu Santo, which had received a donation of legally granted land from Bernabé Carabajal west of Cleto Creek, Béxar's missions occupied land by virtue of the vague language of their founding documents. To the townspeople's way of thinking, civilian ranchers were just as entitled to the lands as the missions.[18]

The missions often won the formal battles. Protests in the late 1770s by the families of Martín Lorenzo de Armas, Juan José Flores, and Miguel Guerra that they had occupied lands which had been obtained illegally by Mission Espíritu Santo in 1761, proved of no avail. When in 1792 Vicente Flores asked the town council to certify that the lands known as Rancho de Nuestra Señora de los Dolores were public lands, the council refused, stating that Espíritu Santo's records showed that the mission owned the land. Moreover, the same request previously made by the Granado family had been turned down.[19]

On the other hand, persistent encroachment by Spanish ranchers onto mission-claimed lands led to de facto occupations. Despite the limited amount of land left to Miguel Guerra in the Bernabé Carabajal–Mission Espíritu Santo transaction of 1759–61, his widow continued to claim a much larger ranch in succeeding decades, as did Juan José Flores and the widow of Martín Lorenzo de Armas. The de la Peña family, which had been in litigation over the part of their ranch that Mission Valero claimed encroached on mission lands, ultimately retained possession of their full claim and transferred ownership to parts of it on two occasions. As late as 1809 Governor Manuel Salcedo reported that the Arocha and Travieso families' ranches covered parts of Mission San Juan Capistrano's ranch lands.[20]

Unfortunately for Béxar's ranchers, cases concerning contested land could not be settled within the province. Neither the missions' claims, the verbal permits, nor the grants by governors formed legal titles. Any action taken by a governor, whether a grant of land or settlement of a dispute, was subject to confirmation at the *audiencia* level.[21] Consequently, all disputes not settled through compromise *per force* wound up before a judge. Since most individuals were too poor to undertake the costly litigation, not to mention too poor to pay for the land if they won the contest, no more than four individuals ever took the matter before *audiencia* authorities.[22]

Compromise was therefore the most frequent solution to quarrels be-

tween ranchers. Luis Antonio Menchaca, one of two Bexareños to successfully petition for a ranch before the *juez privativo*, purchased fifteen
sitios and twelve *caballerías* for one hundred pesos in the mid-1750s. Andrés
Hernández challenged the title, stating that his father had received a grant
of this land from Governor Franquis twenty-two years earlier. Citing,
among other factors, the high costs of litigation, the two parties agreed to
a compromise by which Hernández received four *sitios*, eight *caballerías* in
return for recognizing Menchaca's title.[23] In the early 1770s Juan José
Montes instituted a claim against Martín de la Peña, declaring he had been
in possession of the disputed land between 1764 and 1769, when he abandoned it because of Indian hostilities. Peña, on the other hand, claimed
legal possession since 1768. Fifteen years later, the case, which had begun
under Governor Ripperdá and continued under Governor Cabello, was
turned over to the new governor. Apparently, Peña was allowed to remain
on the ranch while Montes took possession of a tract further up stream on
the San Antonio River.[24]

The case of "Rancho San Lucas" demonstrates both the power of the
missions at their apogee and the vagaries to which settlers who sought the
protection of the *juez privativo* exposed themselves. Early in 1764 Domingo Castelo, former ensign at Presidio de San Sabá married to a Béxar
woman and serving as council member, requested a grant to a large tract
of land west of town. Early in 1765 the *juez privativo* in Mexico City
determined that the land should be appraised and posted for auction, with
Castelo or the highest bidder receiving title. The proceedings were formally begun in Béxar early in 1765, at which time the missionary at San
José stepped forward to claim the land, stating that the area had served as
pasture for his mission's flocks in the past but had been abandoned due to
Indian hostilities. He also stated that Castelo had been denied occupation
of the land by Governor Martos and had twice been thrown off by Captain
Menchaca at the request of the mission. The insignificant value placed on
Texas land is made clear in the appraisal: "All the land is pasture, there
being no good water supply, and the land being exposed to attacks by
Indians of the North and thefts by Apaches and escaped Indians, it was
valued at one-half peso per sitio." The eleven *sitios* were thus appraised at
five and a half pesos, but if Castelo calculated that the missionaries would
be unwilling to spend money on the tract, he was wrong. Mission San José
bid one hundred pesos for the land and Castelo was forced to concede. In
accepting the bid, the land court declared, among other things, that the
laws favored Indian communities.[25]

Local arrangements mutually agreed to were indispensible in allowing
Béxar's informal rural land system to work. Although disagreements did

not disappear, as the century came to a close they became more infrequent. A 1787 agreement between settlers and missions concerning livestock roundups demonstrates the growth in compromise and cooperation in ranch land matters; the boundary lines drawn by Governor Martínez Pacheco created sectors for groups of ranchers which did not adhere to ranch boundaries. Mission Espíritu Santo, in particular, gave up a substantial amount of land it claimed under the Bernabé Carabajal deed.[26] The agreement also demonstrates that land use (the search for wild cattle) superseded land tenure (the secure holding of a clearly described tract) for all parties making claims to the Texas countryside.

Compromise and cooperation is also evinced in multiple ownership and sharing of ranch land. By the 1770s Béxar's ranches were group affairs in which family members and renters participated as fully as the recognized owner.[27] In some cases the owner allowed kin to share in use of the land. José Félix Menchaca was such a prominent participant in his brother Luis's ranch that Fray Pedro Ramírez de Arellano believed him to be the owner. After Vicente Alvarez Travieso's death there was considerable difficulty figuring out what parts of his ranch, Las Mulas, belonged to which heirs, especially since part of the ranch had been bought by his son Tomás from one of the heirs to the neighboring Hernández ranch. Juana de Ollos, Andrés Hernández's widow, leased Rancho San Bartolo to José Macario Zambrano, but continued to keep her own stock and that of her sons there. In 1782 this ranch had eight *parcioneros* (users sharing the ranch) and Las Mulas had eleven.[28]

Such multiple participation in ranch use surprisingly did not foster subdivision of the land, nor did the secularization of San Antonio's missions, which made mission ranch lands part of the public domain. Despite the free bequeathals and sales of some property, there were no more ranches in the 1790s—in 1791 there were only fourteen recognized ranch properties—than there had been in the late 1760s. If individuals stepped in to occupy former mission lands, they did so as extrajudicially as when they had occupied most of their own ranches.[29] At the beginning of the nineteenth century Béxar's countryside had yet to be formally organized.

It should also be noted that the occupation of the countryside is the only aspect of life in Béxar that appears to have escaped early Isleño–*agregado* conflict. Other than Bernabé Carabajal's remarks quoted above, which probably refers to lands close to town, there is no documentation of any Isleño attempt at exclusive possession of rural lands. To the contrary, the first two rural grants were to military settlers, Francisco Hernández and Luis Antonio Menchaca.

III

Béxar's most important agricultural product, along with maize, was cattle. Béxar's settlers, like most frontiersmen, were livestock raisers at least on a small scale from the beginning. Each of the Canary Islands families received five breeding cows and a bull, and five mares and a stallion as part of their entitlement. The *agregados* must also have had domestic cattle, as well as a number of horses available for military service: Mateo Pérez's 1748 will listed ownership of over two hundred head of cattle and fifty horses and mares. From the Reglamento of 1729 and other early records, it is clear that meat was an important part of the local diet. Disputes among townspeople, missions, and presidio over crop damage by loose livestock and frequent cattle slaughters are a prominent part of San Antonio's early history.[30] Formation of a significant livestock economy, however, became possible only after townspeople attempted to move their stock raising operations into the countryside following the peace with the Apaches in the late 1740s.

By the early 1750s, when the first San Antonio ranches were established, there was already sizable economic activity based on livestock in the countryside. Although most of the products taken were for local consumption, the slaughter of wild cattle for meat as well as other products was already on a scale sufficient to permit exports as far south as Saltillo. The same mule trains that brought flour, chocolate, and cloth into Béxar left with jerked meat, candle tallow, and hides.[31] During these mid-century decades some Bexareños made the first efforts to establish standing herds. Monsieur de Pagés, a French traveler through Texas in the late 1760s, has left us a clear picture of this activity before the onset of cattle drives.

Their principal employment is to rear horses, mules, cows, and sheep. Their cattle, commonly allowed to roam at large in the woods, are once in two months driven into fields adjoining to the houses of their owners, where every means is used to render them tame and tractable. After having been subjected to hunger and confinement, they receive their liberty, and are succeeded by others, which experience in their turn a similar course of discipline. Such of the inhabitants as are at pains to prevent their herds from running entirely wild, are found to possess five or six thousand head of cattle.

After describing the "hunting or lacing" of wild animals, he continues: "Having only one or two keepers for all the cattle of the settlement, even their domestic animals run day and night in the woods."[32]

New Spain's expanding silver economy in the eighteenth century stimulated the demand for live cattle exports. Increased investments, new discoveries, and a growing labor force in the silver mining industry increased the demand for cattle and mules. The frontier garrisons, themselves large consumers of cattle and cattle byproducts, had to compete with the mines for livestock. It is not surprising, therefore, that by the 1770s the demand for hides and beef allowed even remote Béxar to participate in this economy. In that decade, cattle on the hoof first began to be herded from the province with drives to Rio Grande settlements, Coahuila, and to Saltillo for sale at the annual fair. During this period another market temporarily opened in Louisiana, in part as a result of the American war of independence.[33]

Before cattle became an export commodity, it helped feed the population. Cattle prices during the first decades reflect limited availability—mostly from the missions—and the impact of Indian depredations. Beginning in the late 1760s or early 1770s there was a steady drop in cattle prices until they stabilized at about four pesos a head for a full-grown cow or bull. The prices in Table 5.1 represent what may be considered full retail price, that is, the value of animals sold to the garrison or to the government for feeding visiting Indians. There is much evidence to suggest that the price in the field was considerably lower, however. For instance, in 1778 José Padrón obtained 348 animals at two and three quarters pesos a head. In his livestock ordinance of 1783, Governor Cabello set a price of two and a half pesos per head on wild cattle captured. The 367 bulls obtained for Mission Refugio in 1795 cost just over two and a quarter pesos each.[34] As in the price of maize, the fixed presidial market resulted in an artificially high retail price for cattle.

Prices at Saltillo were considerably lower than at Béxar, but more cattle could be sold and the greater volume created larger profits. The cattle of three Béxar ranchers who failed to pay the *alcabala* tax at the Saltillo customs house in 1788 averaged just over three pesos per head for their 1,357 animals. The three claimed, however, that they had lost many head on the road and had received considerably less than the 4,452 peso appraised value and that the tax-appraisal value should therefore be reconsidered.[35]

The demand for heavy export of cattle and cattle products in the late 1770s first brought into focus the shortcomings in ranching methods as they had developed in Texas, where stock raising was little more than a harvesting operation. Indian hostilities did not permit the development and control of herds until late in the century, and then only in very

Table 5.1: Béxar Cattle Prices, 1729–1799

Year	Beef per Pesos	Beef per Year	Pesos
1729	12	1791	4
1735	12	1792	4
1767	10	1793	4
1774	5	1794	4
1779	5	1795	4*
1780	4.5	1796	4*
1789	4.25	1797	4*
1790	4	1799	4 to 5*

*Only bulls sold to the garrison that year.

precarious terms. Most ranchers were content to brand or slaughter whatever cattle grazed within the pasture lands they claimed, and to collectively assert their communal rights to all the other unbranded cattle in the region. Such haphazard methods led to the quick decline in breeding stock, so much so that by 1780 Governor Cabello felt compelled to ban the export of cows, allowing only bulls and steers to be exported out of the province.[36]

In the last year of his governorship, Cabello reported that the ranchers refused to participate in formal branding roundups under the supervision of an overseer appointed by the governor. The roundups were intended to curtail cattle theft and fraud to the public purse, but the ranchers instead preferred to claim and brand all the wild cattle as they came across individual animals in order to avoid paying taxes.[37] Nearly a decade after the 1785 peace with the Norteño Indians, Governor Muñoz voiced alarm at a system so shortsighted.

Since the time they made their representation [claiming all wild cattle] they have not stopped rounding up unbranded stock, to the great detriment of the species. For this reason, I have not spoken to them of the ordered end to the collection of the tax, which would bring about the extinction of cattle in this province because of how it is destroyed. . . . The stock raisers have not taken advantage of their roundups to brand or increase their tame stock, with the exception of one or two, and there are no more than ten who maintain a standing herd. Even these I had to force to brand and pay the tithe.[38]

Improvident slaughter or export of what appeared to many to be an inexhaustible natural resource was a major issue throughout the century. The spoilage resulting from inefficient and wanton slaughter, both by settlers and Indians, was a problem recognized early in the century. In 1751 *Alcalde* José Padrón, citing the problems and outrages caused by indiscriminate killing, issued an ordinance forbidding slaughters within a radius of eighty miles of town by anyone not a cattle owner.[39] The cattle drives out of the province, which began in the 1770s, provided additional sources of depletion of both privately owned and unbranded stock.

Although friction between the missions and Béxar's settlers over cattle dated back to the town's earliest days, the latter group never committed a wholesale violation against mission property until the potential profits to be derived from driving cattle into the interior or Louisiana sent ranchers searching for wild stock wherever it might be found. The ranchers justified their actions by claiming that the cattle were descended from animals brought by their forebears into the province; the missionaries claimed that their ranches predated the settlers' operations and that the missions' herds had been larger and, therefore, the true source of the province's wild cattle.

When Commandant General Teodoro Croix arrived in Béxar in January 1778 during an inspection tour of the *Provincias Internas*, he faced a number of serious issues: conflicting claims to cattle foraging between the San Antonio and Guadalupe rivers; rapid depletion of a valuable natural resource; and the lack of public revenues being raised in Texas. He attempted to tackle all three problems at once through a general ordinance retaining ownership of unbranded stock by the Crown. Besides answering the ownership question by denying the wild stock to both ranchers and missions, he ordered stiff fines for the slaughter of unbranded stock, "in order to stop the abuses committed in the field against the wild cattle, which is property of the king, because they are killed in the field and left there, only the tallow used for soap being taken."[40] He also attempted to control live cattle exports by requiring licenses and the payment of a half-peso tax on each head of unbranded cattle. Taxation thus became a means of raising revenue while solving the ownership problem and slowing down the depletion of wild stock.[41]

Ten years later the bishop of Nuevo León, Fray Rafael Josef, added his voice to those of officials seeking to control the excesses of Béxar ranchers. He refused to rescind a special assessment on breeding cows, claiming that the killing of five to six head of cattle by settlers to obtain one mule load of meat, as well as their uncontrolled export of large herds, would eliminate this source of income. If the available evidence is trustworthy, the bishop's protests paid off for the diocese. While tithe assessments were collected on all agricultural production, it was the livestock portion of the collection that was of consequence in Texas. The province as a whole (there are no separate numbers for Béxar) contributed four hundred pesos as its annual tithe assessment between 1783 and 1791. In 1792 the province's offering was 766 pesos, and over fifteen hundred pesos for each of the next three years. Between 1796 and 1800, Texas tithes amounted to just under or just over one thousand pesos annually.[42]

Béxar's ranchers used lawsuits and appeals as tactics to delay the inevitable implementation of the decree retaining ownership of wild cattle by the Crown, but by 1795 they faced the government's final verdict. Commandant General Pedro de Nava, basing his decision on a previous resolution of the *junta superior* (Superior Council), determined that the taxes on unbranded stock assessed during the administrations of Domingo Cabello and Rafael Martínez Pacheco would be forgiven, but all unbranded cattle in the province would, in one year's time, become property of the Crown and could only be appropriated through payment of one-half peso per head. Governor Muñoz founded his comprehensive sixteen-point ordinance regulating the Béxar cattle industry based on his superior's decision.[43] He addressed the problem of indiscriminate slaughters:

10. Due to the unprecedented and wasteful slaughter of cattle by some, which may be seen in the large amounts of soap available, and this by people who are not known as stock raisers, I order that all captures be licensed, with each family getting one or two beeves depending on [family] size. . . .

11. Because the secrecy with which the sale of tallow by the slaughterers to those who make soap allows them to go unpunished, I order all sales of tallow be reported to the authorities . . .

12. Anyone denouncing an illegal slaughter is to get the meat and tallow and half the amount of the fine.

The number of convictions under the various ordinances is undeterminable, and the only surviving evidence of transgressions is from attempts to enforce Crown law late in the century by the governors residing at Béxar. The ill-gotten gains of Francisco Guerra, unlucky enough to be arrested for having slaughtered cattle without the governor's license, consisted only of the salted meat, tallow, and fat from four head of cattle. Governor Cabello, "wishing to make an example of him to other *vecinos* who are breaking the law," sentenced him to pay the penalty imposed by the commandant general for the offense. The fine included four pesos per head because it was a first offense, the value of the four animals—two and a half pesos per head—and the time employed by a corporal and four soldiers in tracking down the miscreant. In all, the fine totaled thirty-five pesos, which Guerra did not have, so the confiscated products had to be sold at auction. Later the same year Guerra was caught again, and this time fined eight pesos per animal as a second offender.[44]

Guerra's case demonstrates that the profits to be derived from Texas's wild cattle were not limited to ranch owners. An undeterminable number of townspeople derived at least part of their income by manufacturing items from cattle byproducts. Among the cattle-derived items produced in Béxar by the 1770s were soap and candles. Leather items for the garrison were also crafted locally; in his 1779 inspection of the company, Governor Cabello noted that the soldiers' protective *cueras* (leather doublets) and *adargas* (shields) were made in Béxar and were of good quality. The only problem was that the *adargas* could not be uniformly painted for lack of a painter, "it being necessary, in order for them to be painted as prescribed, that they be sent to San Luis Potosí, which adds somewhat to the cost. . . ."[45] Aside from this, many settlers hunted cattle for subsistence purposes, much as they hunted bison, bear, and deer.

As the number of Bexareños dependent upon the unbranded cattle population grew toward the end of the eighteenth century, taxation became more attractive as a fiscal measure. The small impost paid on wild cattle made unnecessary the actual ownership of a ranch, since with no more investment than a license and a minor payment anyone could run livestock. Governor Muñoz argued:

> The duty collected of [one-half peso] on cattle and [one-quarter peso] on horses is not excessive, as shown by the fact that [the townspeople] are continually asking for licenses, which they would not if the tax were too great a burden. . . . and there is no reason for them to consider this small contribution to His Majesty a hardship.[46]

Even at the height of tensions between ranchers and royal officials over stock ownership (during Domingo Cabello's administration, 1778–86), a considerable amount of legal trade continued to be conducted with neighboring provinces. Between 1779 and 1786 there were sixty-eight legal drives totaling more than eighteen thousand head of cattle. Of the total number of drives, only nineteen were made with cattle belonging only to the driver. On the other hand, twenty-seven drives included unbranded stock.[47] The profits of driving wild cattle to Coahuila and Nuevo Santander outweighed any potential tax liability resulting from the loss of the ranchers' lawsuit over ownership.

The half-peso-per-head fee charged by the Crown left a considerable profit to stockmen when the animals were slaughtered or sold outside the province. Governor Muñoz reported that individuals who slaughtered cattle could recover their expenses from the byproducts alone. The money received from sale of the meat was all profit; salted beef brought four to six pesos per animal. Unfortunately, there is little documentation on the volume and price of the various raw products derived from cattle, but when the confiscated products of Francisco Guerra's four head of cattle were auctioned off they brought in thirty-six pesos.[48]

Thus, with the proper license and tax payment, large *carneadas* (meat hunts) on public lands were common until wild cattle began to disappear. Santiago Pérez slaughtered thirty-seven beeves in January 1787 and another twenty-four in March, paying a total of twenty-seven and three quarter pesos. José María Lugo, a *vecino* of Saltillo, paid nineteen pesos for taking thirty-eight head of cattle. Even the prominent ranch owner, Simón de Arocha, ventured onto public lands that year to slaughter thirty-one head of unbranded cattle.[49]

By the 1790s the reduced availability of wild cattle was evident by the reduction in the sizes of the herds being exported. The largest drive for which a license was sought in 1793 consisted of 120 bulls and steers plus ten oxen. No permits were granted for the export of cows. In that same year, Governor Muñoz brought charges against two groups, one of townspeople and the other of Mission Concepción Indians, for slaughtering without a license. In February 1794 Muñoz documented the deplorable state of the area's cattle population, citing the residents' inability to provision the garrison with meat since early December, the small number of captures despite the issuance of many licenses, and the need to slaughter what few they could find. In the midst of the crisis, the governor sought and received approval from the *cabildo* to impose a quota on the number of animals that could be taken for family needs and banned the slaughter of breeding cows in an attempt to reduce illegal slaughters.[50]

Despite Muñoz's efforts, the condition of the cattle herds, both branded and unbranded, remained critical well into the nineteenth century. In 1803 Governor Juan Bautista Elguézabal reported:

> There is a notable scarcity of cattle. For this reason, a lack of meat is almost continuously experienced; and so it is that, if the semi-annual slaughter of buffaloes which takes place in the months of May and October did not in a measure relieve the misery, the majority of the families would no doubt starve. The catching of wild horses—and there is a great abundance in the province—is the second thing which attracts the attention of the settlers.[51]

IV

The greater the dearth in cattle, the more the people of Béxar turned to trading in horses. While the horse was probably introduced into Texas somewhat before cattle, economic interest in it lagged far behind because of the greater effort required to make use of the province's wild horse stock as compared to its cattle: the horse had to be captured, broken, pastured, cared for, and often recaptured after stampedes or Indian raids.

The civilian population looked upon horses as a mixed blessing. No one could get about without them, but horses increased Indian depredations and entailed much hard work. Efforts in the 1790s to separate the civilian horse herd from the military's (which had often borne responsibility for the town's horses after the Isleños' arrival) were met with waves of protest that doomed the projects to failure. Commandant General Croix's 1778 imposition of a three-quarter-peso tax on each unbranded horse captured caused the residents either to stop capturing the animals or to break the law. A year after the tax was ordered Governor Cabello explained that no one thought it worth the risk to their saddle horses, nor the trouble, to go after wild horses at that tax rate. He suggested that an assessment of a quarter of a peso per animal would be more amenable to the townspeople and would, therefore, raise revenue.[52]

Although most horses were captured wild, some were raised domestically as part of Béxar's livestock economy. As early as 1734 Miguel Núñez Morillo, a military settler, was providing a significant number of horses to the military for six to seven pesos per head. In his will, Mateo Pérez left six horses to each of his four sons; his estate also included sixteen mares[53] and debts owed to him for purchases of other of his horses. A good horse could have considerable value under the right circumstances. Matías Treviño, hired to guard the cattle in the mid-1730s, had a difficult time collecting part of his salary—a horse from each stockman. In 1747 Marcos Cabrera sold a lot facing the town plaza for two saddle horses, the same price for which Andrés Hernández sold his inheritance in San Bartolo ranch to Tomás Travieso.[54]

Domestic horse raising was, however, a small-time operation that, by the late 1770s, was not able to provide sufficient mounts to Béxar's garrison. The settlement's remount herd was kept in open pastures because there was no large-scale growing of fodder in Béxar. Rotation of pasturage, often requiring the transfer of the herd forty to sixty miles in order to find fresh grass, resulted in many stampedes and created conditions favorable for horse raids by Apaches and other Indian bands. Moreover, pursuit of an enemy usually required abandoning tired mounts along the way, many of which were not recaptured.[55]

As the garrison grew toward the end of the century, so did the demand for horses. One source for horses was the ranches of the Rio Grande valley in the province of Nuevo Santander, where by 1780 large purchases were being made to meet garrison needs. When drought and Indian depredations led the governors of Nuevo León and Nuevo Santander to prohibit horse exports from their provinces, Governor Cabello established a program of roundups by soldiers and vecinos. In 1784 the number of captured wild horses increased to over four hundred, and in 1787 more than three hundred were captured. Overall, however, it seems that the economic potential of the horse was not exploited to any great degree until drives of equine stock out of the province began after the turn of the nineteenth century.[56]

Aside from horses, draft animals were also readily available from fairly early in the century, as attested to by the documentation of prices. By 1779 a yoke of oxen brought as little as twelve pesos. Four years later, Fernando Veramendi's five yoke of oxen were worth ten pesos each. The price of mules in the course of the century dropped from between twenty to twenty-five pesos per animal in the early years to between ten and twelve pesos in the last three decades, strongly suggesting that Béxar had a local source of supply.[57] This could well have been Luis Antonio Menchaca and his brother Félix, who maintained the large numbers of mares and jackasses necessary for a mule-breeding operation.[58]

Little else can be said about other livestock raising activities in Béxar, however. *Ganado menor* (sheep and goats) appear in numerous paymaster reports and testamentary records, but there is little evidence of their com-

Table 5.2: Livestock Ownership in Béxar, 1779

	Military Households (total 80)		Male-Led Households (total-241)		Female-Led Households (total-53)		Total Civilian Households (total-294)	
	Number of Households	Number of Animals	Number of Households	Number of Animals	Number of Households	Number of Animals	Number of Households	Number of Animals
Mares	21	72	64	475	7	24	71	499
Horses	78	615	133	456	20	64	153	520
Mules	30	33	33	217	5	24*	38	241
Asses	0	0	3	36	0	0	3	36
Cows	41	231	113	2,473	27	562	140	3,035
Bulls/ steers	24	104	84	999	15	270	99	1,269
Yoke oxen	10	16	73	176	17	31	90	207
Sheep/ goats	0	0	5	1,635	1	30	6	1,665

*One household owned twenty mules.
Source: Provincia de Texas: Estado General de la Tropa del Presidio de San Antonio de Béxar, AGI:G legajo 283.

mercial importance within the settlement. In 1779 six families owned the 1,665 head of sheep and goats reported for the settlement, and Luis Antonio Menchaca, the retired commander of Presidio de Béxar, owned 1,500 of them. The missions seem to have been the more important producers, maintaining herds of up to five thousand animals during the 1760s, the wool being consumed in their own looms. As late as 1803 Governor Juan Bautista Elguézabal reported that there were not over one thousand head of sheep in the whole province.[59]

V

Béxar's livestock trade had an important commercial aspect, aside from providing an income to a significant portion of the population. Those individuals who took cattle, and later horses, out of the province often brought back merchandise. While the basis for most of these families' wealth continued to be their livestock and farming operations, some individuals raised their commercial transactions to a par with their livestock and farming pursuits. Among the most successful families were the Canary Islander Arochas and Traviesos, the military Menchaca, and the late-arriving Zambranos.

The Travieso family took an interest in cattle at an early date. Vicente Alvarez Travieso, one of the original Canary Islanders, had tried to establish a ranch as early as the mid-1750s, and ultimately came to acquire one on Cíbolo Creek called Las Mulas. At his death in 1778, Travieso's widow, María Ana Curbelo, became one of the leading cattle owners of Béxar, while his son Tomás was well on his way to even greater success. A part-owner of the Las Mulas ranch with his father, Tomás was so successful in his early shipment of cattle products to Saltillo that by the mid-1770s he had married into a Saltillo family and established part of his operations there. He continued the practice of bringing mule trains to Texas, perhaps loaded with textiles, ironware, and flour, and taking back dried meat, tallow, pecans, and whatever merchandise he could trade for along the way. In effect, Travieso was a traveling merchant, prosperous enough to maintain homes at both ends of his trade circuit. While in 1779 he was still considered a farmer, he appeared in the 1793 houselist of Béxar as an *hacendero*, a rank not achieved by any other livestock raiser to that time. But he also put in an appearance in the same year's census for Saltillo as a merchant and muleteer.[60]

Like the Traviesos, the Arocha family had a number of thriving repre-

Table 5.3: Top-Ten Béxar Cattle Owners, 1779

Luis Antonio Menchaca	850 head
María Ana Curbelo	300
Simón de Arocha	250
Macario Zambrano	230
Leonor Delgado	150
Félix Menchaca	150
Francisco Flores	120
Marcos de Castro	100
José Ignacio de la Peña	95
Jacinto Delgado	80

Source: Provincia de Texas: Estado General . . . , AGI: G, legajo 283.

sentatives, the most successful of whom was Simón. Simón de Arocha took mule trains to Saltillo but, unlike Travieso, he also exported cattle out of the province. Between 1780 and 1786, Arocha drove one herd each year, except in 1784. The licenses were issued in August or the beginning of September, indicating that the cattle were intended for the Saltillo fair. He also owned a considerable amount of farmland and was listed as a farmer in the 1793 census. Arocha differed from Travieso in other respects as well; he did not seek his fortune away from Béxar, but was content to be a "big fish in a small pond." The status-conscious Arocha served both as lieutenant governor of the province and commander of the town's militia, and he sent his son, José Clemente de Arocha, to Mexico City to study for the priesthood, a not-inconsiderable expense.[61]

Luis Antonio Menchaca, Béxar's commander during the 1760s and a prominent ranch owner, likewise linked livestock and commerce. By the 1770s he had become the settlement's wealthiest citizen, as attested by his ownership of the largest holdings of cattle, equine stock, and sheep and goats in Béxar. In 1785 his son, Luis Mariano Menchaca, was running what must have been one of San Antonio's three or four stores. The Menchacas also established an important commercial link with the Presidio de Aguaverde when one of Menchaca's sons, who had previously served at Béxar, was appointed commander there. By 1786 Captain José Menchaca was sending his soldiers to collect shipments of cattle products and cattle on the hoof from his brother Luis Mariano at Béxar.[62]

Macario Zambrano, a native of Saltillo, arrived in Béxar in the 1760s or 1770s. Like other outsiders looking to become insiders, he married Juana de Ocón y Trillo, who descended on both sides from some of the settlement's early setters. By 1779, although he did not yet have his own ranch, Zambrano boasted of owning 230 head of cattle. His knowledge of cattle must have been considerable, for during the early 1780s he was entrusted with overseeing the annual brandings authorized by Governor Cabello. Having been an original grantee in the upper farm, he was also one of the community's more substantial farmers, and did business with the garrison. Whether as a reward for his services or through his own devices, Zambrano did not remain landless, for by 1791 he had managed to acquire a ranch called Nuestra Señora de la Candelaria de las Calaveras. Although he died that year, his children, among whom one studied for the priesthood and served as Béxar's parish priest in the early nineteenth century and another served as a deacon, built on his work and became prominent livestock owners in their own right. Unlike the other prominent ranchers, at least one of the Zambranos, Juan Manuel, turned his attention to the wool market by the turn of the century.[63]

VI

Crop and livestock agriculture faced the same problem in expanding beyond the settlement's immediate vicinity as had the growth of the town—Indian hostilities and the presence of missions. In the most peaceful of times farmers and ranchers were subject to theft of crops and animals, and occasionally death. As a result, much ranch land was held tentatively throughout the century, forestalling the development of formal, well-organized estates *(haciendas)*. In many instances, missions and settlers battled over pastures and animals, keeping open the question of ownership. Consequently, at the end of the eighteenth century Béxar's countryside was tenuously organized into properties enjoying little legal or economic status, most of which were only temporarily occupied each year.

Maize and cattle, the most distinguishing features of New Spain's economy after silver, were Béxar's chief products. While both found markets in San Antonio's garrison, for a time cattle became the basis of Béxar's only export activity, tying San Antonio to the colonial economy. Ironically, while maize production (and agricultural production in general) was always restrained and never functioned at full capacity, the area's cattle were exploited to the point of real scarcity.

Livestock raising, an early small-scale activity, experienced a dramatic boom in the 1770s and 1780s. The previous small exports of cattle products—dried meat, hides, tallow, fat—were replaced for a time by large cattle drives to frontier presidios and towns below the Rio Grande as far south as Saltillo and for a time into Louisiana. Thus, late-eighteenth-century Béxar became a part of New Spain's silver economy, if only marginally. Bexareños attempted to reap too many cattle crops in the last three decades of the century, however. Wanton slaughter and large exports of beeves resulted in a critical shortage of the wild stock on which so many depended.

6

Making a Living

The establishment of any royal monopoly is made impractical because coin does not circulate, and all sales and purchases are made by the barter of one set of goods for another. Also, the poverty of this citizenry being so great, consumption is restricted and it is paid in fruit, chickens, eggs, soap, and by those who have the most, with beeves and horses.

—GOVERNOR JUAN MARÍA, BARÓN DE RIPPERDÁ, 1771[1]

San Antonio was not a village where each family merely farmed its own plot and herded a handful of cattle. A certain degree of self-sufficiency was common to all Bexareños, but a market, outside the family, did exist for local produce. The presidio's presence combined with the town's growth, slow as it often was, brought increasing numbers of artisans and merchants to Béxar, contributing to the economy's diversity. The more important farmers, ranchers, and the presidio all required manpower, contributing to the emergence of a substantial labor sector in the population. In the money-scarce environment of the frontier, most of this economic activity relied heavily on barter and on one form or another of credit. This limited economic growth, however, was neither extensive nor intensive, perpetuating Béxar's sense of backwardness throughout the colonial period.

I

Study of the early development of manual labor in San Antonio must begin with the arrival of the Canary Islanders. During the 1720s there were "helpers" present at Mission Valero and the presidio, but what functions these individuals performed is not known. At least in the case of the mission, the helpers were soldiers stationed there to assist the missionaries in the training of the Indians in agriculture and herding practices.[2] It is probable that, by the late 1720s, at least some of those identified as helpers of the presidio were involved in farming the garrison's irrigated fields.

Although scanty, the surviving evidence suggests that from the town's earliest days there were men available to perform agricultural and other manual labor. Some of these men were employed as *sirvientes* (servants), *mozos* (hands) or *campistas* (field hands), or as *jornaleros* (day laborers).[3] The presence of men hired by families of such limited means as those of Béxar should not be surprising in light of the evidence from other parts of the frontier, where even individuals considered to be vagabonds employed servants.[4] Such a practice was a natural outgrowth both of the family's quest for an adequate labor supply without expending a disproportionate amount of its resources, and of the need of other individuals to subsist.

The labor situation during the mid-century period is confused by alternating periods of scarcity and plenty. As early as Franquis de Lugo's administration, the Isleños sought to meet their labor needs with mission Indians. The missionaries' protests resulted in a lawsuit that was settled out of court in 1745. Among the terms of the agreement, the townspeople dropped their demand that mission Indians be allowed to work for them, indicating the availability of workers from other sources. And, indeed, in that same year *Alcalde* Juan José Montes de Oca issued an ordinance requiring the unemployed and transients to find employers. Other orders on the same subject were issued in 1754, 1756, and 1761, but in 1771 the town council complained that the foundings of San Xavier, San Sabá, and Orcoquisac presidios had drained the town of workers. During the 1770s new ordinances were issued requiring the registration of new arrivals and gainful employment by all able-bodied men.[5]

Toward the end of the century Béxar appears to have enjoyed an adequate labor supply. In the absence of consistent information gathered by those entrusted with census taking, it is difficult to say much more. Lack of property ownership by the majority of family heads appearing in the 1779 census makes it clear that most men worked for others or rented the land on which they worked for themselves. The number of servants employed by artisans and tradesmen is also indicative of an available pool of laborers, most probably consisting of those listed as *jornaleros*. The summary census of 1792 makes this clear—only twenty-five men were listed as farmers, probably those who owned farmland, but there were 556 laborers listed, probably adult sons, servants, day laborers, and tenants without farmland of their own.[6] The availability of labor is also attested to by the absence at the end of the century of any ordinances requiring the physically fit to find employment.

Coerced or not, manual labor barely commanded a subsistence wage. Field work was probably paid in kind, as was most ranch work. In terms of value, agricultural pay probably differed little from the pay for other manual labor in town. The standard wage for unskilled labor was one-quarter peso (two *reales*) per day. This included such work as quarrying stone, helping on construction projects, and menial work. For example, the two men usually hired by the governor to cook and tend to the needs of visiting Indians received the standard wage. Laborers were not paid when they did not work.[7]

Livestock work was an entirely different matter. As early as 1735 livestock raisers paid a premium to those who worked with their cattle. Matías Treviño earned twelve pesos per month (three *reales* per day), two *almudes* of maize per week (the equivalent of another peso per month), and a horse from each stockman, for guarding the cattle of the town.[8] The premium increased when livestock operations were removed from the town's immediate vicinity. Beginning in the 1770s and lasting through the end of the century, numerous documents point to a daily wage of one peso, sometimes paid in goods, as the standard for roundups and cattle drives. Some individuals received somewhat less, and on occasion participants received shares of the cattle gathered.[9]

The high cost of ranching labor was due to the Indian menace and the difficulty of the job, which probably resulted in a limited labor pool. In 1787 Governor Martínez commented that the town's *vecinos* paid *vaqueros* (cowboys) one peso daily for more than a month sometimes, without catching anything. And, even if captured, the cattle might stampede and be lost.[10] At about the same time some ranchers complained against the imposition of yet another tax on the grounds that, aside from those taxes they already paid, they had to pay "mozos one peso daily to go as far as fifty to one hundred leagues away to get [cattle], often without success."[11]

The degree to which most hired workers were subject to an insecure existence is outlined in a complaint lodged against Governor Muñoz. In late 1790 he was accused of forcing the workingmen of Béxar to labor on public works and to watch over the horse herd without timely pay. "The working *vecinos* and poor wretched peons have not been paid by him in the last three months, so that the day the latter do not work for themselves or their masters they do not eat."[12] Other evidence also points to the unhappy circumstances of many laborers. In 1760 Juan Enrique Otón was

beaten by his employer, Pedro Ocón y Trillo. Otón filed charges against
Ocón, who was sentenced to cover the expenses of Otón's treatment and
of the proceedings. Governor Navarrete overturned the sentence, however, on Ocón's appeal that he beat Otón for not obeying him while
working on his field.[13] Payments in kind and advances on salary meant that
laborers sometimes found themselves in debt to their employers. Manuel
Castro, a thirty year-old *español* accused of stealing horses and running
away from his employer, claimed that all he wanted was to find his father
to obtain enough money to pay a thirty-peso debt to his master, Clemente
Delgado. Found guilty, he was sentenced to time served plus one month
at public works and ordered to find "a master in whom he [Castro] may
have the highest confidence, so that with his salary he may dress and
maintain his family."[14]

The cost of labor may be one reason why ranchers themselves took to
the field. Often they relied on their sons for much of the work involved,
but participation in field operations by the younger ranchers was common.
Often the ranchers worked in teams, assisting each other. And, in at least
one case, a herd owner participated in a roundup because he was offered
pay. Cattle drives were generally made by more than one rancher, undoubtedly to cut costs.[15]

Although job status and ethnicity were related to some degree, there
were no clear racial boundaries in work. Many *mozos* on cattle drives were
the sons of prominent families; they worked side-by-side with mission
Indians and the settlement's mixed-blood residents. In 1779 a third of all
campistas, those who did agricultural and ranching work for others, were
españoles, and seven of them even employed their own servants. Some
within the group owned their own homes and agricultural land. Only
among *jornaleros*, those hired on a day-to-day basis, was there a clear
absence of *españoles* as well as of property ownership.

II

Aside from family members, domestic work was done by servants, as
well as slaves and *criados* (literally brought up, that is, domestics raised by
the household). Indian captives, some of whom were *criados*, constituted
another source of household labor. By the time Béxar was founded, the
practice of taking captured young Indians into individual households as
servants was well established. During the early hostilities with the
Apaches, Béxar's missionaries accused townspeople of conducting slave-

hunting expeditions. Criticizing the motives and execution of a 1739 campaign, Fr. Benito Fernández de Santa Ana wrote to the guardian of his college:

> . . . the expedition was profitable only to those who had horses and other goods, which they sold at excessively high prices; and it is ridiculous that these same persons should claim certificates as servants of the King our Lord, when they were interested in what I have stated, and had greater hopes of a considerable prize of horses, hides, and Indian men and women to serve them.[16]

Upon his return to San Antonio, after a campaign against the Apaches in 1745, Captain Toribio de Urrutia brought back numerous hostages.[17] Fourteen of them, all between the ages of one and seven years, were baptized immediately after their arrival.[18] These, like young Apaches captured during previous campaigns, were raised as servants in the homes of townspeople. The practice of taking in non-mission Indians continued into the latter part of the century, and beginning in the late 1750s, Bexareños took Comanches as well as Apaches into their homes.[19]

Aside from the inexpensive labor provided by these "adopted" Indian servants, slavery was also present in Béxar from the settlement's early years but should be considered more a matter of status than of economics, since the cost of Indian servitude was much less. An exchange of male slaves between Josefa Flores y Valdez and Governor Justo Boneo y Morales in 1743 mentions that Flores's husband, Miguel Núñez Morillo, had bought Luis, a twenty-one year old black slave, for two hundred pesos in 1736 while visiting Mexico City.[20] The presence of black and mulatto slaves in Béxar is also documented in the parish's baptismal and burial records. By 1777 there were fifteen slaves living in Béxar, four male and eleven female;[21] in 1796 there were fifteen slaves in six households. Merchant Antonio Baca's slaves included females thirty, five, and two years old, and an eleven-year-old male.[22]

Servitude was not limited to Indians and slaves, however. As in other parts of northern New Spain, many households relied on mixed-blood and Spanish servants. The census of 1796 records the variety and extent of servitude in Béxar: of the sixty-five extended family groups recorded that year, thirty contained servants. Juan José de la Santa, a merchant, had an assortment of races among his servants, including Spanish and mulatto males and mestizo and Indian females. The Indian shoemaker, Juan

Blanco de Sierra Guadalcazar, had three journeymen of different races in his household, a *coyote*, a *mulato*, and an Indian. Curiously enough, the single largest group of domestic servants consisted of male *españoles* (eleven) followed by female Indians (ten).[23]

III

For those who tired of the difficult life on the range and in the fields, there was always military service. Enlistments lasted ten years and were usually served in the same company. During Béxar's first decade, when the civilian population was too small for the military to draw from, recruitment was difficult. Governor Fernando Pérez de Almazán complained in 1724 that replacing troops was costly and time consuming because of the reluctance of people to move to Texas.[24] But as the civilian population increased, military service became an attractive alternative to the uncertainties of farming and herding. Leading the way were four Canary Islanders who, soon after their arrival, sold their property and enlisted in garrisons around the province; two entered service at Béxar. By the last quarter of the century the garrison had become San Antonio's largest employer of local manpower.[25]

As the settlement's population stabilized, it became the major source of new recruits for the presidio.[26] Sons followed fathers into military service and, in turn, sent their sons to serve the King. Throughout the century Coahuila remained an important source of recruits, but some soldiers came from as far away as Puebla, New Orleans, and France. Not surprisingly, most of those who signed up for service came from an agricultural background, although desperate times drove an occasional artisan into the financial security of military life.

The case of Tomás del Toro offers a good study of a fairly regular practice until the 1770s. Toro, a native of Coahuila, was first recruited for military service at the Presidio de San Sabá in 1769, was part of the garrison transferred to serve at Béxar in 1770, and was among those discharged when the Béxar garrison was reorganized in 1773. He remained in Béxar working as a field hand, at least part of the time working as a *mozo* of Francisco Flores, and participating in cattle drives out of the province. Less than five years after his discharge, Toro once again enlisted for service.[27] After weighing the vagaries and dangers of civilian life on the frontier against the perils and regimentation of military life, he opted for the latter.

Movement to and from military service was easy because in many respects life in a presidial company differed little from civilian life on the frontier. Soldiers on horse herd or convoy duty practiced the arts of the cowboy and muleteer. The town's defense and the larger campaigns against hostile Indians were joint ventures between the military and civilians. Construction work in the presidio fell upon soldiers not otherwise occupied, and their service at the missions often meant supervising agricultural and irrigation work. Furthermore, soldiers who married lived in their own homes and often acquired town lots, where they could grow at least some of their food.[28] In all these respects, the differences between military and civilian life blurred.

Despite the unscrupulous practices of some officers who controlled provisioning up to the 1770s, soldiers usually had access to a steady, if expensive, source of supplies and provisions. Matters improved toward the end of the century with the introduction of regulations for the election of company *habilitados* (paymasters). The soldiers' pay, four hundred pesos annually in the 1720s, reduced to 365 pesos by the Regulation of 1729 and further reduced to 290 pesos in 1772, averaged out at a much higher rate than the annual wages day laborers could expect owing to their unsteady work source. That the reforms of the 1770s did some good is evinced by the few soldiers found to be in debt to the garrison store when Governor Cabello inspected the books in 1779, as compared to the situation earlier in the century.[29] Moreover, the ten-year enlistment offered significant insulation from the vagaries of the frontier economy. It is not surprising, therefore, that military service constituted an attractive option for many frontiersmen.

IV

If, at least by the latter part of the century, Béxar's garrison was composed mostly of local men, the reverse was true in the crafts sector of the economy. Béxar's land-based, essentially subsistence economy, which relied on family effort, probably limited the opportunities for young boys to be involved in crafts. Consequently, throughout the century San Antonio imported most of its artisans, some from French Louisiana, Spain, and France. Francisco Guadalupe Calaorra, a carpenter, came from Ireland, according to the 1779 census. The predominance of outsiders and non-*españoles* within the ranks of the craftsmen attests to opportunities available on the frontier at a time of economic instability for artisans in more

central parts of the Spanish empire, particularly for those who were not
españoles.[30]

The financial success of the artisans could not have been great, however.
The incidence of artisans entering military service, and their limited property ownership as a group, attests to their inability to make a living from
practicing their crafts. Just as in other parts of colonial Latin America,
artisans in Béxar turned to other economic activities to supplement their
craft income. Many of them farmed or tended gardens. One tailor, Sebastián Monjaras, became tithe collector for the province in 1776 and led
cattle drives to Saltillo. The carpenter Juan Jupier, a native of France, set
up an impressive shop that, from the inventory of tools, must have been
capable of turning out sophisticated work. Yet Jupier practiced other occupations. His ownership of lancets, dentist's forceps, and scraper marked
him as a practical surgeon, the only type available in Béxar until the second
decade of the nineteenth century. He was also a tinker. At the time of his
death in 1783, Jupier owed three doors with frames, the boards for another
door, a small window, and three chairs. He was owed ten large boards,
one-quarter peso for fixing a pot, and one-quarter peso for a bloodletting.
An exception to multiple activities was José Lambremon. A New Orleans
native who came to "Béxar to seek my fortune," he appears to have practiced no other profession than that of tailor in the 1790s.[31]

Perhaps the most important trade practiced was that of blacksmith or
gunsmith, occupations often practiced by the same individual in Béxar.
Marcos Ruiz, hired in Querétaro to serve as gunsmith and blacksmith at
Los Adaes, spent a short time in San Antonio, during which the garrison
accrued a debt of more than sixteen hundred pesos. One of the earliest
French artisans was the blacksmith Juan Banul. He arrived in Béxar shortly
before the Canary Islanders, hired to work at Mission Valero. Soon, however, he set up shop in town, where his services were, it seems, considered
indispensable. When the commandant general advised Governor Cabello
in 1780 that a gunsmith was being hired in Coahuila to whom all broken
guns should be sent for repair, the latter replied that not only did he have
a qualified gunsmith for his company, but that a knowledgeable assistant
had also been hired. Another blacksmith, Juan Leal, was one of the few
home-grown artisans.[32]

Expertise in construction was always in demand. Béxar seems to have
had one or two masons and carpenters from the earliest days, but other,
more skilled craftsmen from the interior were brought in for the parish
and mission churches, reflecting on the skill of local masons. In one of the
biggest setbacks to Canary Islander ascendance, Antonio Rodríguez Me-

deros failed to live up to his 1742 promise to build a stone town hall and jail for 270 pesos, and the following year the town council turned to two *agregados*, Manuel de Carabajal to haul the stone, and Alberto López to supervise the work. By the 1770s the town hall was in need of reconstruction. Despite the services of one master mason and four associates, as well as one carpenter, major work on the town hall was again required in the early 1790s.[33]

Versatility was also found in the transport business. The movement of building materials and goods into, around, and out of San Antonio, was in the hands of two distinct groups of individuals. One group was involved in local transportation. By the latter part of the eighteenth century a small handful of individuals who considered themselves teamsters had appeared. Many teamsters were, however, farmers who took advantage of their oxen and carts to provide needed hauling. Carters quarried and hauled stone for public works and homes. After lumber became scarce in the San Antonio area, cart owners and others formed lumbering expeditions to the Medina and Guadalupe rivers. Some made a living providing the community with firewood, which was often sold by the cartload.[34]

The town hall's reconstruction in 1790 offers a good deal of evidence about the carting business. Although much of the work was donated, the prices assigned to work were the going rate and provide an accurate gauge of the value of such activities. Sixteen men provided the carting for 361 loads of stone needed for the project at a rate of one-half peso each. The quarrying itself was done at a rate of one-eighth peso per load. The three men who hauled the twenty-one carts of wood shingles were paid just under two pesos per load, yet the lumberers themselves were paid just one-quarter peso per day.[35] The difference in prices between the transporting of stone and wood was due to the distances traveled.

Long-distance hauling was in the hands of a second group of individuals, *arrieros* (muleteers). Primitive roads, most no more than trails, made pack mules the only reasonable form of transport into and out of the province. A number of townspeople were involved in the freighting business. Some were independent muleteers, others merchants who maintained their own droves, others the employees of the first two. There seems to have been enough business, at least during relatively peaceful times, for some mule skinners to make a living from freight charges. Others supplemented their income by participating in roundups and other work.[36]

For most of the century mule driving was a dangerous occupation.[37] In April 1770 Captain Menchaca informed the viceroy of the death of four muleteers about fifty miles from the presidio and of the extraordinary measures necessary to protect the presidio's supply train.

> [The Nations of the North] have the land so obstructed that no one can traverse it. For this reason the governor saw himself forced to reinforce with salaried men, twenty-five armed Indians and fifteen soldiers, the twenty-six man escort that was conducting this presidio's convoy; which is something that has never been seen until now.[38]

In 1779 Miguel de la Garza lost, to Apaches, thirty-eight mules he was pasturing.[39]

The dangers and difficulties of travel in the north were reflected in the high freight rates charged. The usual price of one peso per mule over the ninety or so mile course to La Bahía added as much as fifty percent to the cost of a *fanega* of maize at Béxar. Freight costs between the Saltillo area and San Antonio remained as high late in the century as they had been earlier. The forty-five mules that brought the garrison's supplies in 1735 cost the captain five hundred pesos, just over eleven pesos each. Fifty-three years later, the cost of one mule load to Real de los Alamos, approximately one hundred miles west of Saltillo, was sixteen pesos, and the freight from San Luis Potosí was eighteen pesos per mule.[40]

V

Distance and high transportation costs were only two of the obstacles residents faced in meeting their supply needs. Shoddy goods, price gouging, specie scarcity, lack of commercial competition, and the disruptions occasioned by hostile Indians contributed to the problem. Although San Antonio's commercial activity expanded throughout the century, the limitations imposed by Béxar's remoteness, as well as the province's small population, created no great fortunes and few moderate ones.

Through at least the 1740s, the civilian sector accounted for very little of Béxar's commercial activity; most merchandise was available through the presidio. The commander received a power of attorney from the company to collect their salaries, which he transmitted to his agent in Mexico City; the latter collected the money and sent back a shipment of goods. Local farmers who provided maize and other produce were paid in *libranzas* (bills of exchange) made against the supplier or some other merchant with whom the commander had dealings. At the presidio store, after an initial distribution of arriving merchandise, soldiers and their families obtained what they needed and the price of the goods was charged against the soldiers' salaries. This process was modified by the Regulation only to the extent of making the presidial commander responsible for business and prohibiting the governor from interfering.[41]

Because the garrison payroll was converted to supplies and provisions, the whole company underwrote the governors' or commanders' commercial activities. Miscellaneous and incidental expenses and purchases from the company store were paid by the captain (and later by the paymaster) and debited to the soldiers' accounts. As all soldiers received the same pay, those with few expenses subsidized those with large families and greater needs. Moreover, because the merchandise in the convoy might include more than the soldiers needed, the garrison store was also open to the public.[42]

In many respects, this system employed the same methods found in other sectors of New Spain's economy, particularly in mining. Powerful commercial houses in Mexico City took advantage of the general scarcity of specie in the viceroyalty to operate a commercial system that relied largely on credit and on the *libranzas* they controlled.[43] The system had an adverse impact on local commerce, however, inhibiting the commercial development of the province by preventing an adequate circulation of specie and making the economic environment inhospitable to independent merchants and local producers. It is not surprising, therefore, that full-time retail merchants did not put in an appearance in Texas until about the 1760s.

Needless to say, the system was open to abuse.[44] The *aviadores* (supply merchants), and consequently the commanders, consistently overcharged the soldiery, often for shoddy and rotten goods. For instance, after a particularly small and poor quality shipment in 1743, the commander, Urrutia, found it expedient to put his *aviador* in Mexico City, Juan de Angulo, on trial *in absentia*. Among the testimony taken was that of Pedro Ocón y Trillo, who claimed to have been in the province since the time of Martín de Alarcón (ca. 1718) without ever witnessing such a small or poor shipment. In the first shipment in more than two years, during which time some families had stopped going to church "because they are naked," only twenty-seven of the forty-three soldiers had received goods. Francisco Hernández and others declared that the civilian population had not received even a pair of shoes from the shipment and that, instead of conditions improving, they were getting worse. All the witnesses told stories regarding the poor quality of the goods. Although the outcome of the case is unknown, the proceedings of the company, Captain Urrutia, and his family against Juan de Angulo, the supplying merchant, were still in progress in 1747, and Angulo was still the commander's supplier two years later.[45]

Charges of excessive profits were also made against Urrutia's successors, Captain Luis Antonio Menchaca and Governor Ripperdá. The Marqués de Rubí, during his inspection tour, chastised Menchaca for the company's lack of cleanliness and uniformity, and for the poor quality and scantiness of the goods in which the soldiers' salaries were paid. Rubí also found fault in the high prices charged for these goods, as well as in the excessive distribution of *piloncillo* (brown sugar in cone form), soap, laces, trims and silks. The inspector did find, however, that the company was well equipped and mounted and that the prices on locally available produce, as well as some of the more important imports, had been reduced. Governor Ripperdá was the target of criticism during his successor's review of the company paymaster's activities. The soldiers complained that, because Ripperdá had undertaken the supply shipments at his own risk, he had overcharged on many items, as well as forced soldiers to take useless items. Ripperdá was subsequently charged with the relatively minor overcharging for some cows he sold to one soldier, and with forcing others to take twelve pesos in items they did not need.[46]

The paymaster system instituted in 1773 seems to have worked somewhat better in San Antonio than in many other parts of the frontier. The new procedure allowed the paymaster to collect a 2 percent commission for handling the garrison's outfitting. In 1779 the soldiers reported that they were receiving their daily allowance of one-quarter peso and their monthly ration of maize, beef, sugar, and soap, and that their accounts were being settled every four months. The prices being charged for goods from the company store were fair, being no more than what was being charged at their point of purchase in Saltillo or San Luis Potosí. A small invoice from 1788 reflects the limited margin of profit allowed in prices under the new system. Because part of the shipment was coin, the retail price for the other goods was not enough to cover the costs of packing, transport, and the paymaster's commission.[47]

Although the new system worked, it was not without its intrigues. In his first year in office, Governor Cabello faced a plot by former captain Luis Antonio Menchaca to have his son elected paymaster. The plan was an attempt to get around Cabello's order that *vecinos* and merchants not extend credit to the soldiers. The governor moved to block Menchaca's election by forcing a tie vote and explaining the matter to the commandant general, who chose another officer. A couple of years later, when Sergeant Mariano Rodríguez spread rumors that paymaster Francisco Amangual was transferring merchandise to Angel Navarro's store, Amangual went to great lengths to prove his innocence and insisted on stiff punishment for Rodríguez.[48]

Despite its shortcomings, the *habilitación* (garrison store) continued to exercise a public commercial function into the 1790s. For most of the century the garrison store also handled the various *estancos* (public monopolies) over tobacco, stamped paper, and playing cards, as no private merchant in town was able to afford the bonds required to assume the concessions. Available inventories from the 1790s also reveal that the company store continued to serve broad needs. The presence of a wide range of cloth, laces, women's and children's shoes, and even plows indicates that the store served the needs of the soldiers' dependents as well. The garrison store was also responsible for maintaining a supply of gifts for the Indians.[49]

VI

The establishment of the paymaster system also affected the town's developing civilian commerce. As early as the mid-1730s there were individuals in Béxar who were involved in commerce, at least on a part-time basis. The slight evidence available suggests that they handled only a limited amount of goods, which they acquired through sale of hides and, later, of dried meat and tallow. Some of their goods were probably acquired with the proceeds from their sale of maize to the presidio. At least some of these limited goods being sold by individuals were marketed through the presidio store.[50] The very limited nature of commercial activity in Béxar as late as the 1750s is indicated in the town council's own declaration that Béxar was suffering from the "the lack of commerce that this province offers."[51] It is also of note that none of the town's early records mentions a store and that the first ordinance regarding commercial transactions—the certification of weights and measures—does not appear until 1752.[52]

Fray Benito Fernández's 1741 representation in a complaint by the Isleños against the missions, offers one of the few glimpses at civilian commercial activity in Béxar. According to the Franciscan, the *agregados* Miguel Núñez Morillo and José Antonio Rodríguez, as well as the Isleño

Vicente Alvarez Travieso, maintained "themselves quite comfortably by trading." The Leal men were more merchant and Antonio Santos more a stonemason than they were farmers. One Isleño was a carpenter and four had become soldiers. Also, some of the town's public officials were not farmers.[53] Fray Fernández's comments may be excused as somewhat exaggerated, yet it is nevertheless apparent that many men exercised a number of economic roles simultaneously. Early merchants and tradesmen were often the same men who controlled the town's agricultural and livestock resources; their commercial activities were part of their agricultural endeavors.

Records of merchants who were not principally farmers or ranchers do not appear until the 1770s. These mercantile specialists, attracted by the population boom that followed the garrison's expansion and the transfer of the East Texas population to San Antonio, and aided by the establishment of the paymaster system, opened stores and derived their principal income from trade. As in the case of artisans, however, most of the important merchants were outsiders, some of them Spaniards.[54] Like the artisans and those townspeople with commercial interests, the merchants often participated in other economic activities.

The only Béxar-born man listed as a merchant who did not have an interest in farming or ranching—as the evidence to date reveals—was Antonio Rodríguez Baca. The son of Marcos Rodríguez y Baca and María Teresa Ximénez, Antonio grew up in obscurity. He first appears in the public record as a soldier in the garrison. What Baca did between the end of his enlistment in December 1783 and his election as one of the sponsors of the feast of the Virgin of Guadalupe for 1789 is not known, but to be chosen for such an honor required some status in the community and a reasonable source of income with which to meet the obligations. Among Baca's commercial activities were supplying maize, meat, and *aguardiente* (brandy) to visiting Indians. The maize apparently was bought from the growers, while the meat he captured and slaughtered. He employed a number of men whom the records show he kept fairly busy. He had his own drove of mules, which he used to collect and transport pecans and maize. He also had a commercial interest in buffalo hides.[55] Baca's success endured well into the nineteenth century, when he bought substantial amounts of farmland at Valero and later made a substantial monetary contribution to the Mexican insurgency in Texas.[56]

Reorganization of Texas in the early 1770s brought the first merchants from outside the province into Béxar, many of them, apparently, seeking to escape difficult pasts. Marcos Vidal, whose 1773 account book survives, operated an establishment that sold a little of everything. Although most of his business was in brandy and wine, other products included bananas, chocolate, raisins, flour, soap, shoes, and cloth. Vidal's stay in Béxar was not long, however. Having been caught with a wide assortment of contraband goods in the area of Nacogdoches, he attempted to make his escape into the interior and was drowned in the Nueces River in 1775 or 1776.[57]

Other merchants who arrived in Béxar about this time included: Santiago Villaseñor, who opened a store on the presidial plaza; Juan Baptista de Isurieta, who was implicated in a contraband case in 1780 and fled Béxar; and José de la Santa, a traveling petty merchant who, by 1777, had worked his way into the inner circles of Béxar society, been elected to the post of regidor for 1778, and been reelected several times. By 1784 Santa's outstanding debts outside the province began to catch up with him, and Governor Cabello reported that Santa maintained himself in a rented house by the work of his two daughters. Within two years, Santa's daughters had moved to Saltillo and Governor Cabello was convinced Santa would never return to Béxar.[58]

The most successful and prominent of the 1770s merchants was Fernando Veramendi, born in Pamplona, Spain, in 1743 or 1744. He first established himself in Texas at Presidio La Bahía sometime around 1770.[59] Business brought him on occasion to San Antonio, where in 1776 he married María Josefa Granados, a Canary Islander descendant, and thus guaranteed his acceptance in the community. Once established in San Antonio, Veramendi's business thrived. He opened a store, acted as moneylender, and bought extensive tracts of agricultural land. He served in the city's militia, as *regidor* in the *cabildo* of 1779, and was elected senior *regidor* for the year 1783. That same year, while on a business trip to Mexico City, he was killed by Mescalero Apaches near the presidio of San Juan Bautista, Coahuila.[60]

Veramendi's shop was well stocked and remained so for years after his death. Toward the end of 1785 it could still offer merchandise less expensively than did Luis Mariano Menchaca's store. The store inventory reveals that Veramendi was basically a draper. With the exception of some cups and bowls, fair amounts of chickpeas, sugar, and rice, and a larger amount of chocolate, his stock consisted of a wide assortment of cloth, silks, laces, buttons, needles, and other sewing needs. His account book included debts owed by other Béxar merchants, Tomás Travieso, Simón de Arocha, Luis Mariano Menchaca, and even the garrison store. On the other hand, Veramendi had only two debts at the time he made his will, one in Mexico City for 2,283 pesos, and another of 74 pesos to a merchant of Candela, Coahuila.[61]

The 1793 census recorded a total of seven men whose principal occupation was commerce. All but two—Angel Navarro and Manuel Berasadi—have previously been mentioned. Of Berasadi nothing is known; apparently his stay in Béxar was brief and uneventful. Navarro, a native of Corsica, left his home at age fourteen. He traveled in Italy and Spain before coming to New Spain in the late 1760s. He worked for a merchant of Nuevo León for eight years before coming to Béxar as a merchant in his own right in 1776 or 1777. Navarro was another shop-owning merchant who had substantial dealings in cloth. While Navarro's business success was more limited than Veramendi's, he did acquire considerable social status and was elected to the town council on numerous occasions between 1783 and the end of the century. He too married a Béxar native, probably for love rather than social gain, since it appears she was of humble parentage.[62]

VII

The stories of these men of commerce should not obscure the fact that Béxar, and Texas in general, suffered from an economic backwardness that was often a source of comment. In 1771, after being informed that Tejanos would have to pay for the salt they gathered below the Nueces River, Governor Ripperdá responded that the province had previously been exempted from taxes because of the continuing warfare with the Indians and the lack of means of the citizenry.[63] A dozen years later, at the height of the cattle exports, the town council was asked to make a list of the *pulperías* (grocery stores) in San Antonio. Its response was that it

> could not carry out the order because there are none at the moment. Most of the vecinos maintain themselves from their own fields and ranches, and when there is some little surplus to be sold, the amounts are so small as to not merit attention, and furthermore, the goods are generally exchanged for others since the majority of the vecinos are very poor and only barely manage to exist in the face of the Indians.[64]

In 1794 Governor Muñoz made a similar, if stronger, observation. Asked to recommend some individual in Béxar with the resources to handle the tobacco monopoly, he could only suggest a merchant of La Bahía, stating:

The other citizens have no other goods than their houses, their not very valuable pieces of land, and they are indebted to one another; for although some of them have small herds of cattle, these are exposed to the hazards of the countryside.

This capital's few merchants have few assets and are indebted to those of Saltillo, and aside from not being able to guarantee the proceeds from the monopoly on their own, they cannot even be received as bondsmen. And to prove what has been stated, Your Grace may receive information in the said town of Saltillo from D. José Francisco Pereyra, D. Miguel Lobo, and D. Felipe Calsado.[65]

Credit and debt, therefore, were the economic principles which made possible even the little commerce that existed. All too often debts were compounded by payment in worthless *libranzas*. Because coin was scarce throughout the viceroyalty, many commercial transactions were conducted through a complicated system of bills of exchange. A person receiving goods from another would make out a *libranza* to the seller against a third party with whom the buyer had credit. It was the responsibility of the seller to get the *libranza* to the paying party. Over time, these bills even became negotiable through fourth parties—as the original payer might be far removed from the residence of the holder, the latter might endorse the bill to a fourth party selling other commodities, or in payment of a previous debt. It was now this fourth party's responsibility to cash the voucher. In effect, *libranzas* became both a medium of exchange and credit, as the issuer enjoyed the benefits of what he purchased without having to produce anything of immediate value.

Bad debts and bad *libranzas* were ubiquitous throughout the colonial period. Francisco Fernández de Rumayor's case against various Bexareños serves as an example of the tortuous complexities of the system and the problems of debt for economic development. In the spring of 1736 Rumayor's agent, Juan de Barro, arrived in Béxar in an effort to collect bad debts from Juan Curbelo; Martín Lorenzo de Armas; José Antonio Rodríguez, who had given him a bad bill of exchange for four hundred pesos; and Fermín de Ibiricú, the captain's cashier, who owed the balance on a loan of 3,962 pesos. Ibiricú turned over a *libranza* for 120 pesos (payment for twenty horses he had sold) and promised to go to La Bahía to sell some mules and mares to raise more money, and then on to Rio Grande to collect from various debtors who owed him more than the balance.

According to Rodríguez, he had received the *libranza* that Rumayor could not cash from Captain José de Urrutia as payment for some goods. Rumayor could not get Juan de Angulo, the captain's *aviador* to make good the *libranza* and so Rodríguez now faced confiscation of his property. Rodríguez, therefore, demanded from Captain Urrutia that he make good on the bill of exchange and so the officer complied by making out two new notes, one for four hundred pesos and another for ninety-three pesos to cover Barro's costs.[66]

After cattle exports began in the mid-1770s, debt became an often-stated reason for requesting an export license. Juan José Flores, the tithe collector in 1781, requested permission to export some cattle in order to meet his obligation. He had made loans that could not be collected before the tithe was due. Francisco Xavier Rodríguez wanted to build a flour mill but was short on funds, so he asked permission to export three hundred head of cattle. In 1786 Amador Delgado was selected as an assistant sponsor of the feast of Guadalupe; not having the means to cover the costs, he requested permission to export some cattle.[67]

The continued precarious state of Béxar's commercial sector is illustrated by the case of Juan Timoteo Barrera, appointed administrator of the royal monopolies in 1794. Although Governor Muñoz suggested that no one in Béxar had the necessary means to deal effectively with the post, the administrator at Monclova, Juan Ignacio de Arispe, appointed Barrera, perhaps because his father had previously been tithe collector for Texas.[68] Barrera's first two years as administrator of monopolies seemed to flow smoothly, but by 1797 there were signs of trouble. First, Barrera asked to be relieved of his charge. To Arispe's request that he recommend a replacement, Muñoz sarcastically replied that Arispe must know better who could do the job, as Arispe had ignored Muñoz's previous recommendation. Second, when in 1798 Barrera asked for and received permission from Arispe to travel to Nacogdoches on business, Muñoz and the latter once again argued over Barrera's competence. Arispe appealed to Silvestre Díaz de la Vega; the monopoly's director general in Mexico City sided with the governor after Muñoz had an opportunity to explain the matter.[69]

By early 1799 the depth of Barrera's financial woes became apparent. He had not turned over 3,518 pesos in income from the monopoly for 1797 and owed another 4,615 pesos for 1798. When confronted, Barrera disagreed with Arispe's totals and stated that he could only turn over three thousand pesos, the balance having to wait until he sold two hundred head of cattle at Béxar. Arispe pressed the matter, and Muñoz suggested that Barrera's property could be confiscated, even though his goods would not put a dent in the debt. In May 1799 Arispe and Muñoz agreed to accept the three thousand pesos and allow Barrera time to get the money he needed from his father-in-law, Antonio Gil Ybarbo, who was on business at Nacogdoches.[70]

In October, Arispe, once again demanding payment of the 5,311 pesos Barrera still owed, asked Interim Governor Elguézabal to proceed against Barrera's property and that of his father-in-law, who was Barrera's bondsman. Further, the governor was to immediately turn over management of the monopoly to a trustworthy individual. Despite the confiscation, it was not until March 1800 that Arispe and Barrera worked out a plan for paying off the debt. The absence of further correspondence regarding Barrera suggests the debt was retired. Arispe, however, continued to have trouble with Barrera's successors, who also had difficulties meeting the proper requirements for the post.[71]

VIII

San Antonio de Béxar led a marginal economic existence throughout the eighteenth century. Local markets for agricultural products and the export of livestock and cattle byproducts only marginally tied Béxar to the broader colonial economy. Without mineral resources to exploit or cash crops to develop, and because of the difficulties in transportation, San Antonio's economy saw only limited growth throughout the century.

Under such restrictive conditions there was little opportunity for specialization. Most individuals performed two or more economic functions, including cultivation of some of their own food. Those at the bottom of the economic ladder labored under unstable circumstances, and emigration for them was not a viable option, since conditions were similar throughout the north. Most of them were also held to the town by bonds of birth and kinship. Wages, directly tied to work done, sometimes were not paid at all. Livestock work was much more remunerative than farm work or other manual labor, but it was seasonal and dangerous. Compared to the uncertainties of manual labor, the presidio was an oasis of stability. While the work was little different from that done by civilian laborers, the dangers were not much greater, and long enlistment periods afforded relative economic security.

The concentration of local labor in farming and ranching meant that most artisans were outsiders who usually joined the community by marrying into one of the families. Even for those who controlled the most important agricultural and ranching interests, conditions imposed on them the need for personal work. Although the lives of these families were somewhat comfortable, San Antonio had no leisured group of *vecinos*.

Debt was a way of life for all. The worker owed the employer; the soldier owed the provisioning officer; the employer and officer in turn owed the merchants of Saltillo, Mexico City, and elsewhere. The people of Béxar were thus part of the colonialwide economy, which functioned on the basis of credit and the substitution of goods for scarce specie. Most of the soldiers' pay was converted into goods, which the soldiers had to take at set prices, much as Indians in other parts of the empire were forced to accept the *repartimiento de comercio*.

Although the Canary Islanders and their descendants enjoyed a certain degree of social prestige, this did not mean that they were at the top of the economic hierarchy. Indeed, with the exception of the Traviesos and Arochas, the Canary Island families do not appear to have enjoyed any greater degree of economic success than most of the Spanish families of Béxar. Aside from two or three outsiders who enjoyed quick success, most successful families were the result of the mixing of various activities, and of two or three generations of effort. Even so, not even the most successful had the means to venture away from the foundations of their wealth— their small farms and livestock operations—or to live comfortably free of debt.

7

Building a Frontier Community

There is no doubt that almost every year . . . debates occur in this cabildo, *born of ignorance and malice, that force the governor to overlook some nullities in their annual elections in order to avoid complaints.*

—GOVERNOR RAFAEL MARTÍNEZ PACHECO, 1790[1]

In the process of building presidio, town, farms, and ranches the people of San Antonio de Béxar also built community. But community also arose from conflicts among early competing parties and from the compromises necessary to survive on the frontier. Conflicts over rights, privileges, and resources helped define who would be considered members of the community, and on what terms. Compromise allowed the definitions to become stable means of ordering relationships in the community. In eighteenth-century Béxar such conflicts and compromises may be found in the politics of the *cabildo*, public and private religious ritual, and self-identification of individuals and the community as a whole.

I

Until 1731 Béxar had no civilian government. Decisions, both administrative and judicial, were made by the presidial commander in his capacity as *justicia mayor*. This state of affairs was common throughout the frontier at primarily military settlements. For example, at La Bahía the commander governed the town until the last year of Spanish rule, despite the presence of a large civilian population.[2] At San Antonio, after *alcaldes* began to be elected, the presidio's commander shared jurisdiction with them, retaining full authority over soldiers on active duty.[3] Not until 1771, when the seat of government shifted to San Antonio, did the governor assume command of the presidio and acquire the captain's jurisdiction.

The orders for the settling of the Canary Islanders required that the first town government be appointed for life.[4] There were nine permanent members: six *regidores* (councilmen), an *alguacil* (constable), a *síndico procurador* (attorney), and an *escribano* (scribe/notary). The *cabildo*, that is, the *regidores*, annually elected two men to serve as *alcaldes*. The *cabildo* as a whole held responsibility for regulating water supplies from the main acequia, authorizing public works, issuing grants of town lots in the absence of the governor, regulating weights and measures, and other minor duties. They could also serve, under certain circumstances, as *alcaldes* in the absence of the officeholders. The *alcaldes* exercised judicial authority, acting as judges of first instance in both civil and criminal cases, as well as issuing local ordinances. The *alguacil*'s chief occupations were taking charge of prisoners and running the jail, when one was available, and extending possessions to land grantees. The *síndico procurador* collected fees levied by the *cabildo* and oversaw public works. The *escribano* acted as scribe to the *cabildo* and recorded public transactions. After Francisco José de Arocha retired in 1757, the notary's position went unfilled for the rest of the century, perhaps because, Arocha exempted, it required an examination and payment of a licensing fee that Béxar's volume of business could not justify.[5]

Poverty precluded the normal colonial procedure of purchasing municipal offices once the original members died, and the practice of elections for vacant council posts therefore took hold in the late 1730s. Elections were limited to incumbent members; one year's council electing the following year's. In 1741 the first non-Isleño was elected *alcalde*, and later in the decade other *agregados* made it into the *cabildo*. Although the *cabildo* attempted to have permanent replacements appointed in 1749, the plan fell through. Only Antonio Rodríguez Mederos, originally the *síndico procurador* and therefore a life member, succeeded in being appointed by the council to the post of senior *regidor* in 1745. Elections for all councilmen posts were being held by the late 1750s, with the governor certifying the *cabildo*'s actions.[6]

That Béxar's electoral system diverged from the norms of colonial practices should not be surprising. Spanish custom and law were subject to loose interpretation and modification according to local circumstances.[7] Béxar's annual election of *regidores* stood in marked contrast to the standard practice of purchased council seats.[8] Other conventions that developed in Béxar's elections directly violated the *Laws of the Indies*. Reelection of individuals, and sometimes whole councils, election of close relatives to serve in the same year, kinsmen voting for each other, and meetings held outside the town hall were faults generally tolerated by governors.[9]

Those authorities who attempted to enforce strictly the laws governing the *cabildo* found themselves under attack by the municipal corporation. Captain Toribio de Urrutia, in a 1740 report to the viceroy following his appointment as commander at Béxar, was less than kind to the Isleño-monopolized *cabildo*.

> The said Isleños govern themselves through two *alcaldes* whom the *cabildo* elect every year from among themselves [i.e., the Isleños], and at present [the *alcaldes*] are father and son-in-law, the notary also being the son-in-law of one and the brother-in-law of the other. The alcalde elections they hold and run without any approval from a superior, for they say they recognize no other in this province than the governor. Those who exercise the posts often, and at present, cannot read nor write, and they are so backward politically that they make no progress, and any discord that [the Isleños] have among themselves or with others is tolerated by those justices, so that to this day no disorder or scandal has been punished, nor has anyone seeking justice received it.[10]

Within the next few years the *cabildo* attempted to deprive Urrutia of his posts, charging him with failure to execute orders in favor of the town and not showing respect for the rights and privileges of the Isleños.[11]

Reliance on *vecinos*, even the most prosperous and competent, for the administration of justice was a system fraught with pitfalls. Fernando de Veramendi, serving as *alcalde* in 1783, arrested Felipe Flores for adultery on the instruction of the parish priest but did not formally charge him. When the governor chastised him for not complying with the law, Veramendi retorted that He [Veramendi] "did not do it because he did not know whether the circumstances were proper for making [a formal charge], for his profession has solely been that of merchant." Moreover, Veramendi stated, it was not the custom in Béxar for such charges to be filed before the *alcaldes*, nor were there any instructions in the *cabildo's* archives on how *alcaldes* should handle such a matter.[12] Vicente Amador, in less than two months in office, occasioned such turmoil that the rest of the council decided to hold a secret hearing. Amador fled the town, leaving various prisoners in jail without charges, only to turn up less than two months later with an order from the commandant general reinstating him.[13] In 1779 Governor Cabello reported to the viceroy that he worried about leaving on his inspection trip to La Bahía—he did not trust the *alcaldes* elected for that year because the only reason that they had been elected was that they could write. Cabello was convinced that Toribio de Fuentes, the priest's father, had been elected through intrigue. All was not lost, however, for Cabello was planning to leave José Antonio Curbelo, who had done a good job as *alcalde* the previous year, as lieutenant governor.[14]

In the course of the century, as families intermarried and immigration made the *agregado* population boom, the qualifications for participating in municipal government changed. In the last decades of the century, the term *republicano* (apparently a citizen qualified to hold office) began to appear. Although the presumption would be that, as a minimum, the qualifications included being capable of reading and writing, complaints by governors of the election of illiterates attests otherwise. Property ownership in town was an important qualification, as was proof of stable residency. How much property was needed is open to question, however. Governors complained that the town had no men of means who could devote adequate attention to public office. In some instances, the elected official was described as poor and ignorant. It would appear, however, that being a member of a long-standing San Antonio family, or marrying into such a family, improved one's chances. And, although the evidence is sketchy as yet, there are indications of social climbing; some individuals who joined the *cabildo* late in the century came from families long in San Antonio but previously excluded from service.[15]

Keeping the *cabildo* filled with qualified individuals was only one of the problems Texas governors had with the *cabildo*, which most governors found to be very independent minded. For the early governors, the problem was a sporadic one since their residence at Los Adaes precluded extended contacts with Béxar. Matters changed radically during the last three decades of the century after the provincial capital was permanently transferred to Béxar.

Juan María, Barón de Ripperdá, the first governor to make Béxar his official residence, was constantly at odds with the *cabildo*. When the council refused to follow Ripperdá's order to lead the citizenry in reconstructing the barracks and jail, the governor suspended the *cabildo*. The viceroy sided with the council in their appeal and Ripperdá was admonished to restore the *cabildo* "and extend to it the proper respect due it according to the laws and in consideration of their being first settlers of the province."[16]

Immediately following their restoration the council refused to accept Ripperdá's choice of Simón de Arocha, an Isleño, as lieutenant governor; they lodged a complaint with the viceroy and would not attend Mass, which could have shown respect for Arocha.[17] This time the viceroy favored the governor and the *cabildo* backed down.

Over the long term it was governors and other royal authorities who had to adjust to local practices. On more than one occasion troubles between Ripperdá and the council concerned improper election procedures. During Teodoro de Croix's inspection visit in 1778, the governor took the opportunity to complain that the annual *cabildo* elections were both irregular and dishonest. Croix, accepting the local electoral practices, ordered that the election be held on 20 December of each year, which would allow time for the governor to certify the election by 28 December and the *cabildo* to take office on 1 January.[18] Troubles with the *cabildo* continued to hound Ripperdá's successors, however. Governor Cabello was embroiled in a controversy with the council over reconstruction of the guardhouse. At one point, he went so far as to arrest the entire council for disrespect.[19] In the documentation of his dispute with the *cabildo* over elections, Governor Martínez Pacheco wrote of the continual disregard of the law in *cabildo* elections and suggested that election-law offenders should be barred from holding office for ten years.[20] Later in the decade, Governor Muñoz also had election problems with the council.

II

Even aside from disputes with governors, the evolution of the *cabildo* into an annually renewed assembly was not easy. Indeed, much of the attention paid to colonial Béxar is a result of the perceived combativeness of the Canary Islanders.[21] Yet such confrontations must have been frequent when such unrelated groups were brought together under similar circumstances. At the Rio Grande settlement of Laredo, founded in 1755 by Tomás Sánchez as an extension of José Vázquez Borrego's Dolores *hacienda*, the arrival of a large group of new settlers from the downstream town of Revilla led to similar group conflict. The more recent arrivals, who lived on the west bank of the river, received most of the lands distributed in 1767 by a royal commission, and when the town's landowners elected a *cabildo* the following year, all the posts went to the *agregados*. The result was a series of disputes between the Sánchez faction and the west-bank settlers that were not resolved for twenty years—and then to a great extent through intermarriage.[22]

In Béxar, the original exclusion of a large portion of the population from farmland, water rights, and participation in local government, as well as the grant of *hidalguía* and the title of "original settlers" to the Isleños set the stage for conflict between Isleños and military settlers.[23] At first, the *agregados'* reaction was to abandon Béxar to the new arrivals. According to Captain Pérez de Almazán, a number of families did leave the province within months. In asking those who remained about the trouble, they made it clear that the Isleños little understood the need for cooperation. The Isleños, they declared, were "of an unsettled nature and generally a people without unity, not even between fathers and sons."[24] The *agregados* further stated that they wished to be free to stay or go as they pleased.

With little prospect of making a better start elsewhere, a number of families decided to remain in Béxar. By 1733 the *agregados* asked not for permission to leave Béxar but, rather, sought to be included as full members of the settlement. From the viceroy they requested land, water, and privileges on a par with the Isleños. They requested that one of the two *alcaldes* be elected from among their number, as well as half the councilmen, as these positions became vacant on the incumbents' death.[25] Despite a positive response from Mexico City, it was another eight years before the Isleños started sharing authority with the *agregados*.

In the meantime, the Isleños demonstrated considerable lack of unity among themselves. The two principal factions (extended families really), Juan Leal Goraz and his two sons, and Juan Curbelo and his two sons-in-law, prevented town government from acting in a unified manner. It was not uncommon for one *alcalde* to arrest the other, or to have various council members in jail.[26] During one of their various petitions for lands and water, the *agregados* stated that those who held the *cabildo* posts were the "most quarrelsome and trouble-making" of the Isleños. The governor could attest to the fact, having had to use all his prudence to settle the various disputes among the Isleños when he arrived in the province.[27]

Those Isleños interested in retaining control of the *cabildo* had their own arguments for keeping *agregados* out of the town's government. Few, the council claimed, were qualified, and the majority of the non-Isleño population was of mixed race "although they would all like to pass as Spaniards."[28] Yet, as the original Isleños died and alliances were formed between *agregados* and Isleño families, the ability of the latter group to control the *cabildo* was reduced. Beginning in 1741 a series of *agregados* was elected to serve as *alcaldes*, and in 1745 Governor Francisco García Larios appointed two *agregados* as councilmen on a temporary basis.[29]

Not all Isleños accepted the inclusion of *agregados* as full *vecinos* of the town. Some Isleños continued to use the *cabildo* as their own instrument. For instance, a lawsuit brought by the council against Captain Toribio de Urrutia was in reality the work of only a few of the Isleños. And there is evidence that the Curbelo faction, now headed by his two sons-in-law, Vicente Alvarez Travieso and Francisco José de Arocha, continued to look upon the *cabildo* as an Isleño prerogative. The disputes of the Isleños with the governor, Captain Urrutia, the *agregados*, and the missionaries were in reality the work of two or three individuals. Antonio Rodríguez Mederos, an Isleño who sided with Captain Urrutia and the *agregados*, blamed all the troubles on Travieso and Arocha, who manipulated the council to their own ends. The *cabildo*, in turn, accused Rodríguez Mederos of lying before the viceroy's court, manipulating the *alcalde* elections in order to gain control over the incumbents, and acting irresponsibly as senior *regidor*. But the charges apparently had not been made by the full council, and José Leal, an *alcalde* who signed the complaint, later testified that four of the six *regidores* had not signed the complaint nor even known about it, and that Travieso and Arocha had "pursued me to make a complaint against Mederos."[30]

These were among the last battles in which the terms "Isleño" and "*agregado*" were employed to label opponents. Under the increasing strength of social, economic, and kinship ties between Isleños and *agregados*, such divisions became increasingly difficult to maintain. This is not to say that differences disappeared among the people of Béxar, only that the group label "Isleño" could no longer easily be used by individuals as a cover for their actions.

One indication of the growing union between Isleño and *agregado* groups into a single community was the kinship structure of the council members. Most *agregados* who entered the corporation, beginning in the 1740s were not directly related to the Isleños. Through 1758 there was only Martín Flores y Valdez, who had married a Leal. He was joined that year by Juan José Flores de Abrego, whose second marriage in 1750 was to Leonor Delgado. Of the twenty-seven different *agregados* who served on *cabildos* during the 1760s, just seven were married to Isleñas. During that same decade, only fifteen Isleños served in public office and almost half were married to *agregadas*.[31] The last three decades of the century tell a similar story. As previous unions between Isleños and *agregados* produced a number of individuals of joint descent, the presence of an Isleño surname no longer represented a separate biological group. Of more than ninety-four men who held council posts between 1771 and 1800, two-thirds were non-Isleños by male descent. While twenty-three of the thirty-one Isleñosurnamed councilmen married *agregado*-surnamed women, only fourteen or so *agregados* married Isleño descendants.[32]

The quickly-formed marriage bonds between the Isleño and *agregado* populations noted earlier could not help but have repercussions on the *cabildo*, many of whose important Isleño members were either married to or descended in part from *agregados*. The important mid-century councilman José Curbelo, born in the Canary Islands and ten-time member of the corporation between 1745 and 1758, was married to the *agregada* Rafaela de la Garza. His son and grandson also found wives in the *agregado* population. The Arocha men, prominent members of the *cabildo* after mid-century, all married outside the Isleño families. The Travieso men, who entered *cabildo* service in the mid-1760s, also married out of the group.[33]

Other Isleño families took longer to mix with the *agregado* population. The first two generations of Delgados, who were well represented in the *cabildo*, married Isleño daughters; not until the third generation did the Delgados form unions with non-Isleños. The large Leal family, on the other hand, was apparently represented by only three members after Juan Leal Alvarez's resignation in 1742 and his father's death the following year; two of these three Leals married Isleño daughters.[34]

Most important, however, is that by the end of the century Isleño status was no longer an issue on the *cabildo*. For instance, in March 1790 Béxar's male population qualified to hold office, the *republicanos*, presented a grievance to the governor against that year's council for using trickery to reelect some of its members. Although the *republicanos* blamed the trouble on Francisco de Arocha, whose father Simón was one of the most prosperous second-generation Isleños, at no time was his Isleño status mentioned. Rather, Francisco's "natural mean-spiritedness and troublemaking attitude . . . that he inherits from his ancestors" was cited.[35] Conflict within Béxar's municipal government was no longer between Canary Islanders and *agregados* but between individuals or, at most, families. To Governor Muñoz's 1793 protest against the election of relatives to the *cabildo*, the council argued: "Here we are all kinfolk, so that if we fixed on that, it would not be possible to form a *cabildo*."[36]

III

If the *cabildo's* evolution reflected independent attitudes with regard to how Bexareños governed themselves and the emergence of a single Islander–*agregado* community, the townspeople's religious and ceremonial practices reflected their understanding of their collective place in the world and their obligations toward one another. Celebrating "both majesties" (God and King) represented the people's efforts to participate in the greater Spanish society as a group. Undertaking religious obligations, both of a personal or public nature, represented acceptance of one's place in local society.

The first opportunity, or more accurately the first necessity, for the residents of San Antonio to act collectively came in regards to constructing a parish church.[37] In the first years after their arrival in 1731, the Canary Islanders had found it necessary to attend services either at the presidio's provisional chapel or at one of the missions. Following the complaints of the parish priest about the rapidly deteriorating presidio chapel, the governor decided to act in February 1738 and called on the Islander controlled *cabildo* to work on the matter. Although they made all the decisions among themselves and appointed two of their own to act as overseers for the project, they did not shy away from asking the presidial and *agregado* communities to contribute to the project. The *agregados* and soldiers responded by donating between one and ten pesos each. Miguel Núñez Morillo, a retired soldier and livestock raiser, led the way, donating thirty pesos, the single largest contribution, aside from those of the governor and presidio commander. A sign of conciliation, intentional or unintentional, came at the formal laying of the corner stone, where Juan Recio de León, parish curate, declared: "In the exercise of my ecclesiastical jurisdiction I pronounce the said building, the parish church of this Villa *and the royal Presidio of San Antonio.*"[38] In addressing the viceroy for assistance in meeting the expenses for the church, the Islander town council stressed that all the residents and soldiers had cooperated in establishing the church fund, but that the settlement's poverty precluded its being able to meet more than one-fourth of the construction expenses.

As the authorities in Mexico City pondered assisting the people of San Antonio in building their church, the work proceeded as quickly as the community's resources permitted. By 1745 the church was only half built and the need for completing it was greater than ever, as the presidial chapel was falling in. *Alcalde* Antonio Rodríguez Mederos decided to take the heavy-handed approach and called on all citizens of the *villa* of San Fernando to contribute to the construction project, regardless of caste or station, on penalty of a twenty-five peso fine, to be applied to the church fund, and fifteen days in jail.[39] Various delays in obtaining the funds promised by the viceroy and disputes among the overseers, the *cabildo*, and Rodríguez Mederos prevented completion of the project for another decade, but when it was done, the church represented the efforts of the entire community—Islanders, *agregados*, and military.

It is not surprising that the establishment of organized religious feasts for the town dates from the mid-1750s. It was the period during which the parish church was completed. The decade was also marked by a general peace with the Apaches, the opening of the countryside to occupation, and increased involvement of the *agregado* population in the town's affairs. In short, it was a time of prosperity for the settlement.

The townspeople probably could think of no better way to display their newfound harmony and prosperity than to organize their public religious life.[40] Consequently, in 1755 the *cabildo* and Captain Toribio de Urrutia, as *justicia mayor*, took an oath before the citizenry to observe annually the feast of Our Lady of Guadalupe, the church's patroness, the feast of Our Lady of Candlemas, and the feast of San Fernando Rey de España (Saint Ferdinand, King of Spain), the town's patron. Within a few years, the feast of the Immaculate Conception had been added to the town's religious calendar. Within the following two decades, the town's public ceremonial religious activity assumed considerable proportions. Not only were the church costs of the feasts of Saint Ferdinand, Saint Anthony of Padua, the Immaculate Conception, and Our Ladies of Guadalupe and Candlemas paid for by the citizenry, so were the expenses for the Paschal candle, for capturing bulls and fencing the plazas for the attendant bullfights, and for constructing the frames and altars for the Corpus Christi procession.[41]

In the absence of guilds or *cofradías* (lay religious brotherhoods), which in large urban centers sponsored and organized religious festivities,[42] Béxar's town council organized the town's public celebrations. The *cabildo* selected two captains and two assistants each for the feasts of Guadalupe and the Immaculate Conception. The captains had principal responsibility for meeting the costs of the official celebrations. The assistants provided monetary support to the captains. In the 1780s each assistant was required to contribute twelve pesos to the cause.[43]

The pressures on the town's more well-off individuals to put on a good show were considerable, even at an early date. In 1767 Juan José Montes de Oca, who had already been carrying the cost of Saint Ferdinand's feast, was selected captain for the feast of the Immaculate Conception.

> He accepted the charge without any excuse, and on the eve and day [of the feast] he gladly and cheerfully manifested his fervent Christian devotion with grace and generosity, thus occasioning among the citizenry much satisfaction and the spirit for each to do

just as well when it is their turn to serve in such holy ministry to the Immaculate Queen of Heaven and earth, Our Lady Patroness and Advocate.[44]

The hefty costs of the celebrations could be quite taxing on the finances of those individuals chosen as captains or assistants. In 1777 Francisco Xavier Rodríguez went into debt and participated in a dubiously legal roundup to raise the funds to meet his obligation, "finding himself short of funds for the feast of the Immaculate Conception."[45] The deal included receiving liquor, cloth, soap, sugar, and chocolate from Juan José Flores in return for selling Flores a share of the captured cattle at a low price. Other individuals also took advantage of the province's cattle to meet their feast obligations.[46]

The *cabildo* was directly responsible for the feasts of the church and town patron saints because the town had not received episcopal permission to cover the costs from parish funds. Not surprisingly, the council limited expenses on these celebrations and, as individuals, would only bear the expenses "on condition that the functions do not carry excessive costs but moderate ones and only for the church [celebrations]; those who contribute being rewarded."[47] Father Pedro Fuentes' receipt for payment of his services in celebrating Saint Ferdinand's feast in 1783 (just under twelve pesos) attests to the *cabildo*'s resoluteness.[48] Juan José Montes de Oca bore the expense for the feast of Saint Ferdinand for over a decade beginning in 1761, an action that equally reflects the limited cost of this function and the acceptance of *agregados* as leading members of the emerging community.

December marked the most socially active month of the year for the community. After the feasts of the Immaculate Conception and Our Lady of Guadalupe, bullfights and games were held in the plazas and there were numerous dances throughout the town. Timed to coincide with the break between the late maize harvest and the early-year cattle branding and planting preparations, the festivities allowed Béxar's population to celebrate another year of survival as a community. The custom of a month-long celebration in December lasted until the end of Mexican rule in Texas.[49]

Connected with the year-end festivities were religious ceremonies reinforcing the town's social hierarchy and its association with the rest of the empire. From the earliest days and until 1778, the council's elections were held on 1 January, and from that year on they were held on 20 December.

Following the installation of the new *cabildo* on the first day of the new year, the group marched to the church, where it was received by the parish priest. By the 1750s there was already a customary ceremony at the church associated with the new council's installation.[50] The importance of this formality is evident in a 1778 complaint against the parish priest for failing to receive the *cabildo* after its installation.

> Having made the elections the first day of January, as is the custom, the new *cabildo* left for mass, and the priest instead of waiting to receive us, as he should and as is the custom in all towns and places, even in Indian settlements, did the contrary and began saying Mass, leaving us without it. We have felt this rebuff very deeply, principally for having been a public act, in which he should have attended to us with the same honor as to His Majesty.[51]

Religious practices of a more private nature also had an important role in building community. One way the corporate emphasis of Catholicism expressed itself was in the requirement that individuals receiving the sacraments of baptism, confirmation, and holy matrimony have sponsors.[52] In the Hispanic world this practice of ritual kinship, *compadrazgo* (co-parenthood), became an instrument for community formation and maintenance, as it bound individuals with formal ties of obligations and privileges under the authority of God. In the ceremonies that admitted individuals to fuller participation in the faith, biological parents and sponsors became *compadres* (co-parents), that is, a form of kinfolk. *Compadrazgo* within the sacrament of baptism played a very important role, because the godparents were expected to replace the biological parents in case the former died. Godparents also had a responsibility to see to it that the child received a good Christian education and was properly socialized.

Unlike other forms of kinship, however, *compadrazgo* was voluntary. Because of the element of choice, *compadrazgo* reveals the nature of social relations in the community. Individuals would not chose co-parents for their children who were not their social equals, were incapable of fulfilling religious obligations and financial expectations, or who represented some type of moral weakness. For the chosen godparents, the honor represented a token of friendship, respect, and even deference. Godparenthood, although technically only a religious practice, acquired a broad range of social characteristics. It was an instrument through which alienated friends or family could be brought together; it served as a means of expressing social status or as a way of cementing important interfamily ties; and it could even function as a system of social consolidation in which an individual "is part of a network in which the community acts, feels, and thinks as one group."[53]

These processes were at work in San Antonio from the earliest days.[54] As might be expected, the bonds of friendship among military families appear to have been the principal factor in choosing godparents. In many instances, soldiers and residents of the presidio and their wives served as godparents for each other. On only six occasions did higher status individuals, presidio officers or the governor, serve as godparents within the presidial community.

Numerous cases reveal the importance of status, despite the primitive conditions of an emerging frontier society. In 1727 Lieutenant Governor Juan Pérez de Almazán served as godfather to the daughter of Captain Nicolás Flores, commander of the presidio.[55] For Governor Juan María, Barón de Ripperdá, the problem of choosing godparents for his children born in Texas was a serious one. No one in San Antonio, or the whole province for that matter, had the necessary social status to serve, and in choosing any civilian his family would be dishonored. A solution was found in the clergy. Four of his children were sponsored by the parish priest, Pedro Fuentes, and one by the president of the Zacatecas Franciscan missions of Texas, Fray Pedro Ramírez.[56]

Even among locals, those with some ranking in the community had to choose godparents carefully. Joaquín Urrutia, son and brother of Béxar presidio commanders and already a corporal in the company at the time of his first child's birth in 1744, appears to have made very calculated choices. His firstborn, a son, had the Canary Islander town notary Francisco de Arocha and his wife Juana Curbelo as godparents. The parish priest, Francisco Polanco, sponsored the second son. Daughter Joaquina, born in 1749, had her uncle, Captain Toribio Urrutia, and his wife Josefa Hernández, as godparents. By the time his fourth child was born in 1752, Joaquín was company sergeant and his status to the broader community had been consolidated; the choice of godparents fell on Martín Flores, a long-time *vecino* who had served on the town council on numerous occasions and who was married to María Leal, a member of one of the Islander families. Similarly, his last child, born in 1758, had Juan José Montes de Oca, a rancher who had risen to a high rank in Béxar society, having served both in the presidio and in the *cabildo*, and his wife Marcela de la Peña. The least status conscious of all of Urrutia's godparent choices was for daughter María Luisa, born in 1756. Her godfather was Cristóbal

Chirino, a native of San Antonio and one-time fellow soldier with Joaquín.[57]

The capacities of *compadrazgo* for building community and strengthening interfamily bonds are evident in the first generation of baptisms following the founding of the town in 1731.[58] The first handful of children born to Isleños had members of the presidio or *agregado* communities as godparents. There followed over the course of the next twenty years an exchange of *compadrazgo* bonds between *agregados* and Islanders that linked most of the families in the settlement. And, lest one think that the ritual had only personal and family significance, there is the case of Juan Nepomuceno Travieso. He was baptized twice, once on 23 February 1745 and again on 9 March because the parents, Vicente Alvarez Travieso and Mariana Curbelo, wanted their good friend Francisco de Arocha to be present. The Arochas would return the favor in folds a few years later, choosing the Traviesos as godparents for their daughter María Gertrudis and their son Fernando José Agustín.[59]

Shared roles, kinship ties, and the frontier experience bound much of Béxar's population by the end of the century. The proximity between presidio and town, and the interdependence between the two, slowly fostered a joint identity for the town's population. In the process of living, working, fighting, dying, and celebrating together, the people of San Antonio came to see themselves as a single community.

IV

As we have seen in previous chapters, during the first decades of Béxar's existence, when the Isleño and presidial population could be said to have no more than coexisted, inhabitants were labeled vecinos either of the presidio or of the town.[60] Both the Isleños and the *agregados* contributed to this early division, clearly distinguishing presidio and town as separate establishments. In a complaint made against Governor Sandoval by the Isleños in early 1735, they mentioned the governor's forcing the Isleño town council to perform guard duty, despite "there being in the said presidio more than twelve residents [*personas agregadas*] who should and could occupy themselves in said function and not the justices."[61] In 1743 Captain Urrutia, in his capacity as *justicia mayor*, had to issue an order requiring the *vecinos agregados* to obey the town's authorities.

Having come to my attention that since the founding of the town of San Fernando some of its *agregado*s have said that they do not have to recognize the town's justices, and knowing that such [an opinion] emanates from the ignorance that comes from the residents of this presidio, who lived here before the town's founding, having had no other justices than the captains. . . .[62]

By the 1770s the people of Béxar were calling themselves *vecinos* of the presidio and town or using the terms indiscriminately. It also became common just to call oneself a *vecino* of Béxar.[63] A 1787 accord between the townspeople and missions over roundups was labeled "Agreement celebrated by the *cabildo* and citizenry of this Presidio of San Antonio de Béxar of the Province of Texas with its Missions, concerning the gathering of livestock, bovine and equine. . . ."[64] The incorporation of many soldiers into the civilian population, including their election to public office, contributed to this merging of identities.

At the same time, labels used to divide the population into Isleños and *agregados* slowly fell into disuse. The terms *primeros* (original) and *principales* (principal) *pobladores*, which in the early years had been part of the polemic concerning rights and privileges, became interchangeable appellations for both groups.[65] Shortly after their arrival on the frontier, the Canary Islanders had gone so far as to contend that they had pacified the area. They based the claim on the king's order for their settlement in Texas, which granted them the privileges of original settlers.

And the *Laws of the Indies* do not concede the same privilege to those who come to reside as to those who settled the area, nor is there any reason for it when the latter, abandoning their own fatherland . . . traveled to such distant and remote lands with untold perils to their lives, while the former found the land quiet, and to some degree safe.[66]

The *agregados* challenged this view, and as late as 1745 declared that the Canary Islanders, becoming "conceited by the title of [original] settlers, wish to be the only [settlers] of that land, scorning the *agregados* who at no cost to His Majesty were and are the true and most ancient settlers and conquerors of that land."[67]

These arguments disappeared in the course of the 1750s. By 1762, when the non-landholding residents asked for the distribution of lands and water from the San Antonio River, they did so without reference to the Isleños.[68] In his 1778 petition for a town lot José Martín de la Garza claimed to be both a descendant of Canary Islanders (on his mother's side) and of the original settlers of the presidio.[69] Francisco Xavier Rodríguez claimed to be the son of original settlers (his father had been a soldier in the 1720s) and married to the daughter of one of the principal settlers (the Isleño Vicente Alvarez Travieso). The second-generation Isleño Joaquín Leal called himself the son of original settlers while declaring his wife, also an Isleño descendant, as the daughter of principal settlers.[70] The descendants of Isleños and *agregados* thus formed a new identity that, though somewhat confused, recognized that the settlement had existed prior to 1731 and that the original inhabitants had been frontiersmen from New Spain's northern provinces.

The *cabildo's* 1787 *"Representación"* illustrates the emergence of a community that accepted both the *agregados* and the Isleños within a single historical framework. A long memorial intended to prove that the province's wild livestock belonged to the *vecinos* of Béxar, the *"Representación"* ignores the early divisions in favor of a concensus outlook. In effect, Béxar's people provided us with a brief history of themselves. The facts surrounding San Antonio's founding by the Martín de Alarcón expedition in 1718 were totally lost by 1787; only the vague idea of Béxar's being settled by a group of families from Nuevo León and Coahuila "desiring glory or advancing their own particular interests" was retained. The presidio, according to the memorialists, was not established until 1721 or 1722, during which time Mission San Antonio de Valero was also founded. In the years that followed, various presidios and missions were established.

And finally, at the expense of His Majesty, this town of San Fernando [was founded] with fourteen Canary Island families along with the said creoles, who had already started the settlement; and it has grown until today it counts more than one thousand and almost four hundred persons, including the children.[71]

This is not to say that Isleño descendants were not proud of their heritage. Various examples in this section demonstrate that individuals with Isleño blood quite willingly made reference to it, but there appears to have been just as much pride in descent from military settlers. Nor does the overarching unity of the community mean that some Isleños did not continue their forebears' contentious ways. Indeed, the Arocha clan, as explained above, although only partially of Isleño descent by the 1790s, was considered by many locals the town's biggest troublemaking group.[72] .

In 1762 Governor Martos y Navarrete cited the existence of a previous viceregal order banishing Vicente Alvarez Travieso and Francisco José de Arocha "as the spring of all the troubles and disputes" in Béxar.[73] However, in the latter part of the century, disputes among residents had nothing, or at most very little, to do with being or not being an Isleño. Instead, they had to do with being insiders, those who traced their lineages to the town's earliest inhabitants and for whom the term Isleño served as a convenient label, and outsiders, those late arrivals seeking to work their way into the local power structure.

Governor Muñoz described the situation to the viceroy in 1792 in asking, like many of his successors, for the abolition of the *cabildo*. The citizenry was divided into two groups, Muñoz claimed, those descended from the Isleño families and those from the provinces of Coahuila, Nuevo León, and New Spain. All relied on their personal labor in farming and ranching to make a living. "The bonds of kinship, with the former wishing to be more than the latter, occasion all the discord which [Governor] Pacheco found." Efforts to elect one *alcalde* from each of the two groups had failed because poverty and illiteracy prevented all but a few from serving, with the result that "in many years the staff of justice and regidor posts are found in a single family of brothers and sons, as has happened with the Arochas."[74] But, as stated earlier, the Arocha men had all long since married *agregadas*, a trend which continued in subsequent generations. Consequently, the Isleño label served more to define status within the community than to identify a separate ethnic socioeconomic group.

v

Canary Islander predominance in the political sphere was short-lived. Within a decade of their arrival, the administration of justice was shared by *alcaldes* from both the Isleño and *agregado* populations. Five years later, *agregados* held three *regidor* posts. By 1750 attempts by a faction of Isleños to continue using the town council to achieve their own purposes ended, exposed by fellow Canary Islanders who sided with the *agregado* population. Beginning about 1760, the growth in population and intermarriage resulted in a municipal corporation that no longer defined itself in terms of its Isleño origins. At the same time, the form taken by local government during the years that Isleños controlled the *cabildo* survived. The annual elections that began to take place when the original life-members started dying out were continued for the rest of the century. Also surviving were numerous irregularities in the electoral process.

The emergence of the *cabildo* from the early years of division and divisiveness coincided with the onset of peace with the Apache and the creation of economic opportunities. The council marked this happy, if temporary, situation by formally committing itself and the town to undertake the costs of public religious functions. Through such celebrations, the *cabildo*, in particular, and the townspeople, in general, exhibited their group membership in the broader colonial society. The feasts thus symbolized religious devotion, patriotism, and civic pride.

Finally, the emergence of a single community in Béxar is evidenced by the labels people assumed and by the way they portrayed their own history. The confused view of San Antonio's early history, in which the founding of the Isleño-controlled town was no more than a part of the already developing settlement, is one sign of consensus among townspeople, and so too is the interchangeability of ascriptive labels. Had antagonisms between Isleños and *agregados* survived into later generations, the terms original settler and principal settler would not have been handled as loosely as they were. By the latter part of the century, it no longer mattered whether the Isleños or military settlers were first, since through a whole series of social and economic bonds many of Béxar's people enjoyed joint ancestry. As a result, such labels served to place individuals within the historical framework of the community as descendants of the earliest Bexareños.

Conclusion

Béxar entered the nineteenth century with little expectation that the province of Texas would receive more than the cursory attention it had received during the previous eighty years. Events worlds away, in Paris, Madrid, and the capital of the upstart United States of America, conspired to change royal policies toward Texas and expectations in the province. As the nebulous boundary between the Spanish provinces of Texas and Louisiana, which lay somewhere east of the Sabine River, became an international boundary between the Spanish empire and the United States, colonial officials were forced to move decisively. Troops from neighboring provinces occupied key positions in the province. Governor Antonio Cordero organized a colonization effort that included founding two new settlements along the Camino Real between Béxar and Nacogdoches, along with plans for others.[1]

For the people of Béxar the changes, while welcome at first, soon turned stressful and eventually disastrous. Soldiers, settlers, and their families constituted important new markets for the limited products of the Béxar economy, which must have pleased the town's leading men. Unfortunately, the more intense scrutiny of royal officials, particularly Governors Cordero and Manuel Salcedo, also brought new rules and more vigorous law enforcement. Battles between the *cabildo*, representing the town's elite, and governors were not tolerated by the no-nonsense Cordero, who reduced the size of the council with the approval of the commandant general. Worse soon came, however, as Father Hidalgo's *grito* reached frontier Texas in January 1811 and brought on a brief insurrection led by a retired militia officer. The distractions of the rebellion also brought on

new depredations by the Comanches, not only in the countryside around
Béxar, but even to the extent that the recently established settlement on
the San Marcos River was abandoned by July 1812. The worst of Béxar's
troubles came between August 1812 and August 1813, when the province
was invaded by a combined force of Mexican insurgents and Anglo-American filibusters. Defeated by a royalist army at the Battle of Medina, the
invaders left behind a legacy of destruction and desolation which threat-
ened to undo all the work of the previous century.[2]

San Antonio de Béxar's role in the chain of events that commenced with
the retrocession of Louisiana to France in 1800 and concluded with the
Texian victory at San Jacinto on 21 April 1836, is another story. Previous
to that, Béxar had endured, and occasionally thrived, as a military outpost
on the fringes of a sprawling empire. Consequently, Béxar's development
from an agglomeration of soldiers and settlers into a well-defined community in the course of the eighteenth century has eluded historians of
early Texas.

A static view of Béxar society has prevailed—one that sees the early
Isleño predominance continuing among subsequent generations of Bexareños; one that looks upon Spanish colonial Texas as a mere prelude to
the Anglo-American rescue of the region from barbarism. As a result, the
settlement's social and economic dynamics have often been ignored or
misinterpreted. Intermarriage with the *agregado* families began a little
more than a decade after the Canary Islanders' arrival in 1731, so that by
the third generation most "Isleño" descendants were of mixed parentage.
Isolated and subject to the social and economic forces at work throughout
the Mexican colonial north, the mixing went beyond Isleños and *agregados*
to include assimilated Indians and mixed-bloods from the interior of the
viceroyalty.

Limited economic opportunities also contributed to the social mix. Although the distribution of land and water resources early favored the
Isleños, the determination of governors and *agregados* to expand the town's
population ultimately led to compromises. Town lots were eventually
distributed to *agregados*, and access to San Pedro *acequia* water was gen-
eralized. Through sale, a considerable quantity of farmland in the Isleños'
farm became the property of *agregados* and, ultimately, other irrigated
farmland was opened to meet the town's growing needs. By the end of the
1770s, those holding the greatest concentrations of urban land were non-
Isleños. In the countryside, acquisition of ranch land never favored the
Isleños as a group and, if anything, the dangers of the range, human and
otherwise, gave something of an advantage to the *agregados*.

The evidence suggests that the true keystone of Béxar's economy was the presidio, which the Isleños never dominated. The presidio provided the town a market for labor, agricultural products, and artisanal services. Because it recruited locally, the garrison was the most important and most stable source of work for a considerable portion of the male population. Presidial salaries were turned into capital that the provisioning officer employed to purchase supplies for both troops and civilians. The presidio, through its store, served the consumer needs of the entire settlement while it provided a livelihood to local farmers and ranchers who sold their produce there, and to tailors, smiths, and other artisans who worked for the garrison. The result was a clearly defined economic hierarchy, one in which, because of close interdependence, the extremes of wealth and poverty were not too far distant from one another, and in which Isleños and *agregados* could be found at every step.

An emerging Béxar community is also visible in the town's *cabildo*, where the early struggle by the Isleños to create a political monopoly over Béxar did not outlast the original immigrant members. Complaints by the *agregados*, infighting among Isleño members, and the development of kinship and *compadrazgo* ties with non-Isleño families led to *agregado* membership as early as 1741. By mid-century, the *agregados* were at least equal partners in the town's management. All the evidence, then, points to the absence of a separate Isleño socio-economic status group by the 1750s.

Rather than disappearing, the term Isleño took on a new meaning toward the latter part of the eighteenth century. If it did not define a distinct ethnic or socioeconomic group, it did serve as a useful way of separating older families from new arrivals. By employing such other contrivances as "principal settlers" and "original settlers," the early military families, who may or may not have been related to Isleños, could also distance themselves from latecomers. Thus, the people of Béxar gave themselves a history in which families had assigned places either at the core or at the fringes of the community.

The people of San Antonio de Béxar also shared the perspective of many subjects of the Crown, although Bexareños certainly did not recognize it.[3] Poor and isolated, they often saw themselves as neglected and abused. They considered themselves to be good subjects of the King, who suffered mistreatment at the hands of arbitrary governors and greedy friars. Despite the hardships, the economic backwardness, and the isolation, Bexareños held on to their homes in the wilderness. There were threats of abandoning the province on more than one occasion, but few actually left. Bexareños identified themselves with the place and each other.

Community in San Antonio de Béxar did not spring up overnight. It was
the product of a shared struggle for survival among people who originally
had little in common. By applying this more specific definition of community across a range of social and economic aspects of Béxar, the variety
and pace of change in the settlement has come to light. This perspective
has permitted a reinterpretation of early conflict and later discord, without
recourse to the static view that there existed an Isleño–*agregado* schism
throughout the colonial period. The Isleños who had received land and
water from the King, and the *agregados* who had defended town and missions against Indian enemies, were joined into one community. The mark
of their success is the continuity of their legacy to the present day.

Notes

PREFACE

1. A number of scholars have addressed what Carey McWilliams labeled the "fantasy heritage," among them: Arthur L. Campa, *Hispanic Culture in the Southwest* (reprint, Norman: University of Oklahoma Press, 1993), 3–9; John R. Chávez, *The Lost Land: The Chicano Image of the Southwest* (Albuquerque: University of New Mexico Press, 1984), 85–106; Carey McWilliams, *North From Mexico: The Spanish-Speaking People of the United States* (rev ed., New York: Praeger, 1990), 43–53.

2. Two historiographical essays dealing with the impact of Bolton and his "school" on borderlands studies are "Turner, the Boltonians, and the Spanish Borderlands," and "John Francis Bannon and the Historiography of the Spanish Borderlands: Retrospect and Prospect," in David J. Weber, *Myth and the History of the Hispanic Southwest: Essays by David J. Weber* (Albuquerque: University of New Mexico Press, 1988).

3. Gilbert R. Cruz, *Let There Be Towns: Spanish Municipal Origins in the American Southwest, 1610–1810* (College Station: Texas A&M University Press, 1988).

4. David J. Weber, ed., *New Spain's Far Northern Frontier: Essays on Spain in the American West, 1540–1821* (reprint, Dallas: Southern Methodist University Press, 1989), xvi.

5. Oakah L. Jones, *Los Paisanos: Spanish Settlers on the Northern Frontier of New Spain* (Norman: University of Oklahoma Press, 1979), xi.

6. Douglas Monroy, *Thrown Among Strangers: The Making of Mexican Culture in Frontier California* (Berkeley: University of California Press, 1990); Ramón A. Gutiérrez, *When Jesus Came the Corn Mothers Went Away: Marriage, Sexuality, and Power in New Mexico, 1500–1846* (Stanford: Stanford University Press, 1991).

7. Marc Simmons, *Albuquerque: A Narrative History* (Albuquerque: University of New Mexico Press, 1982); W. H. Timmons, *El Paso: A Borderlands History* (El Paso: Texas Western Press, 1990).

8. Gilberto Miguel Hinojosa, *A Borderlands Town in Transition: Laredo, 1755–*

1870 (College Station: Texas A&M University Press, 1983); Antonio Ríos-Busta-mante, *Los Angeles, pueblo y región*, 1781–1850: *continuidad y adaptación en la periferia del norte mexicano* (Mexico: Instituto Nacional de Antropología e Historia, 1991).

9. Gerald E. Poyo and Gilberto M. Hinojosa, eds., *Tejano Origins in Eighteenth Century San Antonio* (Austin: University of Texas Press, 1991); María Esther Domínguez, *San Antonio, Texas, en la época colonial* (1718–1821) (Madrid: Ediciones de Cultura Hispanica, 1989).

10. Jesús F. de la Teja, "Indians, Soldiers, and Canary Islanders: The Making of a Texas Frontier Community," *Locus* 3 (Fall 1990): 82.

11. Yi-Fu Tuan, *Space and Place: The Perspective of Experience* (Minneapolis: University of Minnesota Press, 1977), 154.

12. Ibid., 166–74.

13. Thomas Bender, *Community and Social Change in America* (New Brunswick: Rutgers University Press, 1978), 7–10; Tuan, *Space and Place*, 166–67; Helena M. Wall, *Fierce Communion: Family and Community in Early America* (Cambridge, Mass.: Harvard University Press, 1990), 16–18.

14. John R. Van Ness, *Hispanos in Northern New Mexico: The Development of Corporate Community and Multicommunity* (New York: AMS Press, 1991).

15. Thomas Bender, *Community and Social Change*, 64–65.

16. Peter Alan Stern, "Social Marginality and Acculturation on the Northern Frontier of New Spain" (Ph.D. dissertation, The University of California, Berkeley, 1984).

17. Gerald E. Poyo and Gilberto M. Hinojosa, "Spanish Texas and Borderlands Historiography in Transition: Implications for United States History," *Journal of American History* 75 (September 1988): 393–416. In this essay the authors review the literature on colonial Texas and find it wanting in many respects on these topics.

CHAPTER ONE

1. "Título de gobernador e instrucciones a don Martín de Alarcón para su expedición a Texas," *Archivo General de la Nación de México: Boletín* 6, 4 (1935): 536 (hereafter cited as AGN: Boletín).

2. An able survey of early Texas history is Donald E. Chipman, *Spanish Texas, 1519–1821* (Austin: University of Texas Press, 1992).

3. Chipman, *Spanish Texas*, 207–9.

4. An excellent treatment of the Spanish and French experiences in the late seventeenth and early eighteenth centuries in the area of the northern Gulf of Mexico is Robert S. Weddle, *The French Thorn: Rival Explorers in the Spanish Sea, 1682–1762* (College Station: Texas A&M University Press, 1991). The sources of Spanish unfamiliarity with the region are treated in the same author's earlier work, *Spanish Sea: The Gulf of Mexico in North American Discovery, 1500–1685* (College Station: Texas A&M University Press, 1985).

5. AGN: Boletín 28, 1 (1957): 64; 28, 2 (1957): 357–58.

6. Ibid., 29, 1 (1958): 153–54.

7. Carlos E. Castañeda, *Our Catholic Heritage in Texas*, 1519–1936, (7 vols., reprint, New York: Arno, 1976) 2: 71.

8. Castañeda, *Our Catholic Heritage* 2: 71–72.

9. AGN: Boletín 29, 2 (1958): 305.

10. In his recommendation, the viceroy's fiscal wrote: "If possible, all the sixty soldiers should be Spaniards, not mulattoes, coyotes, or mestizos, so that the occurrences of 1693, will not be repeated."AGN: Boletín 29, 2 (1958): 339. The missionaries had previously complained of the ill effects caused by the behavior of low-caste soldiers toward the Indians on the first occupation.

11. Ibid., 537.

12. Castañeda, *Our Catholic Heritage*, 2: 76–77. There was little concern that discharged soldiers would abandon the frontier, for they already had farms and homes and would remain freemen in the settlements adjoining their former presidios (AGN: Boletín, 29, 2 (1958): 339–40).

13. Olivares to Viceroy, 22 June 1718, Archivo General de la Nación de Mexico, Ramo Provincias Internas, vol. 181 (hereafter cited as AGN:PI).

14. *Universidad de México* 5, 25–26 (1933): 62–63; Castañeda, *Our Catholic Heritage*, 2: 94.

15. *Universidad de México*, 5, 25–26 (1933): 62–63, 66–67; 5, 27–28 (1933): 233.

16. W. W. Newcomb, Jr., *The Indians of Texas: From Prehistoric to Modern Times* (Austin: University of Texas Press, 1961), 107–8; Castañeda, *Our Catholic Heritage*, 2: 188; Robert S. Weddle, *The San Sabá Mission: Spanish Pivot in Texas* (Austin: University of Texas Press, 1964), 10.

17. Elizabeth A. H. John, *Storms Brewed in Other Men's Worlds: The Confrontation of Indians, Spanish and French in the Southwest*, 1540–1795 (reprint, Lincoln: University of Nebraska Press, 1981), 258–60.

18. Castañeda, *Our Catholic Heritage* 2: 146–47.

19. The Colegio de Propaganda Fide de Nuestra Señora de Guadalupe de Zacatecas was one of two Franciscan missionary colleges that had mission fields in Texas; the other was the Colegio de la Santa Cruz de Querétaro, to which belonged Mission San Antonio de Valero.

20. "Fundación del pueblo y misión de San José y de San Miguel de Aguayo," Spanish Collection, General Land Office, Austin, Texas (hereafter cited as GLO).

21. Thomas H. Naylor and Charles W. Polzer, S.J., eds. and comps., *Pedro de Rivera and the Military Regulations for Northern New Spain*, 1724–1729 (Tucson: The University of Arizona Press, 1988), 161.

22. John, *Storms Brewed*, 263–75.

23. Ibid., 275–76.

24. Castañeda, *Our Catholic Heritage*, 2: 237–43; Marion A. Habig, *The Alamo Chain of Missions: A History of San Antonio's Five Old Missions* (rev. ed., Chicago: Franciscan Herald Press, 1976), 123–24.

25. "Testimonio de asiento de Misiones," [22 September 1730], GLO.

26. Castañeda, *Our Catholic Heritage* 2: 271–72.

27. Ibid, 301–2.

28. Castañeda, *Our Catholic Heritage*, 2: 275–76, 283–84; "Auto en que se da razón de haber ospedado a los Ysleños y otras providencias," 10 March 1731, AGN: PI, vol. 32.

29. Quoted in Juan Agustín Morfi, *History of Texas*, 1673–1779, trans. Carlos E. Castañeda (2 vols.; Albuquerque: Quivira Society, 1935), 2: 293.

30. John, *Storms Brewed*, 284–88.

31. Newcomb, *The Indians of Texas*, 156–57; Castañeda, *Our Catholic Heritage*, 3: 343–44.

32. John, *Storms Brewed*, 380–82, 397–98. The story of the San Sabá mission and presidio is told in colorful detail in Robert S. Weddle, *The San Sabá Mission: Spanish Pivot in Texas* (Austin: University of Texas Press, 1964).

33. Chipman, *Spanish Texas*, 178–81.

34. O'Conor to Viceroy, 8 August 1768, Archivo General de la Nación de México, Ramo Historia, vol. 91 (hereafter cited as AGN:H).

35. Castañeda, *Our Catholic Heritage* 4: 278–80; John, *Storms Brewed*, 438–39, 621, 630. A recent survey of the Cíbolo outpost is Robert H. Thonhoff, *El Fuerte del Cíbolo: Sentinel of the Bexar–La Bahía Ranches* (Austin: Eakin Press, 1992).

36. "Estado de la fuerza . . . ," 31 July 1786, Bexar Archives, University of Texas Archives, Austin (hereafter cited as BA); Bernardo Fernández to Muñoz, 6 January 1791, ibid; Joseph Menchaca to Muñoz, 12 January 1791, ibid; Commandant General Nava to Muñoz, 21 August 1795, ibid; Town Council to Muñoz, 22 September 1796, ibid.

37. Unless otherwise noted, the discussion that follows regarding Texas's bordering provinces is based on Oakah L. Jones, Jr., *Los Paisanos: Spanish Settlers on the Northern Frontier of New Spain* (Norman: University of Oklahoma Press, 1979), and Peter Gerhard, *The North Frontier of New Spain* (Princeton: Princeton University Press, 1982).

CHAPTER TWO

1. Governor Pérez de Almazán to the Viceroy, 24 March 1724, AGN: PI, vol. 183.

2. "Autos sobre diferentes noticias . . . 1715," AGN: PI, vol. 181.

3. Richard G. Santos, comp., trans., ed., *Aguayo Expedition Into Texas, 1721: An Annotated Translation of the Five Versions of the Diary Kept by Br. Juan Antonio de la Peña* (Austin, Texas: Jenkins Publishing Co., 1981), 25, 30–31, 79; Isidro Félix Espinosa, *Chrónica apostólica, y seráphica de todos los colegios de propaganda fide de esta Nueva España* (Madrid, 1746), 452–57; Castañeda, *Our Catholic Heritage* 2: 115–19.

4. Comparison of the list made of those present in 1718, and the list of officers and soldiers of the Presidio of San Antonio de Béxar, 25 April 1722, in "Autos a

consulta hecha del padre fray José González, Misionero del Presidio de San Antonio Valero contra el capitán don Nicolás Flores por los motivos que expresa," AGN: PI, 32.

5. Fernando Pérez de Almazán to Viceroy, 11 July 1726, in "Carpeta de correspondencia de las Provincias Internas por los años de 1726 a 1731 con los excelentísimos señores, Marqués de Casa y Fuerte y Conde de Fuenclara," AGN: PI, vol. 236.

6. Morfi, *History of Texas*, 2: 257.

7. The number of households is based on examination of Mission Valero's baptismal and marriage records. The population total is based on a multiplier of 4.5 persons per household, which appears reasonable based on other available studies. Gilberto Miguel Hinojosa, *A Borderlands Town in Transition: Laredo, 1755–1870* (College Station: Texas A&M Press, 1983), 20, found Laredo's household size stable at about four persons per unit in the years 1757–1789; Henry F. Dobyns, *Spanish Colonial Tucson: A Demographic History* (Tucson: University of Arizona Press, 1976), 147, calculated Tucson's military households to average 4.4 persons in 1797; James Michael McReynolds, "Family Life in a Borderland Community: Nacogdoches, Texas, 1779–1861," (Ph.D. dissertation, Texas Tech University, 1978), 153, estimated Nacogdoches's average household size at 4.5 members during the Spanish period; Michael M. Swann, *Tierra Adentro: Settlement and Society in Colonial Durango* (Boulder, Colo.: Westview Press, 1982), 247–57, reports Nueva Vizcaya's average in 1760 to be 5.1 persons per household, declining to 4.6 in the late 1770s. All estimates of Béxar's Spanish population before 1777 have, therefore, been worked out on the basis of the 4.5 multiplier.

8. Canary Islanders, however, were sent at royal expense to other areas of the Spanish borderlands—in the first half of the eighteenth century to Florida, and after the Seven Years' War to Louisiana. Susan Lois Pickman, "Life on the Spanish American Colonial Frontier: A Study in the Social and Economic History of Mid-Eighteenth Century St. Augustine, Florida" (Ph.D. dissertation, State University of New York, Stony Brook, 1980), 115; Gilbert C. Din, "The Immigration Policy of Governor Esteban Miró in Spanish Louisiana." *Southwestern Historical Quarterly* 83 (October 1969): 155–56 (hereafter cited as *SWHQ*).

9. For narratives of those events, see: Mattie Alice Austin, "The Municipal Government of San Fernando de Béxar, 1730–1800," *SWHQ* 8 (April 1905): 286–303; Castañeda, *Our Catholic Heritage*, 2: 268–310.

10. David J. Weber, *The Spanish Frontier in North America* (New Haven: Yale University Press, 1992), 307–8. The subject of these captives' roles in the community is more fully treated in Chapter 6.

11. "Inspection of public books, weights, and measures by Governor Pedro del Barrio Junco y Espriella," 14 May 1749, Nacogdoches Archives, Transcripts, University of Texas Archives, Austin (hereafter cited NA). A count of individuals who appear on lists from both before and after the inspection reveals another twenty-five adult male inhabitants.

12. Representation of the cabildo, 7 July 1770, in "Correspondencia con el gobernador de Texas Barón de Ripperdá en los años de 1770 hasta 1773 inclusive," AGN: PI, vol. 100; William Edward Dunn, "The Apache Mission on the San Sabá River; Its Founding and Failure," *SWHQ* 17 (April 1914): 390.

13. Certification of Petition of cabildo, 25 August 1756, BA; Petition of cabildo, 28 November 1759, in "Testimonio de los autos formados sobre la entrega del presidio de San Sabá al capitán don Felipe de Rabago y Terán," Archivo General de Indias, Ramo Audiencia de México, Transcripts, Spanish Material from Various Sources, University of Texas Archives, Austin, vol. 100 (hereafter cited as AGI: M); Petition of Fray Pedro Ramírez, 6 June 1762, BA; Auto of Governor Angel de Martos y Navarrete, 19 August 1762, in "Correspondencia con el gobernador de Texas don Jacinto de Barrios en los años de 1755 hasta el de 1758 inclusive," AGN: H, vol. 91; Representation of the Cabildo, 7 July 1770, in Carpeta 1a, AGN:PI vol. 100; Antonio de Rivas to viceroy, 12 July 1770, in Correspondencia del gobernador don Manuel Antonio de Oca de los meses de junio, julio y diciembre, año de 1770," AGN: PI, vol. 99; Cabildo to Ripperdá, 31 July 1771, Carpeta 1a, AGN: PI, vol. 100.

14. Inspection of town by Governor Navarrete, 20 June 1762, BA.

15. These events are narrated in, among others: Herbert E. Bolton, *Texas in the Middle Eighteenth Century: Studies in Spanish Colonial History and Administration* (reprint, Austin: University of Texas Press, 1970), 325–93; Dunn, "The Apache Mission"; and Robert S. Weddle, *The San Sabá Mission*. The rise in Indian attacks along the frontier also occasioned population increases at Santa Fe, New Mexico. Some settlements, on the other hand, were almost completely abandoned (Alicia V. Tjarks, "Demographic, Ethnic and Occupational Structure of New Mexico, 1790," *The Americas* 35 (July 1978): 57.

16. At various times in the 1760s Béxar's commanders requested and received reinforcements. See, e.g., Viceroy to Governor Navarrete, 6 January 1764, BA; Viceroy to Governor O'Conor, 7 February 1769, ibid.; Viceroy to Captain Menchaca, 5 May 1769, ibid.; Antonio de Rivas to Viceroy, 12 July 1770, in "Correspondencia del gobernador don Manuel Antonio de Oca de los meses de junio, julio, y diciembre, año 1770," AGN: PI, vol. 99.

17. Representation of cabildo, 7 July 1770, Carpeta 1a, AGN: PI, vol. 100.

18. Bolton, *Texas in the Middle Eighteenth Century*, 107–8.

19. *Reglamento e instrucción*, 80–82; "Testimonio de la instrucción formada por el coronel de infantería don Hugo Oconor," a fin del arreglo de los presidios de los Adaes y Orcoquiz, 6 May 1773, Archivo General de Indias, Ramo Audiencia de Guadalajara, Transcripts, Spanish Materials from Various Sources, University of Texas Archives, Austin, vol. 47 (hereafter cited as AGI: G).

20. For the story of the abandonment and reoccupation of East Texas see Bolton, *Texas in the Middle Eighteenth Century*, 375–446.

21. "Expediente promovido por los vecinos del extinguido presidio de los Adaes

para que se les conceda algún establecimiento donde puedan subsistir con sus familias," 4 January 1778, AGI: G, vol. 48.

22. "Provincia de Texas: Estado general de la tropa de el presidio y vecindario de la Villa de San Fernando, empadronado y revisado por mi, el coronel de los reales ejércitos, don Domingo Cabello, gobernador de dicha provincia, en los dias 10, 20 y 30 del mes de julio de 1779," Archivo General de Indias, Ramo Audiencia de Guadalajara, microfilm, legajo 283 (hereafter cited as AGI: Provincia de Texas).

23. Governor Cabello to Commandant General, 20 November 1780, BA; "Estado de la fuerza efectiva de hombres y caballos que tenía esta compañía en primero de enero de 1781," 31 January 1781, ibid.; "Noticia que el coronel don Domingo Cabello," 31 December 1785, ibid.; Governor Cabello to Commandant General, 5 November 1786, ibid.; "Representación, apologia, o escudo, que la República de la Villa de San Fernando, Real Presidio de San Antonio de Béxar," [1787], ibid.; Tjarks, "Comparative Demographic Analysis," 301.

24. "Padrón de las almas que hay en esta villa de San Fernando de Austria [sic]," 31 December 1793, BA. This census revealed 1,271 civilians. Adding the roughly 330 soldiers and dependents of the presidial company, Béxar's total population in that year amounted to approximately 1,600 men, women, and children.

25. Hinojosa, *A Borderlands Town*, 20; Jones, *Los Paisanos*, 22–23, 34, 66–67, 110–16.

26. Swann, *Tierra Adentro*, 207–14; McReynolds, "Family Life," 117; Tjarks, "Demographic Structure of New Mexico," table 2, p. 63.

27. "Diario de la conquista y entrada a los Thejas," *Universidad de México* 5, 27–28 (Jan.–Feb. 1933): 58; "Autos sobre diferentes noticias que se han participado a su excelencia de las entradas que en estos dominios hacen los franceses por la parte de Coahuila," 1715, AGN: PI, vol. 181; Espinosa, *Chrónica apostólica*, 449.

28. Colin M. MacLachlan and Jaime E. Rodríguez O., *The Forging of the Cosmic Race: A Reinterpretation of Colonial Mexico* (Berkeley: University of California Press, 1980), 233. The bishop of Durango's 1730 schedule of fees provided that New Mexicans pay for nuptials with local produce in the absence of specie. Those in deep poverty were allowed to pay what they could (Ramón Arturo Gutiérrez, "Marriage, Sex and the Family: Social Change in Colonial New Mexico, 1690–1846" (Ph.D. dissertation, University of Wisconsin–Madison, 1980), 129.

29. José Martínez to Juana de Carabajal, 8 May 1721, Valero Marriages, Transcript, San Fernando Cathedral Archives, San Antonio (hereafter cited as SF); Cristóbal Basques to Ana de Carabajal, 20 February 1722, ibid.; Diego Camacho to Juana Antonia de Carabajal, 24 June 1723, ibid.

30. Estimate based on the appearance of married couples as witnesses or participants in Valero Mission marriages and baptisms between 1719 and 1730.

31. Tjarks, "Comparative Demographic Analysis," table 7, p. 311. Tjarks ("Demographic Structure of New Mexico," table 7, p. 71) also arrives at similar figures for New Mexico towns of this period. Dobyns (*Spanish Colonial Tucson*, 146–47),

although not specifically looking at numbers of marriages for the entire Hispanic population of Tucson, indicates an even higher marriage rate there.

32. MacLachlan, *Forging of the Cosmic Race*, 233–34. The older marriage ages for both men and women in the latter part of the century match those found in New Mexican settlements of the period (Gutiérrez, "Marriage, Sex and the Family," Appendix II: Mean Age of Males and Females at First Marriage by Place and Year, 456–62).

33. Neither the 929 baptisms nor the 268 burials should be confused with total numbers of births and deaths. The registers upon which these numbers are based are incomplete and sometimes illegible, thereby excluding an undeterminable number of entries.

34. Swann, *Tierra Adentro*, 214–25.

35. Tjarks, "Comparative Demographic Analysis," 313.

36. Schuetz, "The Indians of the San Antonio Missions, 1718–1821" (Ph.D. dissertation, University of Texas at Austin, 1980), 316–17.

37. Tjarks, "Comparative Demographic Analysis," 310.

38. Jones, *Los Paisanos*, 246–47.

39. "Una cuadrilla de trapientos de todos colores;" Juan Agustín de Morfi, *Viaje de indios y diario del Nuevo México* (reprint, Mexico: Manuel Porrua, 1980), 351.

40. A similar process took place in New Mexico at the end of the seventeenth century (Tjarks, "Demographic Structure of New Mexico," 79; Jones, *Los Paisanos*, 130).

41. Leslie Scott Offutt, "Urban and Rural Society in the Mexican North: Saltillo in the late Colonial Period," (PH.D. dissertation, University of California, Los Angeles, 1982), 196.

42. Unlike some other parts of New Spain where the practice was to maintain different parish registers for the different ethnic groups, in Béxar the priest maintained only one set of books. David A. Brading, "Grupos étnicos; clases y estructura ocupaciónal en Guanajuato (1792)," *Historia mexicana* 21 (1972): 461; John K. Chance and William B. Taylor, "Estate and Class in a Colonial City: Oaxaca in 1792," *Comparative Studies in Society and History* 19 (1977): 461.

43. Swann, *Tierra Adentro*, 119; Dobyns, *Spanish Colonial Tucson*, 65, and Appendix Table 3. For a general discussion of colonial racial schemes, see Magnus Mörner, *Race Mixture in the History of Latin America* (Boston: Little, Brown and Company, 1967), 56–62.

44. Alicia Tjarks claims that "in proportion to their actual number, mestizos were so classified very infrequently, probably because such a name still carried with it, at least in the popular mind, a meaning of illegitimacy" ("Comparative Demographic Analysis," 323).

45. Where the authors differ is in deciding whether late colonial society continued to be bound by the caste system or was increasingly based on an emerging class structure. While the debate falls outside the scope of this dissertation, primarily because I have not discovered a relationship between race and occupation, the observations concerning "passing" are extremely helpful in understanding the

social aspects of racial patterns in Béxar. Chance and Taylor, "Estate and Class in a Colonial City," 461–66; Chance and Taylor, "Estate and Class: A Reply," *Comparative Studies in Society and History* 21 (1979): 436–40; Robert McCaa, Stuart B. Schwartz, and Arturo Grubessich, "Race and Class in Colonial Latin America: A Critique," ibid., 422–23; Patricia Seed, "Social Dimensions of Race: Mexico City, 1753," *Hispanic American Historical Review* 62 (November 1982): 591–600. In his 1986 review article ("Urban Society in Colonial Spanish America: Research Trends", *Latin American Research Review* 21 (1986): 32), Fred Bronner points out that "in their quest for analysis, historians compound the confusion by adopting three, four, or more occupational tiers and by conjoining, omitting, or inventing races."

46. "Razón e informe que el padre presidente de las misiones de la provincia de Texas, o Nuevas Filipinas, remite al ilustrísimo señor don fray Rafael José Verger," Transcript, Spanish Materials from Various Sources, University of Texas Archives, Austin, vol. 764 (hereafter cited as SM).

47. For a breakdown of Béxar's ethnic structure in the period when censuses are available, see Tjarks, "Comparative Demographic Analysis," 317–37.

48. Bando of José Padrón, 5 January 1751, BA; Ordinances of Governor Muñoz, 24 October 1793, ibid.

49. Brading, "Grupos étnicos," 461; Chance and Taylor, "Estate and Class," 462; Stern, "Social Marginality," 414–17.

50. Cabello to Commandant General, 16 August 1780, BA.

51. Case against Vicente Amador, 30 May 1768, BA; "Diligencias practicadas por el coronel don Domingo Cabello, gobernador de esta provincia a instancia de Fernando Arocha, carabinero de la compañía de caballería de este presidio," 5 November 1785, ibid.

52. Petition of Francisco Rodríguez, 20 October 1783, BA; see also "Diligencias practicadas sobre la oposición hecha por José Miguel y Francisco de Sales Games; Carlos y Pedro Hernández, tios y hermanos de María de la Trinidad Hernández," 4 June 1784, ibid.; in this case, Ana María Trinidad Hernández's uncles and brothers, all soldiers, attempted to stop her marriage to Urbano Hinojosa, a mission Indian, on the grounds that it would be unseemly because they were in the military. While Hinojosa argued that they should have no objections because they all had mulatto blood, and that his betrothed's aunt had married an Indian without any opposition from the family, the uncles declared they were not mulattos, but that even if they were, they would still be more worthy—having spilt their blood for the king—than any mission Indian, especially an illegitimate one.

53. There are any number of other examples of this type of racial "transformation." The two house lists used for comparison are: "Padrón de las almas que hay en esta Villa de San Fernando de Austria [sic]," 31 December 1793, BA, and "Padrón de las familias y almas que hay en esta Villa de San Fernando de Austria [sic]," 31 December 1796, ibid.

54. See, e.g., "Padrón general de los oficiales, sargentos, tambor, cabos, carabineros y soldados de que se compone la compañía de caballería del Real Presidio

de San Antonio de Béxar," 31 December 1784, BA; Provincia de Texas, Jurisdicción de San Antonio de Béxar, n.d., ibid.

55. Galbán-Vargas, 30 October 1772, Marriage Petitions, SF.

56. Marion A. Habig, O.F.M., *San Antonio's Mission San José: State and National Historic Site, 1720–1968* (Chicago: Franciscan Herald Press, 1968), 215–17; AGI: Provincia de Texas; "Padrón de las almas que hay en esta villa de San Fernando de Austria [sic]," 31 December 1793, BA; census list of Mission San José, 24 January 1798, NA.

CHAPTER THREE

1. Winthuisen to the Viceroy, 19 August 1744, BA.

2. "Título de gobernador e instrucciones a Don Martín de Alarcón para su expedición a Texas," AGN: Boletín 6:4 (1935), 537.

3. "Diario de la conquista y entrada a los Thejas," *Universidad de México*, 62–63.

4. Jones, *Los Paisanos*, 84, 116, 174, 177–78.

5. Morfi, *History of Texas*, I: 225.

6. Sale of lot and house, 25 June 1745, and sale of lot and house 30 April 1746, in Notary protocol, 22 March 1738, BA; Pérez de Almazán to Viceroy, 24 and 25 October 1724, AGN: PI, vol. 183; Case against Felipe de Avila for the murder of Nicolás Pasqual, 12 April 1730, AGN: PI, vol. 32; Schuetz, "The People of San Antonio," 81; Max L. Moorhead, *The Presidio: Bastion of the Spanish Borderlands* (Norman: University of Oklahoma Press, 1975), 42. The nineteenth century scholars who indexed Provincias Internas combined two related *expedientes* into a single document: The documentation on land distribution to the Canary Islanders is in "Testimonio de autos y Diligencias ejecutadas . . . en razón de la subplantación de la villa de San Fernando con quince familias de las Islas de Canarias: Repartimiento de solares, ejidos, dehesas, tierras de labor y aguas y fundación de propios con lo demas que contiene este testimonio," which is in turn listed under: "Testimonio de Autos seguidos sobre, escrito, presentado por las familias isleñas pidiendo merced y posesión del ojo de agua de San Antonio; y contradicción puesta por el reverendo padre presidente de las misiones de la Santa Cruz de Querétaro," 1731, AGN: PI, vol. 163. The former *expediente* will hereafter be cited as "Repartimiento de solares," and the latter as "Merced y posesión del ojo de agua de San Antonio."

7. Moorhead, *The Presidio*, 222.

8. Mattie Alice Austin, "The Municipal Government of San Fernando de Béxar," 286–94; Elizabeth Howard West, trans., "Bonilla's Brief Compendium of the History of Texas, 1772," *SWHQ* 8 (1904), 35–36, 37–40.

9. Marqués de San Miguel de Aguayo to Viceroy, n.d., and Pedro de Rivera to Viceroy, 30 September 1730, AGN: PI, v. 236.

10. Auto of Captain Juan Antonio Pérez de Almazán, 9 March 1731, "Repartimiento de solares," AGN: PI, vol. 163.

11. Auto of that date, ibid.

12. The viceroy's orders for San Fernando de Béxar's layout called for the traditional grid pattern of town blocks with radiating squares for the ejidos, propios, and farmlands. While the historiography of the "grid-pattern" Spanish-American city is long, it has recently been well summarized by Richard M. Morse in "Urban Development," *Colonial Spanish America*, Leslie Bethell, ed. (Cambridge: Cambridge University Press, 1987), 166–70.

13. Juan Francisco Granado's statement of 1774 tends to support this finding. Asking for clear title to a lot he settled in 1761, he stated that he had taken advantage of the fact that the Isleño families were given permission "wherever they thought best, from the San Antonio River's spring to its confluence [with San Pedro Creek]"; "Donación de un solar a favor de Juan Francisco Granado," 18 September 1774, Land Grants, Bexar County Spanish Archives, Transcripts, Bexar County Clerk's Office, San Antonio (hereafter cited as BCSA). For a representation of Almazán's work, see Lota M. Spell, "The Grant and First Survey of the City of San Antonio," *SWHQ* 66 (July 1962); 80.

14. "Testimonio del despacho de Su Excelencia en que mandó a oficiales reales de México pagasen al apoderado de los quince pobladores del Presidio de Béxar la ayuda de costa de 2.250 pesos y replicas hechas al señor virrey por los suso dichos," 4 July 1731, AGI: G, vol. 24.

15. Petition for land by Juan Banul, 12 January 1734, in "Testimonio del decreto de su excelencia en que contiene varios puntos pertenecientes a los vecinos pobladores de esta villa de San Fernando sacado a pedimiento de dichos vecinos para los efectos que les convenga," [1734]. This *expediente* has inadvertently been filed within the following: "Testimonio de las disposiciones del virey respecto a los vecinos y pobladores de la villa de San Fernando y del real presidio de San Antonio de Béxar, en las Provincias de las Nuevas Filipinas," 1735, AGN: PI, vol. 163 (the former testimonio will hereafter be cited as "Puntos pertenecientes a los vecinos," and the latter as "Disposiciones del virey"); Auto of Governor, 29 January 1734, in "Puntos pertenecientes a los vecinos," ibid.

16. "Venta de solar y casa por Matías de la Zerda a favor de José Salinas," 26 July 1761, Land Grants, BCSA.

17. "Donación de un solar a favor de María Cantún," 19 October 1736, Land Grants, BCSA; "Expediente sobre la donación de un solar a favor de Javiera Cantún," 20 October 1736, ibid.; "Petición y donación de un solar a favor de José Antonio Bueno Hernández de Rojas," 13 October 1736, ibid.; "Donación de un solar a José Antonio Rodríguez," 7 October 1736, ibid.; "Donación de tierra a favor de Nicolasa Jiménez," 26 February 1737, ibid.

18. "Expediente sobre denuncia de tierra por Nicolás Benavides," 27 September 1737, Land Grants, BCSA.

19. "Donación de un solar a favor de Domingo Flores de Abrego," 17 May 1738, Land Grants, BCSA.

20. Report on water available from San Pedro, 25 January 1734, in "Puntos pertenecientes a los vecinos," AGN: PI, vol. 163; Bando of Francisco Delgado, 29

April 1752, BA; in 1762 Gerónimo Flores reported that the town's water needs were being met solely from the San Pedro acequia; see Petition of vecinos agregados, 16 August 1762, ibid.

21. A *vara* is approximately 2.8 English feet.

22. "Donación de tierra a favor de Diego Hernández," 20 May 1741, Land Grants BCSA; Donación de tierra a favor de José Montemayor," 21 October 1743, ibid.; "Donación de un solar a Joaquín de Urrutia," 19 July 1742, Land Grants, BCSA; "Donación de un solar a favor de José Miguel de Urrutia," 15 February 1744, ibid.

23. Entry for 25 June 1745, "Libro de cabildo," 11 January 1742, NA.

24. Castañeda, *Our Catholic Heritage* 3: 107; "Ratificación sobre la donación de un solar expedida a favor de José Pérez de Casanova," 28 May 1749, Land Grants, BCSA.

25. "Donación de un solar a favor de Antonio Guerra," 2 January 1744, Land Grants, BCSA; "Donación de un solar a Luis Antonio Menchaca," 18 June 1745, ibid.

26. "Petición para un solar presentada por Marcos Menchaca," 20 December 1760, Land Grants, BCSA; "Solicitud para un solar por Juan de la Cruz del Valle," 20 December 1760, ibid.

27. "Donación de un solar a favor de Jacobo Hernández," 26 June 1762, Land Grants, BCSA; "Donación de un solar a favor de Francisco de Urrutia," 2 August 1762, ibid.

28. "Donación de un solar a Andrés Ramón," 31 August 1762, Land Grants, BCSA; "Donación de un solar a Carlos Ignacio de Uraga," 12 August 1762, ibid.; Auto of Governor Martos y Navarrete, 9 September 1762, in Inspection of Villa by Governor Martos y Navarrete, 20 June 1762, BA.

29. "Donación de un solar a Andrés Ramón," 31 August 1762, Land Grants, BCSA.

30. "Donación de un solar a favor de Juan Leal Alvarez Goraz," 28 December 1768, Land Grants, BCSA; "Donación de un solar a favor de Juliana de la Garza," 6 September 1770, ibid.; "Donación de un solar a favor de Salvador de la Garza," 15 January 1771, ibid.; "Donación de un solar a favor de Leonardo de la Garza," ibid.; "Donación de un solar a Juan José Bueno de Roxas," 6 September 1770, ibid.

31. "Venta de un solar por Juan Leal Goras a Pedro Huizar," 20 February 1783, Land Grants, BCSA; "Venta de un solar por Juliana de la Garza a Pedro Huizar," 13 July 1784, ibid.

32. "Donación de tierra a Ignacio Calvillo," 3 March 1773, Land Grants, BCSA; "Donación de un solar a Francisco Guadalupe Calaorra," 15 February 1778, ibid.; "Mercenamiento de tierra a Josefa Flores," 5 September 1778, ibid.; "Donación de tierra a favor de José Antonio de la Garza," 18 May 1782, ibid.; "Donación de tierra a favor de Bernardo de Soto," 8 October 1794, ibid.

33. "Expediente sobre la donación de un solar a favor de Juan Cantún," 12

November 1749, Land Grants, BCSA; "Donación de un solar a Diego Ramón," 30 January 1745, Land Grants, BCSA; "Donación de un solar a favor de Sebastián Rincón," 12 November 1749, ibid.

34. First mention of the area as "Laredo" is found in "Donación de un solar a favor de Luis Antonio Durán," 12 March 1772, Land Grants, BCSA.

35. "Donación de tierra a Ignacio Calvillo," 3 March 1773, Land Grants, BCSA; Donación de un solar a favor de Luis Antonio Durán," 12 March 1772, ibid.

36. "Venta de tierra por Diego Iríneo Henríquez a favor de Juan José Córdova," 12 May 1791, Land Grants, BCSA.

37. "Donación de un solar a favor de Pedro Miñón," 10 June 1769, Land Grants, BCSA.

38. "Donación de un terreno a Silvestre Joaquín de Soto," 16 July 1762, Land Grants, BCSA; "Donación de tierra a favor de Miguel Santos," 20 August 1767, ibid.; "Donación de un solar a Margarita de la Zerda," 23 February 1785, ibid. The Potrero is first called a *barrio* (neighborhood) in "Expediente sobre la donación de un solar a favor de Francisco Guadalupe Calaorra," 31 August 1784, ibid.

39. "Expediente promovido por los vecinos del extinguido presidio de los Adaes para que se les conceda algún establecimiento donde puedan subsistir con sus familias," Béxar, 4 January 1778, AGI: G, vol. 48; Bando on the creation of barrios, 5 October 1809, in Collection of Governor's *bandos*, 16 January 1809, NA.

40. "Expediente sobre la donación de un solar a favor de Josefa Cadena y venta del mismo a Josefa Menchaca," 3 June 1782, Land Grants, BCSA; "Donación de un solar a favor de Ignacio Estrada," 6 April 1778, ibid.; Domingo Pérez, 8 October 1778, ibid.; "Donación de tierra a favor de María Matiana de los Santos," 17 April 1784, ibid.; "Donación de tierra a José Antonio Bustillo y Zevallos," ibid.; "Donación de un solar a Margarita de la Zerda," 23 February 1785, ibid.

41. "Donación de un solar a favor de María Luisa Guerrero," 18 September 1780, Land Grants, BCSA.

42. "Donación de un solar a Martín Flores y Baldés," 31 August 1762, Land Grants, BCSA; "Donación de tierra a Miguel de Castro," 17 May 1738, ibid.; "Donación de un solar a favor de Manuel Delgado," 16 March 1772, ibid.; "Petición sobre un solar presentada por Rosa Guerra," 16 May 1749, ibid.; "Donación de un solar a Rosalia Flores y Valdés," 24 July 1782, ibid.

43. "Donación de tierra a favor de Francisco de Estrada," 6 October 1739, Land Grants, BCSA.

44. "Donación de un solar a favor de Juan Cortinas," 24 October 1743, Land Grants, BCSA; "Donación de un solar a favor de José Pérez de Casanova," 30 June 1744, ibid.; "Donación de un terreno a favor de Cristóbal Valdez," 8 February 1739, ibid.

45. "Expediente sobre la donación de un solar a favor de Juan Cantún," 12 November 1749, Land Grants, BCSA; "Donación de un solar a favor de Andrés García," 21 September 1761, ibid.; "Donación de un solar a favor de Juan Leal,"

12 March 1772, ibid.; "Donación de tierra a favor de Bernardo de Soto," 8 October 1794, ibid.

46. "Expediente sobre la donación de tierra otorgada a favor de Francisco Luis Charo," 20 August 1751, Land Grants, BCSA.

47. Of 182 eighteenth-century town lot grants from the Béxar County Spanish Archives examined, 122 made mention of family in the petitions. Often, the term used is "large family." Many of the other grants were for scrap pieces of land or for corrals.

48. "Autos hechos a representación de don Antonio Rodríguez Mederos, regidor decano de la villa de San Fernando en la Provincia de Texas," 19 July 1749, BA; "Libro de cuentas de los soldados del real presidio de Nuestra Señora del Pilar de los Adaes destacados en este de San Antonio de Béxar donde consta lo que cada uno va devengando por tercios," 1 January 1771, ibid.; "Donación de un solar a favor de Jacobo Hernández," 26 June 1762, Land Grants, BCSA.

49. "Donación de un solar a favor de Juan Francisco Granado," 18 September 1774, Land Grants, BCSA. See also "Donación de un solar a favor de Juan Bautista Hernández," 28 December 1768, ibid.; and "Donación de un solar a favor de Martín de la Garza," 15 September 1778, ibid.

50. Of seventeen lots granted to women examined, thirteen mention widowhood in their petitions.

51. "Donación de un solar a favor de Gertrudis Guerra," 9 October 1764, Land Grants, BCSA.

52. "Donación de un solar a favor de Gertrudis Sánchez," 6 April 1778, Land Grants, BCSA.

53. "Donación de un solar a Rosalia Flores y Valdés," 24 July 1782, Land Grants, BCSA.

54. "Donación de un solar a favor de Asencio Guadalupe," 20 August 1767, Land Grants, BCSA; "Donación de un solar a favor de Luis Antonio Durán," 12 March 1772, ibid.; "Donación de tierra a favor de Bartolo Seguín," 23 April 1772, ibid.

55. "Donación de tierra a Cristóbal de los Santos Coy," 7 January 1746, Land Grants, BCSA.

56. "Expediente sobre la donación de un solar a favor de Francisco Guadalupe Calaorra," 31 August 1784, Land Grants, BCSA.

57. "Donación de tierra a favor de Juan Antonio de Medina," 12 August 1773, Land Grants, BCSA.

58. See, for instance, "Donación de un solar a Martín Flores y Valdés, 31 August 1762, Land Grants, BCSA; "Expediente sobre la donación de un solar a favor de Francisco Guadalupe Calaorra," 31 August 1784, ibid.; "Donación de un solar a favor de Sebastián Rincón," 12 November 1749, ibid.; "Donación de un solar a Francisco Sánchez," 5 July 1764, ibid.; "Donación de un solar a José Jiménez Cisneros," 24 July 1765, ibid.

59. "Donación de un solar a Diego Ramón," 30 January 1745, Land Grants, BCSA.

60. "Donación de tierra a José Feliciano de la Zerda," 27 April 1797, Land Grants, BCSA.

61. "Expediente sobre la donación de tierra a favor de Nicolás de Carabajal," 3 February 1741, Land Grants, BCSA.

62. "Donación de un solar a favor de Alberto López," 8 March 1740, Land Grants, BCSA.

63. "Donación de un solar a Juan Banul," 24 October 1737, Land Grants, BCSA.

64. "Donación de un solar a favor de Gertrudis Guerra," 9 October 1764, Land Grants, BCSA; "Donación de un solar a favor de Francisco de Urrutia," 19 April 1778, ibid.

65. "Arrendamiento de tierra por el gobierno a Juan Curbelo," 31 May 1736, Land Grants, BCSA; "Donación de tierra a favor de Juan Curbelo," 26 February 1737, ibid.

66. "Donación de un solar a favor de José Curbelo," 5 March 1761, Land Grants, BCSA; "Donación de un solar a favor de Manuel de la Fuente," 5 September 1765, ibid.; "Donación de un solar a favor de Juan José Montes de Oca," 3 September 1762, ibid.; "Donación de un solar a favor de Cristóbal Valdez," 22 April 1742, ibid.

67. "Testamento de Vicente Alvarez Travieso," 16 January 1779, Wills, BCSA.

68. "Venta de un solar por Leonardo de la Garza a favor de Pedro Huizar," 29 December 1784, Land Grants, BCSA; "Venta de un solar por Juan Leal Goraz a Pedro Huizar," 20 February 1783, ibid.; "Venta de un solar por Juliana de la Garza a Pedro Huizar," 13 July 1784, ibid.; "Expediente instruido ante el reparto de las tierras de San Antonio Valero a los vecinos del presidio de los Adaes, año de 1793," GLO.

69. "Testamento de María Josefa Flores," 5 August 1787, Wills, BCSA.

70. "Testamento de María Betancour," 5 January 1779, Wills, BCSA; "Testamento de Mariana Curbelo," 25 September 1784, ibid.; "Testamento de Domingo Delgado," 29 April 1772, ibid.; "Testamento of Pablo Flores," 20 November 1797, ibid.; "Testamento de Juan Manuel de Ruiz," 28 July 1797, ibid.; "Testamento de Ana Santos," 7 April 1778, ibid.; "Venta de tierra por Manuel de Urrutia a favor de Nicolás Carabajal," 3 November 1784, Land Grants, BCSA; "Venta de una casa y solar por Gertrudis de Rosas a favor de Juan José Flores," 5 February 1781, ibid.; "Venta de un jacal y solar por Juan José Flores a favor de Manuel Flores," 15 March 1784, ibid.; "Venta de un jacal por Juan Martín Méndez a favor de Eugenio Mireles," 31 March 1787, ibid.; "Donación de un solar a Jorge de los Santos," 19 October 1774, ibid.

71. "Testamentaria de Jacinto Delgado," 13 July 1799, Wills, BCSA; "Trámites sobre la donación de un solar a favor de Fernando de Arocha y traspasos del mismo," 10 July 1782, Protocol, BCSA; "Venta de una casa y un solar por Antonio

Bustillos y Zevallos a Francisco Amangual," 7 March 1785, Land Grants, BCSA; "Venta de un solar por Luis Antonio Charo a Juan Bautista de Avila," 2 November 1775, ibid.; "Restitución de un solar a Antonio de las Barcenas," 20 October 1777, ibid.; "Venta de un solar por María Andrea Morillo a favor de Dionicio de Jesús González," 28 June 1782, ibid.; "Venta de un terreno por Josefa Flores de Abrego a favor de Nicolás Flores," 24 January 1798, ibid.; "Venta de tierra por Vicente Flores a favor de Francisco Galán," 28 December 1790, ibid.; "Venta de solar, casa, y jacal por Juan Banul a favor de Santiago Pérez," 27 September 1765, ibid.; "Venta de una casa por Francisco Javier Galán al Capitán Francisco José Pereira," 28 April 1800, ibid.; "Venta de un solar por Juan Leal Goraz a Pedro Huizar," 20 February 1783, ibid.; "Venta de un solar por Juliana de la Garza a Pedro Huizar," 13 July 1784, ibid.; "Venta de un solar por Juan Leal Goras a Pedro Huizar," 20 February 1783, ibid.; "Venta de una casa por Gregorio Flores Quiñones a Antonio del Rio," 5 April 1758, ibid.

72. "Diligencias practicadas para la reedificación y recomposición de las casas reales de este real presidio y villa de San Fernando con sus cuentas dadas por don José Antonio Curbelo, primer alcalde ordinario de esta dicha villa y aprobadas por el coronel don Domingo Cabello," 15 February 1779, BA.

73. In at least two cases, Fernando de Veramendi and Joaquín de Orendáin, the owners were married to Isleño descendants; however, at least in Veramendi's case, his wife brought no property into the marriage.

74. A number of grant petitions state that the petitioner had been in Béxar a number of years but without any land of his own; for example, "Having married and living in this town, I have been forced to live in a rented house" ("Donación de un solar a favor de Luis Antonio Durán," 12 March 1772, Land Grants, BCSA).

75. "Testamento de María Ignacia Núñez Morillo," 12 September 1800, BA.

76. Willard B. Robinson, "Colonial Ranch Architecture in the Spanish-American Tradition," *SWHQ* 83 (October 1979): 130–31, provides a detailed description of this type of construction, as do Arnoldo De León, *The Tejano Community, 1836–1900* (Albuquerque: University of New Mexico Press, 1982), 2–3; Jones, *Los Paisanos*, 248; Richard G. Santos, *Aguayo Expedition into Texas*, 74–75.

77. "Diario de la conquista . . ." ; Fernando Pérez de Almazán to Viceroy, 24 October 1724, AGN: PI, vol. 183; *Relación de los méritos y servicios de Don Fernando Pérez de Almazán* (Madrid, 1729).

78. Tomás Felipe de Winthuisen to [Viceroy], 19 August 1744, BA.

79. Morfi, *History of Texas*, 1: 92.

80. Nicolás de Lafora, *Relación del viaje que hizo a los presidios internos situados en la frontera de la América Septentrional* (Mexico: Editorial Pedro Robledo, 1939), 41.

81. Morfi, *Viaje de indios*, 130.

82. Robinson, "Colonial Ranch Architecture," 131–39, describes this type of construction and provides a number of interesting photographs. Perhaps the most significant difference between the ranch and town houses was the inclusion of windows in the latter.

83. Petition of Cayetano Pérez, 24 May 1736, BA; sale of house and lot, 8 July 1739, sale of lot and house, 7 January 1740, sale of lot and house, 25 June 1745, and sale of lot and house, 30 April 1746, in Notary Protocol, 22 March 1738, ibid.; sale of lots and house, 28 May 1748, sale of lot and house, 17 June 1748, exchange of properties, 17 July 1748, and sale of lot, 17 May 1749, in Notary Protocol, 15 September 1747, ibid.; Testamentary proceedings, 5 October 1751, ibid.; "Causa mortual del defunto don Juan José Flores de Abrego, que fallecio en este Presidio de Béxar, y Villa de San Fernando el dia 18 de enero del Presente año de 1779, 9 June 1779," ibid.; petition of various citizens, 15 October 1789, ibid.; Testament of José Curbelo, 28 February 1767, Wills, BCSA; Testament of Pablo Flores, 20 November 1797, ibid.; "Inventarios del finado Juan Leal Goras," 2 March 1743, ibid.; Testament of Juana de Hollos, 13 August 1785, ibid.; Testament of Juan Andrés Travieso, 10 April 1783, ibid.; "Venta de un solar por María Zaragoza Navarro a Francisco Amangual," 18 December 1792, Land Grants, BCSA.

84. Sale of lot and house, 25 June 1745, sale of lot and house, 30 April 1746, in Notary Protocol, 22 March 1738, BA; "Donación de tierra a favor de Diego Menchaca," 25 February 1783, Land Grants, BCSA; "Donación de un solar a Pedro Regalado de Treviño," 14 October 1739, ibid.; "Donación de un solar a favor de Antonio de los Rios," 28 December 1768, ibid.

85. Swann, *Tierra Adentro*, 285.

86. Governor Cabello to Commandant General, 20 July 1784, BA.

87. "Donación de un solar a Pedro Flores de Abrego," 6 September 1770, Land Grants, BCSA; "Donación de un solar a favor de Gregorio Quiñones Flores," 29 July 1765, ibid.

88. "Inventarios de la causa mortual de don Juan Flores, difunto vecino de esta Villa de San Fernando y Real Presidio de San Antonio de Béxar," 10 April 1790, BA; Luis Antonio Menchaca to don Manuel Muñoz, 18 December 1790, ibid.; "Venta de una casa y un solar por Antonio Bustillos y Zevallos a Francisco Amangual," 7 March 1785, Land Grants, BCSA.

89. "Diligencias practicadas sobre la instancia del bachiller don Pedro Fuentes, cura párroco y vicario de esta villa y presidio sobre pretender fabricar una casa de alto de que se le ha dado vista al procurador general y ayuntamiento quienes han asentido a ello," 23 September 1780, BA.

90. In his will Veramendi makes provisions for masses to be said at the presidial church of La Bahía for the souls of all who died there between 1770 and the date of his own death, thus indicating his association with that community from that year. He made similar arrangements for San Antonio's dead from 1776 onward, that is, from the year of his transfer to the capital ("Causa mortual de don Fernando Veramendi, natural del reino de Navarra y vecino de la villa de San Fernando y presidio de San Antonio de Béxar, 28 April 1783, BA).

91. Petition of José Padrón, 26 October 1774, BA; "Causa mortual de don Fernando Veramendi," ibid.; "Diligencias practicadas por el Coronel don Domingo Cabello," 5 November 1785, ibid.; "Expediente promovido por don Juan José

de la Santa y don Francisco Bueno," 18 October 1790, ibid.; "Venta de dos suertes de tierra y agua por Joaquín Menchaca a favor de Fernando de Veramendi," 25 June 1782, Protocol, BCSA; "Veramendi, Juan Martín," *The Handbook of Texas*, 2: 837.

92. "Causa mortual del difunto don Juan José Flores de Abrego, que fallecio en este presidio de Béxar, y villa de San Fernando el dia 18 de enero del presente año de 1779," 9 June 1779, BA; "Venta de una casa y un solar por Antonio Bustillos y Zevallos a Francisco Amangual," 7 March 1785, Land Grants, BCSA; "Venta de una casa y solar por Gertrudis de Rosas a favor de Juan José Flores," 5 February 1781, ibid.; "Venta de una casa por Margarita Falcon a Gavino Valdés, año de 1795, y traspaso de la misma a favor de María Trinidad Gámez, año de 1804," 6 June 1795, ibid.

CHAPTER FOUR

1. Note 3, AGI:Provincia de Texas.

2. Jones, *Los Paisanos*, 47–248; MacLachlan and Rodríguez O., *Cosmic Race*, 155–56; Michael C. Meyer, *Water in the Hispanic Southwest: A Social and Legal History*, 1550–1850 (Tucson: University of Arizona Press, 1983), 29–30, 47–50.

3. Presidio de San Antonio de Béjar, in "Reglamento de Presidios," 1729, Archivo General de la Nación de México, Ramo Bandos, vol. 2, no. 14; "Autos sobre diferentes [asuntos] consultados por el gobernador de la provincia de los Texas: muerte de un correo y otras materias. Año de 1724," AGN: PI, vol. 183.

4. Auto of Alcalde Mayor and Captain Juan Antonio Pérez de Almazán, 9 March 1731, "Repartimiento de solares," AGN: PI, vol. 163; Auto of Captain Almazán, 12 March 1731, ibid.; Auto of Captain Almazán, 13 March 1731, ibid.; Benedict Leuteneger, trans., "Memorial of Father Benito Fernández Concerning the Canary Islanders, 1741," *SWHQ* 82 (January 1979): 277–78.

5. For the various land measures, see Wistano Luis Orozco, *Legislación y jurisprudencia sobre terrenos baldíos* (Mexico, 1895), 1: 758; and J. Villasana Haggard, *Handbook for Translators of Spanish Historical Documents* (University of Texas at Austin, 1941), 71–87 passim.

6. Act of possession for farmland, 10 July 1731, "Repartimiento de solares," AGN: PI, vol. 163.

7. Thomas Glick, *The Old World Background of the Irrigation System of San Antonio, Texas* (Southwestern Studies Series, No. 35, University of Texas at El Paso: Texas Western Press, 1972), 37–40, and Betty E. Dobkins, *The Spanish Element in Texas Water Law* (Austin: University of Texas Press, 1959,) 111, following Edwin P. Arneson in "Early Irrigation in Texas," *SWHQ* 25 (October 1921): 124, incorrectly attribute the building of the town's first acequia to the Isleños.

8. "Autos sobre las providencias dadas por su excelencia al gobernador de la provincia de Texas para la pacificación de los Indios Apaches y sus aliados, 1731,"

1 December 1731, AGN: PI, vol. 32; "Superior despacho del ilustrísimo y excelentísimo señor Arzobispo, virrey de esta Nueva España, ganado en nombre de los vecinos de la villa de San Fernando de la Provincia de Texas," 24 January 1736, AGN: PI, vol. 32; Meyer, *Water in the Hispanic Southwest*, 30, 157.

9. Governor Sandoval to Viceroy, 5 March 1734, "Puntos pertenecientes a los pobladores," AGN: PI, vol. 163.

10. "Puntos pertenecientes a los vecinos," AGN:PI vol. 163; Meyer, *Water in the Hispanic Southwest*, 78–79; Swann, *Tierra Adentro*, 50–51; MacLachlan and Rodríguez O., *Cosmic Race*, 150, 166; Cuello, "Saltillo in the Seventeenth Century," 17, 47–48; Wells A. Hutchins, "The Community Acequia: Its Origin and Development," *SWHQ* 31 (January 1928): 262–64, 272–73.

11. "Autos sobre las providencias dadas por su excelencia al gobernador de la provincia de Texas," 1 December 1731, AGN: PI, vol. 32; "Puntos pertenecientes a los vecinos," AGN: PI, vol. 163.

12. "Puntos pertenecientes a los vecinos," AGN: PI, vol. 163; Petition of Juan Leal Goraz, alcalde ordinario, et al., 4 February 1734, ibid.; Petition of Antonio Rodríguez, mayordomo, 27 February 1734, ibid.; Sandoval to Viceroy, 5 March 1734, ibid.; Petition of Martin Lorenzo de Armas, et al., 14 February 1734, AGN: PI, vol. 236; Order of Viceroy, 24 January 1736, BA.

13. The documentation for the early part of the dispute is contained in: Petition of the Canary Islanders, 27 July 1731; Fray Gabriel de Vergara to [Captain Pérez de Almazán], 20 May 1732, Cabildo to Viceroy, 19 October 1732, "Merzed y posessión de el ojo de Agua de San Antonio," AGN: PI, vol. 163; Order of Viceroy, 12 May 1733, Canary Islanders who settled in San Antonio, SM, vol. 727; Order of Governor Juan Bustillo y Zevallos, 19 October 1733, ibid.; Acknowledgement of Isleños, 21 October 1733, ibid.; Report of Lieutenant and Alcalde Mayor, Don Mateo Pérez, 27 October 1733, ibid.

14. Order of Governor Bustillo, 19 October 1733, ibid.; Report of Lieutenant and Alcalde Mayor, Don Mateo Pérez, 27 October 1733, ibid.

15. Antonio Rodríguez Mederos to Francisco Hernández, 10 April 1739; José Cabrera to Antonio Rodríguez Mederos, 2 January 1740; José Padrón to Gerónimo Flores, 7 October 1740; Manuel de Niz to Pedro Ocón y Trillo, 26 May 1741; Juan Leal Alvarez to Toribio de Urrutia, 25 November 1741; Resignation of office, 28 March 1742; all in Notary Protocol, 22 March 1738, BA.

16. "Inventarios del finado Juan Leal Goraz," 2 March 1743, Wills, BCSA; "Testamentaria de Jacinto Delgado," 13 July 1799, ibid.; "Poder consedido por Juan José Sánchez a Tomás Travieso," 18 December 1791, Protocol, BCSA; Petition of Francisco Javier Rodríguez, 29 March 1784, BA.

17. Petition of Ignacia de Castro, 19 September 1771, BA; Petition of Ignacia de Castro, 17 October 1771, ibid.; Petition of Marcos de Castro, 3 June 1774, ibid.

18. "Testamento de José Curbelo," 28 February 1767, Wills, BCSA.

19. Petition of Juan Leal Goraz, alcalde ordinario, et al., 4 February 1734, AGN: PI, vol. 163.

20. Canary Islanders *v.* agregados, 14 May 1749, NA.

21. "Autos de defensa de don Toribio de Urrutia, Capitán de el presidio de San Antonio de Béxar en la provincia de Texas, contra el gobernador de la misma, año de 1758," Archivo de San Francisco el Grande, Transcripts, Spanish Materials from Various Sources, University of Texas Archives, Austin, vol. 835 (hereafter cited as SFG); petition of vecinos agregados, 16 August 1762, BA; entry for 25 June 1745, "Libro de Cabildo," 11 January 1742, NA.

22. "Autos de defensa de don Toribio de Urrutia," SFG, vol. 835; petition of vecinos agregados, 16 August 1762, BA.

23. Auto of Governor Navarrete, 9 September 1762, in Inspection of town by Governor Navarrete, 20 June 1762, BA.

24. Documents regarding establishment of the upper *labor*, Deed Records, BCSA, book 3: 317–48.

25. Ibid.

26. Hutchins, "The Community Acequia," 271; Meyer, *Water in the Hispanic Southwest*, 70.

27. Documents regarding establishment of the upper *labor*, Deed Records, BCSA, book 3: 317–48.

28. Ibid.

29. The four parcels consisted of one to Pedro Fuentes, the priest, one to his brother-in-law, Ignacio García, and two to his father, Toribio Fuentes, who had directed the construction project in the first few months.

30. Documents regarding establishment of the upper *labor*, Deed Records, BCSA, book 3: 317–48.

31. "Venta de tierra por Manuel de Arocha a Simón de Arocha," 10 August 1776, Land Grants, BCSA.

32. Félix Menchaca to Governor Ripperdá, 7 July 1776, in Documents regarding establishment of the upper *labor*, Deed Records, BCSA, book 3: 317–48.

33. "Permuta de tierras y agua entre Juan José Montes de Oca y Joaquín Flores de Sendeja," 23 March 1782, Land Grants, BCSA.

34. "Causa mortual de don Fernando Veramendi," 28 April 1783, BA.

35. "Venta de tierra y agua por los herederos de Juan Flores a favor de Pedro Flores," 26 March 1788, Land Grants, BCSA; "Venta de un terreno por José María de Veramendi a favor de Pedro Flores," 30 March 1800, ibid.

36. "Venta de tierra y agua por Mariano de la Garza a favor de Macario Zambrano," Land Grants, BCSA.

37. The available evidence indicates the following concentration of suertes: Fernando Veramendi's heirs, 3; the Menchacas, 3; the Fuentes, 4; Macario Zambrano, 4; Joaquín Flores 4; Simón de Arocha, 4; Pedro Flores, 5.

38. Agreement between Querétaro Missions and town of San Fernando, 14 August 1745, GLO.

39. "Carta de Fray Mariano Francisco de los Dolores, respecto a quejas de los indios contra los habitantes de San Fernando de Béxar," 1758, SFG, vol. 835.

40. Proceedings of Juez Privativo, Diego Antonio Cornide y Saavedra, 12 June 1770, GLO.

41. "Expediente promovido por los vecinos del extinguido presidio de los Adaes," 4 January 1778, AGI: G, vol. 48. For a different interpretation of these events, see Castañeda, *Our Catholic Heritage* 4: 344–56.

42. "Expediente promovido por los vecinos," AGI: G, vol. 48.

43. Ibid.

44. Carlos Castañeda argues that Cabello believed such a radical plan should come from the King and that, in any case, the Adaesanos were unworthy of such largess (*Our Catholic Heritage* 4: 356).

45. Castañeda, *Our Catholic Heritage* 5: 36–39.

46. Rullmann, "Historical Map of Old San Antonio," University of Texas Archives, Austin.

47. "Expediente instruido ante el reparto de las tierras de San Antonio Valero a los vecinos del presidio de los Adaes, año de 1793," GLO.

48. The distribution document states that each received enough land to plant one-half fanega of maize. Subsequent grants indicate suertes varying in size from 37,550 to 123,000 square varas. See "Poseción de Catarina Pozos," 4 February 1797, Wills, BCSA; "Donación de tierra a Ignacio de los Santos Coy," 18 September 1797, Land Grants, BCSA; "Donación de tierra a favor de José Pascual Martínez," 9 February 1797, ibid.; "Donación de una suerte de tierra a José Roberto Núñez," 13 February 1797, ibid.

49. "Testamento de Catarina Posos," 14 March 1802, Wills, BCSA.

50. "Donación de un pedazo de tierra a Vicente Amador," 11 April 1793, Land Grants, BCSA; "Donación de un sitio a favor de Francisco Villegas," 18 April 1793, ibid.

51. "Poseción de Catarina Pozos," 4 February 1797, Wills, BCSA; "Donación de tierra a Ignacio de los Santos Coy," 18 September 1797, Land Grants, BCSA; "Donación de tierra a favor de José Pascual Martínez," 9 February 1797, ibid.; "Donación de una suerte de tierra y solar a favor de Miguel Antonio Martínez," 8 February 1797, ibid.; "Donación de tierra a favor de Anastacio Mansolo," 30 April 1797, ibid.; "Donación de una suerte de tierra a José Roberto Núñez," 13 February 1797, ibid.; "Donación de tierra a José Feliciano de la Zerda," 27 April 1797, ibid.

52. "Donación de tierra a favor de José Eduardo Montoya," 5 February 1797, Land Grants, BCSA.

53. Sale of suertes, 10 April 1739; Sale of suertes, 7 October 1740; Sale of suertes, 26 May 1741; all in Notary Protocol, 22 March 1738, BA; Petition of Marcos de Castro, 3 June 1774, ibid.; "Testamentaria de Jacinto Delgado," 13 July 1799, Wills, BCSA.

54. "Venta de tierra y agua por los herederos de Juan Flores a favor de Pedro Flores," 26 March 1788, Land Grants, BCSA; "Venta de tierra y agua por Mariano de la Garza a favor de Macario Zambrano," n.d., ibid.; "Autos seguidos a pedimiento de Juan José Pacheco, vecino de este presidio de Béxar sobre treinta y siete

toros que le demanda a don José Felix Menchaca, también vecino de dicho presidio," 2 June 1780, BA; "Causa mortual de don Fernando Veramendi," 28 April 1783, ibid.

55. Distribution of water from San Pedro, 13 July 1731, "Repartimiento de solares," AGN: PI, vol. 163.

56. Meyer, *Water in the Hispanic Southwest*, 90–92.

57. Petition of Ignacia de Castro, 17 October 1771, BA; "Testamento de Ana Santos," 7 April 1778, Wills, BCSA; "Venta de tres horas de agua por Antonia de Armas a Francisco Amangual y tierra correspondiente a José Antonio Bustillos," 9 August 1800, Land Grants, BCSA.

58. "Auto of Regidor and Alcalde, Juan Leal Goraz, 14 April 1735, BA; Bando of Alberto López, 17 January 1756, ibid.; Bando of Governor Ripperdá, 14 March 1773, ibid.; "Testimonio de diligencias a favor de [la] labor de arriba, llamada de Nuestra Señora de los Dolores, hechas por el Sr. Gobernador D. Domingo Cabello, a pedimiento de los parcioneros de ella," 30 March 1784, ibid.; "Poder consedido por Juan José Sánchez a Tomás Travieso," 18 December 1791, Protocol, BCSA; Entry for 8 June 1747, Libro de Cabildo, 11 January 1742, NA.

59. Entry for 8 June 1747, Libro de cabildo, ibid.

60. Auto of Regidor and alcalde, Juan Leal Goraz, 14 April 1735, BA; Bando of Alberto López, 17 January 1756, ibid.; Bando of Governor Ripperdá, 14 March 1773, ibid.; "Testimonio de diligencias a favor de [la] labor de arriba," 30 March 1784, ibid.; Auto of Governor Cabello, 2 April 1781, in Documents regarding establishment of the upper *labor*, Deed Records, BCSA, book 3: 317–48.

61. Order of Governor José Antonio Fernández de Jáuregui, 28 September 1737, BA.

62. Case against Vicente Amador, 30 May 1768, BA.

63. Glick (*The Irrigation System of San Antonio*, 46–48) argues: "The relative poverty of administrative norms for the control of irrigation in colonial San Antonio is related to the relative infrequency of conflict in irrigation." However, it may be said that the small size of the farming population and the custom of settling all but major disputes through verbal proceedings has greatly contributed to the absence of documentary evidence on water disputes.

64. "Diligencias seguidas a pedimento de Juan José Montes de Oca, vecino de la Villa de San Fernando, para que don Toribio de la Fuente del mismo vecindario no le impida el riego en la parte de tierra que tiene en la labor de arriba," 23 July 1781, BA.

65. "Causa criminal contra don Santiago Seguín, por haber . . . ultrajado al Regidor don Manuel Berbán," 12 August 1796, BA.

66. "Autos a consulta hecha del padre fray José González," AGN: PI, vol. 32.

67. "Autos sobre las providencias dadas por su excelencia al gobernador de la provincia de Texas," 1731, AGN: PI, vol. 32; "Testimonio de las disposiciones del virrey respecto a los vecinos y pobladores de la Villa de San Fernando y del real presidio de San Antonio de Béxar en las provincias de las Nuevas Filipinas. 1735,"

AGN: PI, vol. 163; "Superior gobierno, 1736, Texas No. 18." AGN: PI, vol. 236; Decree of Viceroy, Mexico City, 24 January 1736, BA; "Memorial of Father Benito Fernández Concerning the Canary Islanders, 1741," 266–76.

68. Petition on behalf of Captain Toribio de Urrutia, 7 April 1752, BA; Certification of Petition of town council, 25 August 1756, ibid.; Governor Cabello to Commandant General Croix, 20 February 1779, ibid.; Governor Martínez to Commandant General Ugalde, 30 January 1789 and 28 February 1789, ibid.; Petition of Macario Zambrano to Commandant General, 30 July 1791, ibid.; "Estado que manifiesta los caudales que ha recibido el teniente habilitado don Francisco Amangual en las reales Cajas de San Luis Potosí," 27 April 1792, ibid.; "Autos a consulta de don Toribio de Urrutia Capn," AGN: PI, vol. 32; Agreement between Querétaro Missions and town of San Fernando, 14 August 1745, GLO.

69. Report on Bahía, 17 January 1794, BA.

70. Padrón de Texas, 26 September 1778, SFG, vol. 835; Martínez to Captain Manuel de Espadas, 10 January 1789, BA; José Miguel del Moral to Muñoz, 23 January 1799, ibid.

71. Representation of the Cabildo, Béxar 7 July 1770, AGN: PI, vol. 100; "Diligencias practicadas por el coronel don Domingo Cabello . . . para el número de ganado vacuno orejano que el capitán reformado don Luis Antonio Menchaca ha señalado y herrado en su rancho de San Francisco, fuera de el tiempo prescripto para poderlo ejecutar," 8 August 1786, BA.

72. "Autos a consulta de don Toribio de Urrutia, capitán del presidio de San Antonio de Béxar en la provincia de Texas, sobre aumento de soldados, y otras providencias que pide, para contener los insultos que hacen los Indios Apaches, sobre que también instó don José de Urrutia su padre difunto," 1740, AGN: PI, vol. 32.

73. "Testimonio de los autos hechos sobre la reducción de los indios gentiles de la nación Apaches a las misiones de los rios de San Xavier de la Provincia de Texas," 29 November 1749, AGI: M, 92–6–22.

74. Inspection of town by Governor Navarrete, 20 June 1762, BA; Governor Cabello to Croix, 20 February 1779, ibid.; Cabello to Croix, 31 August 1779, ibid.; "Extracto de la revista de inspección ejecutada por mi el coronel de infanteria don Domingo Cabello," 1 July 1779, Archivo General de Indias, Ramo Audiencia de Guadalajara, Transcript, Texas State Library and Archives, Austin, 104–6–20.

75. Governor Martínez to Viceroy, 6 June 1790, BA.

76. Muñoz to Commandant General, 17 February 1794, in "Cuaderno de correspondencia del señor gobernador comandante general, brigadier don Pedro [de] Nava," 4 January 1794, BA.

77. Cabello to Croix, 20 February 1779, and 29 May 1779, BA; "Diligencias practicadas sobre haber vendido de cuenta de Su Majestad ciento treinta y nueve reses vacunas orejanas a don Francisco Javier Rodríguez," 23 August 1784, ibid.; Martínez to Revillagigedo, 6 June 1790, ibid.

78. "Noticia que el coronel don Domingo Cabello . . . manifiesta de los tem-

porales que se han experimentado en ella en los segundos semestres de el año que espira de 1785, y los efectos que han causado en las cosechas de frutos . . . según real orden de 19 de mayo del año proximo pasado de 1784," 31 December 1785, BA.

79. The most detailed source for the cycle is found in note number 4 in "Padrón de Texas," 26 September 1778, SFG, vol. 835.

80. "Copia de la Carta," AGI: G, vol. 45.

81. Bernardo Fernández to Muñoz, 29 November 1794, BA.

82. That some farmers did have maize storage facilities is certain. Francisco Delgado's 1764 will mentions a jacal that served as granary (Testamento of Francisco Delgado, 7 February 1764, Wills, BCSA). An inventory of the quartermaster's store stated that the company had maize supplies stored with Juan Romero and Vicente Flores (see "expediente promovido por el teniente habilitado de la Compañía de Béxar don Francisco Amangual contra el Sargento Mariano Rodríguez, sobre haber divulgado que se habían extraido efectos de la habilitación," 29 February 1792, BA). For the absence of a public granary, see Intendant to Muñoz, 22 October 1792, ibid.

83. Petition of vecinos, 10 June 1738, BA; Bando of Alberto López, 17 January 1756, ibid.; Order of Governor Ripperdá, 14 October 1772, ibid.; Bando of Governor Ripperdá, 14 March 1773, ibid.; Cabello to Croix, 20 February 1779 and 31 August 1779, ibid.; "Estado de la tropa," 28 February 1782, ibid.; "De las diligencias instruidas por el coronel don Domingo Cabello, gobernador de la provincia de los Texas, justificando no haber en las poblaciones de ella ninguna pulpería para hacer efectivo su empadronamiento," 6 February 1783, ibid.; "Testimonio de diligencias a favor de [la] labor de arriba," 30 March 1784, ibid.; Martínez to Viceroy, 6 June 1790, ibid.

84. For a discussion of agricultural cycles see Enrique Florescano, *Precios del maíz, y crisis agrícolas en México (1708–1810): Ensayo sobre el movimiento de los precios y sus consecuencias económicas y sociales* (Mexico: El Colegio de Mexico, 1969), 112–39.

85. There was no possibility of appealing to neighboring provinces for assistance, for the entire viceroyalty was affected. Unfortunately, no documentation on the drought's impact in Coahuila, Nuevo León, and Nuevo Santander are yet available in published form. Enrique Florescano's compilation on the 1785–1786 crisis *Fuentes para la historia de la crisis agrícola de 1785–1786*, (2 vols., Mexico: Archivo General de la Nación, 1981), extends only as far as Chihuahua and Sonora.

86. "Noticia que el coronel don Domingo Cabello . . . manifiesta de los temporales que se han experimentado en ella en los segundos semestres de el año que espira de 1785," 31 December 1785, BA; Cabello to Rangel, 20 February 1786 and 21 March 1786, ibid.; "Noticia que el coronel don Domingo Cabello, gobernador y comandante de dicha provincia manifiesta de los temporales que se han experimentado en ella en los seis primeros semestres [sic] de este presente año de 1786," 30 June 1786, ibid.

87. "Noticia que el Capitán don Rafael Martínez Pacheco, gobernador interino,

y comandante de las armas de dicha provincia manifiesta del tiempo que se ha experimentado en ella," 30 June 1787, BA; "Estado que manifiesta los víveres con que deve racionarse la tropa de dicha compañía quincenariamente," 19 July 1788, ibid.; Martínez to Captain Manuel de Espadas, 10 January 1789, ibid.; Martínez to Ugalde, 30 January 1789, ibid.; Ugalde to Martínez, 14 February 1789, ibid.; Martínez to Ugalde, 28 February 1789, ibid.; Fr. José Mariano Reyes to [Viceroy], 1 May 1790, ibid.; Martínez to Revillagigedo, 6 June 1790, ibid.

88. "Reglamento de Presidios," 1729, AGN: Bandos, vol. 2, no. 14; Petition of José de Urrutia, 27 April 1735, BA; "Copia de la carta que comprehende las resoluciones tomadas en la Revista de inspección pasada por mi el mariscal de campo Marqués de Rubí, en 12 de Agosto de 1767, a la compañia del presidio de San Antonio de Béxar, gobernación de la provincia de Texas, y cargo de su capitán don Luis Antonio Menchaca," 17 August 1767, AGI: G, vol. 45.

89. Martínez to Revillagigedo, 6 June 1790, BA.

90. See "Cuadro 7. Cronología de los ciclos de la serie 1721–1813," Florescano, *Precios del maíz*, 115–17; "Figure 7. Maize prices in the Guadalajara region, 1700–1825," Eric Van Young, *Hacienda and Market in Eighteenth-Century Mexico* (Berkeley: University of California Press, 1981), 82.

91. "Padrón de las almas que hay en esta villa de San Fernando de Austria [sic]," 31 December 1793, BA.

CHAPTER FIVE

1. Muñoz to Pedro de Nava, 17 February 1794, in "Cuaderno de correspondencia del señor gobernador comandante general brigadier don Pedro de Nava," 4 January 1794, BA.

2. François Chevalier, *Land and Society in Colonial Mexico*; Charles Harris III, *The Latifundio of the Sánchez Navarros*.

3. Enrique Florescano, *Origen y desarrollo de los problemas agrarios de México*, 1500–1821 (6th ed., Mexico: Ediciones Era, 1983), 54.

4. James Ivey and Anne Fox, *Archaeological Survey and Testing at Rancho de las Cabras, Wilson County, Texas* (San Antonio: Center for Archaeological Research, University of Texas at San Antonio, Archaeological Survey Report No. 104, 1981), 44. Among the other archeological reports on Spanish-period ranches is A. Joachim McGraw and Kay Hindes, *Chipped Stone and Adobe: A Cultural Resources Assessment of the Proposed Applewhite Reservoir, Bexar County, Texas* (San Antonio: Center for Archaeological Research, University of Texas at San Antonio, Archaeological Survey Report No. 163, 1987).

5. Frederick C. Chabot, trans. and ed., *Excerpts from the Memorias for the History of the Province of Texas by Juan Agustín Morfi* (Privately published, 1932), 67.

6. Chevalier, *Land and Society*, 287–88; Petition of Andres Hernández, [1 September 1759], BA; AGI: Provincia de Texas; Cabildo's report on the settled ranches in its jurisdiction, 8 November 1791, BA.

7. Chabot, *Excerpts from the Memorias*, 67.

8. "Donación de dos sitios de tierra a favor de Felipe de Luna," 10 September 1773, Land Grants, BCSA; "Diligencias formadas para dar posesión a Luis Pérez, vecino del real presidio de San Antonio de Béxar, de unas tierras para poblar un sitio de ganado mayor," 15 October 1778, GLO; "Expediente promovido por el vecindario," 5 January 1778, ibid.

9. Petition of Andrés Hernández, [1 September 1759], BA.

10. An ordinance issued in January 1751 against the slaughter of cattle in the countryside around Béxar still does not mention private ranches, only missions (Bando of José Padrón, 5 January 1751, BA).

11. Viceroy to Captain Menchaca, 5 May 1769, BA; Auto of Governor Ripperdá, 24 February 1771, ibid.; Cabello to Croix, 17 July 1780, ibid.; Cabello to Croix, 20 October 1780, ibid.; Complaint of the cabildo on conditions in Texas, [1781], ibid.; "Representación, apologia, o escudo," [1787], ibid.; "Expediente promovido por Juan José Montes de Oca, sobre que se le devuelvan unas tierras que pobló en el paraje de la Candelaria," 3 January 1778, GLO; "Expediente promovido por el vecindario," 5 January 1778, ibid.; "Donación de dos sitios de tierra a favor de Felipe de Luna," 10 September 1773, Land Grants, BCSA.

12. "Cabildo's report of the settled ranches in the jurisdiction, in response to the request of the Intendant of Potosí for information on all ciudades, villas, lugares, haciendas and ranchos," 8 November 1791, BA; "Cuaderno de correspondencia del señor gobernador comandante general brigadier don Pedro [de] Nava," 4 January 1794, ibid.; Muñoz to Viceroy, 9 October 1790, "correspondencia con el gobernador don Manuel Muñoz, sobre novedades de indios, año de 1790," AGN: PI, vol. 159.

13. This important document has been inadvertently divided into two parts. It may be found under the following two dates: Proceedings concerning land grants in Nuevo Santander, 12 November 1800, and 1 February 1801, BA.

14. Jack Jackson, *Los Mesteños: Spanish Ranching in Texas, 1721–1821* (College Station: Texas A&M Press, 1986), 69–70, 101–103.

15. Certification of petition of cabildo, 25 August 1756, BA.

16. "Testimonio a la letra de los autos de denuncia de tierras hecha por don Domingo Castelo vecino de la villa de San Fernando jurisdicción de la provincia de Texas; Remate y merced que de dichas tierras que son onze sitios de ganado mayor se hizo a indios del pueblo y misión del Señor San José," [9 February 1764], GLO.

17. "Carta de fray Mariano Francisco de los Dolores, respecto a quejas de los indios contra los habitantes de San Fernando de Béxar," 1758, SFG, vol. 835.

18. "Expediente promovido por el vecindario de la villa de San Fernando sobre pertenencias de tierras y ganados," [5 January 1778], GLO; Jackson, *Los Mesteños*, 38–41, 45–46.

19. "Expediente promovido por el vecindario," GLO; Petition of Vicente Flores for certification of status of rancho Dolores, 29 February 1792, GLO.

20. "Expediente promovido por el vecindario," GLO; "Expediente promovido por Juan José Montes de Oca," 3 January 1778, ibid.; "Causa formada por el

gobernador de esta provincia Barón de Ripperdá, contra Francisco Javier Rodríguez, Juan José Flores, y Nepomuceno Travieso, vecinos de la villa de San Fernando, sobre extracción de reses orejanas," 7 March 1777, BA; "Autos formados contra Juan José Flores de Abrego y otros rancheros por varios robos de ganado orejano en los agostaderos de la misión de Espíritu Santo, con un informe del ayuntamiento de la villa de San Fernando," 23 September 1778, ibid.; "Venta de la mitad de los derechos de un rancho por José Ignacio de la Peña y demas herederos a favor de Pedro Flores," 4 March 1798, Land Grants, BCSA; Jackson, *Los Mesteños*, 328, 510.

21. Orozco, *Legislación y jurisprudencia*, 1: 41n, 48–50, 65–66, 88; John and Henry Sayles, *A Treatise on the Laws of Texas Relating to Real Estate, and Actions to Try Title and for Possession of Lands and Tenements* (St. Louis, 1890), 1: 51–55.

22. Jacinto Delgado's dispute with Manuel de la Fuente was taken to the juez privativo, but there is no record of a decision. Late-century documents record Delgado as the owner of the disputed tract. Bernabé Carabajal obtained confirmation of his grant in 1765, four years after he donated the land to Mission Espíritu Santo. The evidence for both these cases is found in "Expediente promovido por el vecindario," GLO.

23. "Expediente promovido por el vecindario," GLO; Proceedings concerning land grant in Nuevo Santander, 12 November 1800, BA.

24. "Expediente promovido por Juan José Montes de Oca," GLO; "Venta de la mitad de los derechos de un rancho por José Ignacio de la Peña y demas herederos a favor de Pedro Flores," 4 March 1798, Land Grants, BCSA.

25. "Testimonio a la Letra de los autos de Denuncia de tierras hecha por don Domingo Castelo," GLO.

26. Jackson, *Los Mesteños*, 322–30.

27. Ibid., 51–54.

28. "Expediente promovido por el vecindario," GLO; "Autos formados contra Juan José Flores de Abrego y otros rancheros por varios robos de ganado orejano en los agostaderos de la Misión de Espíritu Santo," 23 September 1778, BA; "Diligencias practicadas para que en los herraderos que deben hacer los dueños de ganados de los ranchos del arroyo del Cíbolo y río de San Antonio cumplan, guarden y observen el no correr ni coger ganado orejano," 7 November 1779, ibid.; Petition of Francisco Javier Rodríguez, 29 March 1784, ibid.

29. "Cabildo's report of the settled ranches in the jurisdiction," 8 November 1791, BA; Annual report, 1 January 1794, in "Cuaderno de correspondencia del señor gobernador comandante general brigadier don Pedro [de] Nava," 4 January 1794, ibid.; Cabildo to Viceroy, 4 August 1772, in "correspondencia con el ayuntamiento de la villa de San Fernando y con varios individuos en distintos años desde el de 1771 hasta el de 1793 . . . ," Carpeta 8a, AGN: PI, vol. 99; Jackson, *Los Mesteños*, 412.

30. Last will and testament, n.d., in Notary Protocol, 15 September 1747, BA; Castañeda, *Our Catholic Heritage* 3: 104–5; Jackson, *Los Mesteños*, 16–21.

31. Petition of Francisco Xavier Rodríguez, 29 March 1784, BA; "Diligencias

practicadas por el coronel don Domingo Cabello," 31 July 1786, ibid.; "Expediente promovido por Santiago de Zúñiga sobre cantidad de dinero que demanda contra don Simón de Arocha, de la que están depositados ochenta pesos en don Juan Martín de Amondaráin, y los autos por determinar," 9 May 1788, ibid.; "Expediente promovido contra el caporal de la Purísima Concepción Fernando Martínez, sobre matanza de reses orejanas y dejarlas muertas sobre el campo," 16 May 1793, ibid.; Representation of the cabildo, 7 July 1770, AGN: PI, vol. 100; Jackson, *Los Mesteños*, 17, 42, 76, 127, 131–32.

32. Monsieur de Pagés, *Travels Round the World in the Years* 1767, 1768, 1769, 1770, 1771 (London, 1791–1792), 96–97.

33. Vito Alessio Robles, *Coahuila y Texas en le época colonial* (2nd. ed., Mexico: Editorial Porrua, 1978), 392,609; D. A. Brading *Miners and Merchants in Bourbon Mexico, 1763–1810* (London: Cambridge University Press, 1971), 130–31,157; Sandra Myres, *The Ranch in Spanish Texas, 1691–1800* (El Paso, Texas Western Press, 1969), 47–49; Swann, *Tierra Adentro*, 50–51.

34. Bando of Governor Cabello, 10 July 1783, "Autos y diligencias practicadas por el coronel don Domingo Cabello, gobernador y comandante de las armas de esta provincia de los Texas sobre haberse opuesto los vecinos pobladores de las orillas del Arroyo del Cíbolo a que Sebastián Monjaras, José Padrón y Joaquín Flores llevaran a vender a la provincia de Coahuila 574 reses," 14 December 1778, BA; "Diligencias instruidas sobre la multa impuesta a Francisco Guerra por haber cogido sin licencia del gobernador de esta provincia cuatro reses orejanas," 7 June 1783, ibid.; Petition of Francisco Javier Rodríguez, 29 March 1784, ibid.; "La misión de Nuestra Señora del Refugio, del maíz y toros librados por el señor gobernador de esta provincia, teniente coronel don Manuel Muñoz, para la manutención de los indios de ella consiguiente a orden de 5 de Julio de 1794 del señor comandante general de estas provincias, mariscal de campo don Pedro de Nava a don Antonio Rodríguez Baca del comercio de esta villa de San Fernando y presidio de San Antonio de Béxar," 3 September 1795, ibid.

35. José Pereira de Castro to Martínez, 13 November 1788, no. 1, BA; "Nómina de los vecinos de San Antonio de Béxar que han introducido partidas de reses vacunas en este alcabalatorio . . . Real Aduana del Saltillo," 13 November 1788, no. 2, ibid.; Martínez to Pereira de Castro, 8 December 1788, ibid.; Pereira de Castro to Martínez, 26 December 1788, ibid.

36. Cabello to Croix, 20 December 1780, no. 2, BA.

37. Auto of Governor Cabello, 29 November 1786; "Diligencias practicadas para que en los herraderos que deben hacer," 7 November 1779, BA.

38. Muñoz to Nava, 24 August 1793, "cuaderno de correspondencia del señor comandante general coronel don Ramón de Castro, sigue el señor brigadier don Pedro de Nava," 14 January 1793, BA.

39. Bando of José Padrón, 5 January 1751, BA.

40. "Bando de buen gobierno expedido por el señor comandante general de estas Provincias Internas," 11 January 1778, BA.

41. Jackson, *Los Mesteños*, 152–60.

42. "Fray Rafael José, obispo del Nuevo Reino de León to Martínez," 14 October 1788, BA; Tithe reports for the diocese of Nuevo León between 1774 and 1800, 17 January 1803, Eberstadt Collection, The University of Texas Archives, Austin.

43. Bando of Governor Muñoz, 31 July 1795, in "Copias de las providencias de la junta superior de real hacienda, decretos de conformidad de los excelentísimos señores virreyes, orden del señor comandante general de las Provincias Internas, acuerdos con el ayuntamiento de esta villa y bando publicado en uno y dos de agosto del mismo año, sobre juntas de ganados por los criadores," 27 February 1789, BA; Jackson, *Los Mesteños*, 241–44, 333–45, 394–96, 417–23.

44. "Diligencias instruidas sobre la multa impuesta a Francisco Guerra," 7 June 1783, BA.

45. "Extracto de la revista de inspección," 1 July 1779, Archivo General de Indias, Ramo Audiencia de Guadalajara 104–6–20, Texas State Library and Archives, Austin.

46. Muñoz to Nava, 24 August 1793, in "Cuaderno de correspondencia del señor comandante general coronel don Ramón de Castro," 14 January 1793, BA.

47. "Noticia del número de ganado vacuno herrado y orejano que los vecinos de este real presidio de San Antonio de Béxar y villa de San Fernando, han sacado y llevado a varias provincias colindantes a esta de Texas, consecuente a lo mandado por el señor comandante general de estas Provincias Internas en 11 de Enero de 1778," 29 November 1786, BA.

48. "Diligencias instruidas sobre la multa impuesta a Francisco Guerra," BA; Muñoz to Nava, 24 August 1793, in "Cuaderno de correspondencia del señor comandante general coronel don Ramón de Castro," 14 January 1793, BA; "Relación de los gastos erogados en la manutención de quatro cientos treinta y cinco indios de las naciones Comancha, Taguaya, Taguacana, Tancague y Lipana," 1 January 1794, BA.

49. "Diligencias practicadas por el coronel don Domingo Cabello, gobernador y comandante de las armas de la provincia de los Texas, en que consta haberle impedido a don Luis Mariano Menchaca la extracción de una partida de ganado vacuno," 31 July 1786, BA; "Cuaderno en que se asientan las partidas del derecho que pagan los que cogen reses orejanas del otro lado de Guadalupe, y caballerías mesteñas," 31 December 1787, ibid.

50. "Expediente promovido contra el caporal de la Purísima Concepción Fernando Martínez," 16 May 1793, BA; "Expediente formado contra José Miguel Flores, y demas que adentro se expresan sobre matanza de ganado en el campo contraviniendo a las órdenes dictadas en el asunto," 1 June 1793, ibid.; Petition of Ignacio Calvillo, 18 August 1793, ibid.; Petition of Joaquín Menchaca, 18 August 1793, ibid.; Petition of Gavino Delgado, 18 August 1793, ibid.; Petition of José Miguel Flores, 19 August 1793, ibid.; Petition of Gavino Delgado, 19 August 1793, ibid.; Petition of D. Ignacio Pérez, 22 August 1793, ibid.; Muñoz to Ayuntamiento, 23 August 1793, ibid.; "Contiene tres bandos sobre el buen régimen que deben observar estos vecinos en las corridas del ganado orejano," 15 February 1794, ibid.

51. Mattie Austin Hatcher, *The Opening of Texas to Foreign Settlement*, 1801–1821 (1927, reprint, Philadelphia: Porcupine Press, 1976), Appendix No. 5.

52. Testamentary proceedings, 5 October 1751, BA; Cabello to Croix, 4 April 1779, ibid.; Viceroy Revillagigedo to Muñoz, 26 October 1790, no. 2, ibid.; Muñoz to Nava, 24 May 1797, in Copybook of Muñoz letters, 4 January 1796, ibid.; Nava to Muñoz, 27 June 1797, ibid.; Nava to Elguézabal, 26 December 1797, ibid.; Nava to Muñoz, 18 August 1798, ibid.

53. Only the male horse, often gelded, was put to work. Mares were kept essentially for breeding purposes—both for horse and mule stock.

54. Petition of José de Urrutia, 27 April 1735, BA; Petition of Juan Leal Goraz, alcalde, 7 May 1735, ibid.; Sale of lot, 25 June 1747 and Last will and testament, n.d., in Notary Protocol, 15 September 1747, ibid.; Petition of Francisco Xavier Rodríguez, 29 March 1784, ibid.

55. Viceroy Bucareli to Ripperdá, 9 February 1774, BA; Cabello to Croix, 17 July 1780, ibid.; Cabello to Croix, 1 November 1780, no. 2, ibid.; "Estado de la fuerza efectiba," 31 October 1782, ibid.; Cabello to Rengel, 3 October 1785, no. 1, ibid.

56. Cabello to Croix, 10 August 1780, BA; "Cuaderno en que se sientan las partidas de el derecho que pagan los que cogen reses orejanas y caballerías mesteñas correspondientes al predicho año," 31 December 1784, ibid.; Rengel to Cabello, 5 February 1785, no. 3, ibid.; Cabello to Rengel, 3 October 1785, no. 1, ibid.; "Cuaderno en que se asientan las partidas del derecho que pagan los que cogen reses orejanas del otro lado de Guadalupe, y caballerías mesteñas, 31 December 1787, ibid.; Jackson, *Los Mesteños*, 425.

57. "Causa criminal contra Juan José Sevallos," 17 February 1750, BA; "Causa seguida contra don Marcos Vidal por unos efectos de ropas, barajas y tabaco que introdujo de la provincia de la Luisiana a esta de los Texas en la que se le comisaron por el teniente de gobernador del pueblo de Nuestra Señora del Pilar de Bucareli," 29 January 1779, ibid.; "Causa mortual del difunto don Juan José Flores de Abrego, que fallecío en este presidio de Béxar y villa de San Fernando el dia 18 de enero del presente año de 1779, 9 June 1779," ibid.; "Causa mortual de don Fernando Veramendi," 28 April 1783, ibid.; "Autos sobre las providencias dadas por su excelencia al gobernador de la provincia de Texas para la pacificación de los indios apaches y sus aliados, 1731," [1 December 1731], AGN: PI, vol. 32.

58. AGI: Provincia de Texas.

59. Castañeda, *Our Catholic Heritage* 4: 5–16; Hatcher, *Opening of Texas*, Appendix No. 5.

60. Offutt, "Urban and Rural Society in the Mexican North," Table 1, Individuals Identified as Merchants in 1793, In Order of Appearance in Census, p. 16; Investigation of the death of Juan de Escamilla, 9 October 1776, BA; Testimony concerning fugitives Tomás del Toro and José María de Montes, 21 November 1776, ibid.; Appeal of Tomás Travieso to the Audiencia of Guadalajara, [1777], ibid.; "Diligencias seguidas sobre la causa criminal formada contra Tomás Tra-

vieso, vecino de esta villa de San Fernando y presidio de Béxar, por haber proferido varias palabras denigrativas e indecorosas contra el honor y axendrada conducta del coronel don Domingo Cabello . . . y del alférez don Francisco Amangual," 14 February 1782, ibid.; Petition of Francisco Javier Rodríguez, 29 March 1784, ibid.; "Padrón de las almas que hay en esta villa de San Fernando de Austria [sic]," 31 December 1793, BA; Jackson, *Los Mesteños*, 131–33.

61. "Diligencias practicadas sobre haber vendido de cuenta de Su Majestad 85 toros y 162 toretes orejanos a don Simón de Arocha, vecino," 27 July 1785, BA; "Noticia de el número de ganado vacuno herrado y orejano que los vecinos de este real presidio de San Antonio de Béxar," 29 November 1786, ibid.; "Expediente promovido por Santiago de Zúñiga sobre cantidad de dinero que demanda contra don Simón de Arocha," 9 May 1788, ibid.; Representation of republicanos and *vecinos* of Béxar, 1 March 1790, ibid.; "Expediente promovido por Juan Timoteo Barrera contra don Simón de Arocha, sobre cantidad de dinero que pagó quedándole derecho a salvo," 19 April 1790, ibid.; "Noticia de la distribución que yo don Simón de Arocha, capitán comandante de milicias, doy al señor gobernador interino de esta provincia de los Texas, don Rafael Martínez Pacheco, de los cien fuciles con bayonetas que en el año de 1773 se repartieron entre este vecindario," 13 August 1790, ibid.; Questionnaire for eligibility to study for the priesthood, 17 May 1786, NA; Jackson, *Los Mesteños*, 71–72.

62. Cabello to Croix, 12 April 1779, BA; Felipe de Neve to Cabello, 26 November 1783, ibid.; "Diligencias practicadas por el coronel don Domingo Cabello, gobernador de esta provincia a instancia de Fernando Arocha, carabinero de la compañía de caballería de este presidio, contra la persona de don Luis Mariano Menchaca, por haberle dicho este que era un mulato indigno así el como todos los de su familia," 5 November 1785, ibid.; "Diligencias practicadas por el coronel don Domingo Cabello, gobernador y comandante de las armas de la provincia de los Texas, en que consta haberle impedido a don Luis Mariano Menchaca la extracción de una partida de ganado vacuno," 31 July 1786, ibid.; Revillagigedo to Muñoz, 7 August 1792, ibid.

63. AGI: Provincia de Texas; Robert S. Weddle and Robert H. Thonhoff, *Drama and Conflict: The Texas Saga of 1776* (Austin, Texas: Madrona Press, 1976), 150, 154; Chabot, *With the Makers of San Antonio*, 196–97; Jackson, *Los Mesteños*, 531, 538.

CHAPTER SIX

1. Ripperdá's reply in Melchor de Noriega to Ripperdá, 14 August 1771, BA.
2. Joseph Lorenzo de Castro to María Rosa Camacho, Valero Marriages, SF; José Antonio de Acosta to María Josefa Rodríguez, 25 June 1728, ibid.; Juan Domingo Treviño to María Rita Maldonado, 21 July 1728, ibid.; Asencio to Ana, 29 August 1728, ibid.; Juan Rodríguez to Margarita, 21 January 1729, ibid.; Juan Pasqual to Ana María, 27 February 1729, ibid.; Damián to Juana María, 27 Feb-

ruary 1729, ibid.; Castañeda, *Our Catholic Heritage* 2: 224; Schuetz, "The Indians of the San Antonio Missions," 269–70, Table 5:8, Non-Indian Assistants at San Antonio de Valero, p. 297.

3. José Padrón v. Juan Leal Goraz, 25 June 1733, BA; Petition of Juan Leal Goraz, alcalde, 7 May 1735, ibid.; Petition of Cayetano Pérez, 24 May 1736, ibid.; Last will and testament, 23 April 1745, in Notary Protocol, 22 March 1738, ibid.; Entries for 19 January 1742 and 8 June 1747, in "Libro de Cabildo," 11 January 1742, NA.

4. Stern, "Social Marginality and Acculturation on the Northern Frontier of New Spain," 98.

5. Order of alcalde, don Juan José Montes de Oca, 6 February 1745, BA; Bando of José Curbelo, 12 January 1754, ibid.; Bando of Alberto López, alcalde and juez comisario de la Santa Hermandad, 17 January 1756, ibid.; Bando of Alberto López, alcalde primero, 10 January 1761, ibid.; Order of Governor Ripperdá, 15 March 1772, ibid.; Bando of don Amador Delgado, alcalde primero, 15 January 1775, ibid.; Bando of Alcalde primero, don José Salvador Díaz, 21 January 1776, ibid.; Cabildo to Ripperdá, 31 July 1771, AGN: PI, vol. 100; Agreement between Querétaro Missions and town of San Fernando, 14 August 1745, GLO; "Memorial of Father Benito Fernández Concerning the Canary Islanders, 1741," 266–70; Stern, "Social Marginality and Acculturation on the Northern Frontier of New Spain," discusses the vagabond problem in Chapter 3, 58–89.

6. AGI: Provincia de Texas; "Estado general de la provincia de los Texas," Año de 1792, 31 December 1792, BA.

7. Entry, n.d., in "Libro de Cabildo," 11 January 1742, BA; "Diligencias practicadas para la reedificación y recomposición de las casas reales," 15 February 1779, BA; "Cuenta formal que yo, Don José Antonio de Bustillo y Zevallos, cajero de la habilitacion de la compañía de caballería de este real presidio de San Antonio de Béxar, formó por ausencia de el teniente don Bernardo Fernández, habilitado propietario de dicha compañía," 19 October 1779, ibid.; "Cuenta del gasto hecho por mi don Andrés Benito Courbiere, soldado distinguido . . . en la manutención de setenta y un indios de las naciones del Norte que entraron de paz en este presidio desde 11 de Julio a 13 de agosto," 13 August 1790, ibid.; "Expediente formado sobre el pago de los travajos expendidos por los vecinos de la villa de San Fernando y presidio de San Antonio de Béxar en la obra de las casas reales de esta villa," 11 April 1793, ibid.; Documents regarding establishment of the upper *labor*, Deed Records, BCSA book 3, 317–48.

8. Petition of Juan Leal Goraz, alcalde, 7 May 1735, BA.

9. "Causa formada por el gobernador de esta provincia Barón de Ripperdá, contra Francisco Javier Rodríguez, Juan José Flores, y Nepomuceno Travieso, vecinos de la villa de San Fernando, sobre extracción de reses orejanas," 7 March 1777, BA; "Autos formados contra Juan José Flores de Abrego y otros rancheros por varios robos de ganado orejano en los agostaderos de la misión de Espíritu Santo, con un informe del ayuntamiento de la villa de San Fernando," 23 Sep-

tember 1778, ibid.; "Diligencias practicadas sobre la muerte que dieron los indios comanches a Felipe de Luna residente en este presidio de Béxar con el abaluo de sus bienes y entrega que se hizo del remanente de ellos a José Manuel Pérez Casanova, apoderado de sus herederos, 5 November 1780, ibid.; Expediente promovido por el administrador de diezmos don Joaquín Flores contra su antesesor don Juan Barrera . . . ," 3 July 1793, ibid.; Petition of José Miguel Flores, 19 August 1793, ibid.

10. "Diligencias practicadas para que en los herraderos que deben hacer los dueños de ganados de los ranchos del arroyo del Cíbolo," 7 November 1779, BA; "Diligencias practicadas por el gobernador de la provincia de los Texas sobre haber vendido de cuenta de Su Majetad cuatrocientas y dies reses orejanas a Luis Mariano Menchaca," 17 May 1784, ibid.; Martínez to Juan de Ugalde, 11 November 1787, ibid.

11. Petition of citizenry, 29 January 1788, BA.

12. "Testimonio de los autos de las denuncias hechas contra el governador don Manuel Muñoz, y comisión conferida al del Nuevo Santander Conde de Sierragorda para averiguarlo," Año de 1793, AGI: M, vol. 125.

13. Auto of Martín Lorenzo de Armas, alcalde primero, 13 June 1760, BA.

14. "Causa criminal formada contra Manuel de Castro (alias de a pie) por robo de caballos hecho de los que se hallan en el situado de esta Compañia," 4 July 1793, BA. Another example of both worker debt and violence against workers is "Autos criminales formados por el alcalde de segundo voto de esta villa, don Marcos de Castro, a pedimiento de José María Rodríguez, contra la persona de Pedro José Zambrano, sobre haberlo herido gravemente de el brazo izquierdo," 26 February 1785, ibid.

15. "Causa formada por el gobernador de esta provincia Barón de Ripperdá, contra Francisco Javier Rodríguez, Juan José Flores, y Nepomuceno Travieso, vecinos de la villa de San Fernando," 7 March 1777, BA; "Autos formados contra Juan José Flores de Abrego y otros rancheros," 23 September 1778, ibid.; "Autos seguidos a pedimiento de Juan José Pacheco, vecino de este presidio de Béxar sobre treinta y siete toros que le demanda a don José Félix Menchaca, también vecino de dicho presidio," 2 June 1780, ibid.; "Noticia del número de ganado vacuno herrado y orejano que los vecinos de este real presidio de San Antonio de Béxar y villa de San Fernando, han sacado y llevado a varias provincias, 29 November 1786, ibid.; "Instancia promovida por don José Antonio Bustillo, sobre ciento un pesos que demanda a los bienes del difunto don Joaquín González, la que pago su albacea don Salvador Díaz," 12 August 1788, ibid.; Petition of Ignacio Calvillo, 23 February 1791, ibid.; Petition of alguacil don Amador Delgado, 4 January 1793, ibid.; "Expediente promovido por Juan José Montes de Oca, sobre que se le devuelvan unas tierras qe pobló en el parage de la Candelaria," 3 January 1778, GLO; Jackson, *Los Mesteños*, 135–38, 361–62.

16. Quoted in Castañeda, *Our Catholic Heritage*, 3: 47.

17. Castañeda, *Our Catholic Heritage*, 3: 47–48; John, *Storms Brewed*, 275–76; Dunn, "Apache Relations," 234–42.

18. 12 March 1745, Baptisms, SF.

19. María Rosa de la Luz y Trinidad, 5 August 1757, Burials, SF; Juana Margarita, 14 September 1763, ibid.; Juan Comanche, son of Ana María, 22 November 1789, ibid.

20. Sale of slave, 29 October 1743, in Notary Protocol, 22 March 1738, BA.

21. Padrón de Texas, 26 September 1778, SFG, vol. 835.

22. Padrón de las familias . . . , 31 December 1796, BA.

23. Swann, *Tierra Adentro*, 374–75; Jones, *Los Paisanos*, 134.

24. Governor Pérez de Almazán to Viceroy, 24 March 1724, AGN: PI, vol. 183.

25. This was the case along the entire frontier. See, e.g., Tjarks, "Demographic Structure of New Mexico," 62.

26. This discussion is based on the numerous military reports found in BA and NA for the period 1773–1797.

27. Investigation of the death of Juan de Escamilla, 9 October 1776, BA; Testimony concerning fugitives Tomás del Toro and José María de Montes, vecinos, 21 November 1776, ibid.; Roster change, 3 February 1778, ibid.

28. Order of Gov. Ripperdá, 14 October 1772, BA; "Extracto de la revista," 2 December 1777, ibid.; Cabello to Croix, 17 July 1780, ibid.; Cabello to Croix, 6 December 1780, ibid.; "Diligencias practicadas por el gobernador de la provincia de los Texas, sobre haber vendido de cuenta de Su Majestad cuatrocientas y dies reses orejanas a Luis Mariano Menchaca," 17 May 1784, ibid.; Martínez to Juan de Ugalde, 11 November 1787, ibid.; Revillagigedo to Sierragorda, 23 July 1792, ibid.

29. Reglamento de Presidios, 1729, AGN: Bandos, vol. 2, No. 14; Testamentary proceedings, 27 February 1741, BA; AGI: Provincia de Texas; Moorhead, *The Presidio*, 205 n.9.

30. AGI: Provincia de Texas; "Padrón de las almas que hay en esta villa de San Fernando," 31 December 1793, BA; Louisa Schell Hoberman and Susan Migden Socolow, eds., *Cities & Society in Colonial Latin America* (Albuquerque: University of New Mexico Press, 1986), 246–47.

31. "Testamento de Juan Jupier," 3 April 1783, Wills, BCSA; "Escrito presentado por Manuel González y diligencias practicadas a continuación," 19 September 1780, BA; "Expediente promovido por el vecindario de la villa de San Fernando," [5 January 1778], GLO; Statement of José Lambremon, 12 May 1792, BA; "Noticia de los extranjeros que existen en esta capital y poblaciones," 21 May 1792, BA.

32. "Petition by Marcos Ruiz to be paid the sum for his services as armorer and blacksmith to the presidio," 27 July 1736, NA; Petition of don José de Urrutia, Captain of Presidio and Justicia Mayor, 28 July 1736, ibid.; Cabello to Croix, 27 September 1780, BA; "Noticia de los precios a que hace el armero de la compañía de este presidio de San Antonio de Béxar las piezas de las armas para los individuos de ella," 15 June 1789, ibid.; "Lista de los individuos del ayuntamiento de esta Villa de San Fernando de [Béxar y] vecindario de ella que voluntariamente han de

contribuir con lo que [pueden a la] fatiga de la fábrica del nuevo quartel," 14 October 1793, ibid.; "Donación de un solar a Juan Banul," 24 October 1737, Land Grants, BCSA.

33. Testamentary Proceedings, 27 February 1741, BA; "Diligencias practicadas para la reedificación y recomposición de las casas reales," 15 February 1779, ibid.; "Expediente formado sobre el pago de los trabajos expendidos por los vecinos de la villa de San Fernando y presidio de San Antonio de Béxar en la obra de las casas reales de esta villa," 11 April 1793, ibid.; Entries for 19 January 1742 and n.d., in "Libro de Cabildo," 11 January 1742, NA; Cabildo to Ripperdá, 31 July 1771, AGN: PI, vol. 100.

34. "Criminal case against Roque, Anselmo, Francisco and Mateo, Indians of Mission Valero, for the murder of Miguel Leal," 11 August 1778, BA; "Cuenta formal que yo don José Antonio de Bustillo y Zevallos," 19 October 1779, ibid.; AGI: Provincia de Texas; "Cuenta del gasto hecho por mi don Andrés Benito Courbiere, soldado distinguido," 13 August 1790, ibid.; Bernardo Fernández to Muñoz, 6 January 1791, ibid.; "Relación diaria de la Correduría hecha por el primer teniente de esta compañía don Bernardo Fernández," 14 January 1791, ibid.; Petition of Francisco Xavier Galán, 16 March 1791, ibid.; "Expediente formado sobre el pago de los trabajos expendidos por los vecinos de la villa de San Fernando y presidio de San Antonio de Béxar," 11 April 1793, ibid.

35. "Expediente formado sobre el pago de los trabajos expendidos por los vecinos de la villa de San Fernando y Presidio de San Antonio de Béxar," 11 April 1793, BA.

36. Criminal proceedings against Juan José Zevallos, 17 February 1750, BA; Proceedings against Joaquín Benites, et al., 1 August 1774, ibid.; "Autos formados contra Juan José Flores de Abrego y otros rancheros por varios robos de ganado orejano en los agostaderos de la Misión de Espíritu Santo, con un informe del ayuntamiento de la villa de San Fernando," 23 September 1778, ibid.; "Expediente promovido por Santiago de Zúñiga sobre cantidad de dinero que demanda contra don Simón de Arocha," 9 May 1788, ibid.; Petition of Antonio Baca, 30 March 1791, ibid.

37. Menchaca to Governor Oconor, 18 August 1768, BA; Cabello to Croix, 17 July 1780, ibid.

38. Viceroy to Captain Menchaca, 5 May 1769, BA.

39. Cabello to Croix, 19 August 1779, BA.

40. "Proceso de diligencias seguidas en virtud de superior mandamiento del ilustrísimo y excelentísimo señor arzobispo virrey de esta Nueva España," 1735, AGN: PI, vol. 163; Invoice for tobacco shipment, 6 June 1774, BA; "Memoria de los efectos que lleva para el repuesto de la compañía del Presidio de San Antonio de Béxar el habilitado don Francisco Amangual," 14 April 1788, ibid.; "Expediente promovido por Santiago de Zúñiga sobre cantidad de dinero que demanda contra don Simón de Arocha," 9 May 1788, ibid.; Report to the King, 31 December 1792, in copybook of Muñoz correspondence with the Viceroy, 19 September 1792,

ibid.; Muñoz to Arispe, 6 December 1793, in Juan Ignacio de Arispe to Muñoz, 12 October 1793, ibid.; "La Misión de Nuestra Señora del Refugio del maíz y toros librados por el señor gobernador de esta provincia," 3 September 1795, ibid.

41. Petition of José Antonio Rodríguez, 23 April 1736, BA; Petition on behalf of Captain Toribio de Urrutia, 7 April 1752, ibid.; "Autos sobre diferentes [. . .] consultados por el gobernador de la Provincia de los Texas: muerte de un correo y otras materias, Año de 1724," AGN: PI, vol. 183; Moorhead, *The Presidio*, 205.

42. Testamentary Proceedings, 27 February 1741, BA; Petition of Captain Toribio de Urrutia, 7 May 1743, ibid.; "Libro de cuentas de los soldados del Real Presidio de Nuestra Señora del Pilar de los Adaes destacados en este de San Antonio de Béxar," 1 January 1771, ibid.; "Copia de la carta que comprehende las resoluciones tomadas en la revista de inspección pasada por mi el Mariscal de Campo Marqués de Rubí, en 12 de Agosto de 1767," 17 August 1767, AGI: G, vol. 45.

43. For the history of eighteenth-century New Spain's commercial network, see D. A. Brading, *Miners and Merchants in Bourbon Mexico*, 1763–1810 (Cambridge: Cambridge University Press, 1971); John E. Kicza, *Business and Society in Late Colonial Mexico* (Albuquerque: University of New Mexico Press, 1983); Pedro Pérez Herrero, *Plata y libranzas: la articulación comercial del México borbónico* (Mexico: El Colegio de México, 1988).

44. "Autos sobre diferentes [. . .] consultados por el governador de la Provincia de Texas, Año de 1724," AGN: PI, vol. 183; "Proceso de diligencias seguidas en virtud de superior mandamiento del Ilustrísimo y excelentísimo señor Arzobispo virrey," 1735, ibid, vol. 163.

45. Petition of Captain Toribio de Urrutia, 7 May 1743, BA; Power of attorneys, 18, 22, and 25 September 1747, in Notary Protocol, 15 September 1747, ibid.; Inspection of public books, weights, and measures by Governor Pedro de el Barrio Junco y Espriella, 14 May 1749, NA.

46. "Copia de la carta que comprehende las resoluciones tomadas en la revista de inspección," 17 August 1767, AGI: G, vol. 45; "Testimonio de la sumaria información recibida por el coronel don Domingo Cabello . . . por comisión conferida por el señor comandante general de las Provincias Internas de este Reino de Nueva España," 15 July 1779, BA; "Testimonio de los cargos que se le han formado al coronel Barón de Ripperdá, capitán de dicha compañía de resulta de la revista de inspección que le paso el coronel don Domingo Cabello," 10 May 1781, ibid.

47. "Testimonio de la sumaria información recibida por el coronel don Domingo Cabello," 15 July 1779, BA; "Memoria de los efectos que lleva para el repuesto de la compañía," 14 April 1788, ibid.; Moorhead, *The Presidio*, 208–9, 211–19.

48. Cabello to Croix, 12 April 1779, BA; "Diligencias instruidas por el gobernador de la provincia de los Texas sobre la elección de habilitado para la compañía

de caballería del real presidio de San Antonio de Béxar," 31 May 1786 [sic, should be 1780], ibid.

49. Cabello to Croix, 14 March 1780, BA; "Noticia de los efectos comprados a los sujetos contenidos en cada una de las partidas que se expresarán, para el regalo de los indios," 18 September 1789, ibid.; "Noticia de los efectos que existen en esta habilitación hasta hoy dia de la fecha," 15 August 1790, ibid.; "Expediente promovido por el teniente habilitado de la compañía de Béxar don Francisco Amangual contra el sargento Mariano Rodríguez," 29 February 1792, ibid.; José Luis Barrera to Sierragorda, 23 August 1792, ibid.; "Memoria de los efectos comprados por mi el teniente don José Francisco de Sozaya," 5 October 1797, ibid.

50. Decree of Viceroy, 24 January 1736, BA; Posting of bond by Miguel Núñez Morillo, 4 April 1736, ibid.; Francisco Fernández de Rumayor v. various, 11 April 1736, ibid.; Petition of José Antonio Rodríguez, 23 April 1736, ibid.; Petition on behalf of Captain Toribio de Urrutia, 7 April 1752, ibid.

51. Certification of petition of cabildo, 25 August 1756, BA.

52. Bando of Francisco Delgado and Luis Antonio Menchaca, 29 April 1752, BA.

53. "Memorial of Father Benito Fernández," 280–81.

54. The census of 1779 indicates the recent arrival of the merchants. Of the group of eight none was a native of Béxar, only two owned houses, and another owned a jacal (AGI: Provincia de Texas).

55. "Extracto de la revista," 2 December 1783, BA; Entry, n.d., following that of 20 December 1788, in "Libro en que se asienta lo acordado en el cabildo y da principio en 1 de enero de 1783," 1 January 1783, ibid.; "Duplicados de las cuentas de gastos de indios que se pasaron a el excelentísimo señor virrey Conde de Revilla Gigedo con oficio de 14 de enero de 1793," 26 February 1791, ibid.; Petition of Antonio Baca, 30 March 1791, ibid.; Account of supplies to Indians, 30 April 1793, ibid.; "Relación de los gastos erogados en la manutención de quatrocientos treinta y cinco indios de las naciones comancha, taguaya, taguacana, tancague, y lipana," 1 January 1794, ibid.; "La Misión de Nuestra Señora del Refugio del maíz y toros librados por el señor gobernador de esta provincia teniente coronel don Manuel Muñoz, para la manutensión de los indios de ella," 3 September 1795, ibid.; Petition of Antonio Rodríguez Baca, 30 April 1796, ibid.; Chabot, *With the Makers of San Antonio*, 75.

56. Carlos E. Castañeda, *A Report on the Spanish Archives in San Antonio, Texas* (San Antonio, 1937), 96–97; Jackson, *Los Mesteños*, 538–39.

57. "Cuaderno perteneciente a don Marcos Vidal, Año de 1773," [1773], BA; Proceedings against Joaquín Benites, et al., 1 August 1774, ibid.; "Causa seguida contra don Marcos Vidal por unos efectos de ropas, barajas y tabaco que introdujo de la provincia de la Luisiana a esta de los Texas," 29 January 1779, ibid.

58. "Sumaria del robo hecho a don Santiago Villaseñor, entrando por una ventana de su casa la noche del 24 al 25 de octubre de 1774, de la cantidad de setecientos pesos," 28 October 1774, BA; Order of Governor Ripperdá, 27 March

1775, ibid.; Contract for supplying Bucareli, 10 February 1776, ibid.; Cabildo election, 31 December 1777, ibid.; "Poseciones de oficios de alcaldes y regidores de esta villa de San Fernando," 20 December 1779, ibid.; Cabello to Croix, 14 June and 16 August 1780, ibid.; Neve to Cabello, 10 July 1784, ibid.; Cabello to Neve, 18 September 1784, ibid.; Cabello to Rengel, Béxar 9 April 1786, ibid.

59. In the "Causa mortual" Veramendi makes provisions for masses to be said at the presidial church of La Bahía for the souls of all who died there between 1770 and his own death, thus indicating his association with that community from that year. He made similar arrangements for Béxar's dead from 1776 onward, that is, from the year of his transfer to the capital. (Veramendi is cited as a brandy merchant from La Bahía in Order of Governor Ripperdá, 27 March 1775, BA.)

60. "Noticia que yo don Simón de Arocha, capitán comandante del cuerpo de milicias de la villa de San Fernando, doy al señor don Domingo Cabello," 17 August 1784, BA; "Poseciones de oficios de alcaldes y regidores de esta Villa de San Fernando," 20 December 1779, ibid.; "Libro en que se asienta lo acordado en el cabildo, y da principio en 1 de enero de 1783," 1 January 1783, ibid.; "Causa mortual de don Fernando Veramendi," ibid.

61. "Causa mortual de don Fernando Veramendi," BA; "Diligencias practicadas por el coronel don Domingo Cabello, gobernador de esta provincia a instancia de Fernando Arocha," 5 November 1785, ibid.

62. Statement of Angel Nabarro, 14 May 1792, BA; Election of 20 December 1781, in "Poseciones de oficios de alcaldes y regidores de esta villa de San Fernando," 20 December 1779, ibid.; "Expediente promovido por el teniente habilitado de la compañía de Béxar don Francisco Amangual contra el sargento Mariano Rodríguez," 29 February 1792, ibid.; "Testamento de Juan Manuel de Ruiz," 28 July 1797, Wills, BCSA.

63. Governor Melchor de Noriega to Ripperdá, 14 August 1771, BA.

64. "De las diligencias instruidas por el coronel don Domingo Cabello, gobernador de la provincia de los Texas," 6 February 1783, BA.

65. Muñoz to Arispe, 14 September 1794, in Juan Ignacio de Arispe to Muñoz, 26 August 1794, BA.

66. Posting of bond by Miguel Núñez Morillo, 4 April 1736, BA; Francisco Fernández de Rumayor v. various, 11 April 1736, ibid.; Petition of Cayetano Pérez, 24 May 1736, ibid.

67. "Diligencias practicadas sobre haber extraido Juan José Flores vecino de este presidio y villa de San Fernando ciento y veinte reses vacunas a la provincia de Coahuila," 11 July 1781, BA; "Diligencias practicadas sobre haber extraido Vicente Flores," 13 July 1781, ibid.; "Diligencias practicadas sobre haber vendido . . . a don Santiago Seguín, vecino de este presidio," 6 July 1784, ibid.; "Diligencias practicadas sobre haber vendido . . . a don Francisco Xavier Rodríguez," 23 August 1784, ibid.; "Diligencias practicadas sobre haber vendido . . . a don Simón de Arocha," 27 July 1785, ibid.; "Diligencias practicadas sobre haber vendido . . . a don Manuel de Arocha," 27 July 1786, ibid.; "Diligencias practicadas por el cor-

onel don Domingo Cabello," 31 July 1786, ibid.; "Diligencias practicadas sobre haber vendido . . . a Joaquín Leal," 14 August 1786, ibid.; "Diligencias practicadas por el Coronel don Domingo Cabello . . . ," 22 September 1786, ibid.

68. Juan Ignacio de Arispe to Muñoz, 26 August, 25 November, and 16 December 1794, BA.

69. Arispe to Muñoz, 23 June 1797 and 26 July 1797, 17 February and 30 March 1798, ibid.; Muñoz to Silvestre Díaz de la Vega, 25 July 1798, ibid.; Díaz de la Vega to Muñoz, 12 September 1798, ibid.

70. Arispe to Muñoz, 30 March, 1799, ibid.; Muñoz to Arispe, 17 April 1799, ibid.; Arispe to Muñoz, 26 April 1799, ibid.; Muñoz to Arispe, 15 April 1799, ibid.; Arispe to Muñoz, 25 May 1799, ibid.

71. Arispe to Elguezabal, 8 October 1799, No. 1 and No. 2, ibid.; Elguézabal to cabildo, 22 October 1799, ibid.; Proceedings concerning the estanco administrator, 22 October 1799, ibid.; Elguézabal to Arispe, 30 October 1799, ibid.; Arispe to Elguézabal, 7 December 1799 and 28 February 1800, ibid.

CHAPTER SEVEN

1. Martínez Pacheco to Viceroy, 9 March 1790, no. 1, BA.

2. Jesús F. de la Teja and John Wheat, "Béxar: Profile of a Tejano Community," *SWHQ* 89(July 1985): 13; Tjarks, "Demographic Analysis," Table 1, p.303.

3. "Ordenanzas que han de observar y guardar todos los gobernadores y comandantes de los presidios y Provincias Internas para el mejor gobierno de ellas," [1729], article 50, AGI: M, vol. 81; Toribio de Urrutia to [Viceroy], 17 December 1740, in "Autos a consulta de don Toribio de Urrutia capitán del presidio de San Antonio de Béxar," AGN: PI, vol. 32; cabildo meeting, 25 August 1745, BA; Order of Colonel Angel de Martos y Navarrete, 25 June 1759, in "Order of Viceroy Agustín Ahumada Villalón, Marqués de las Amarillas," 7 April 1758, ibid.; Lt. Governor Ramírez de la Piszina to Cabildo, 21 November 1760, ibid.

4. The viceregal orders for the cabildo's organization and the report on their execution are found in Austin, "The Municipal Government of San Fernando de Béxar," 346–50.

5. Cabildo to Governor, 10 December 1799, in Elguézabal to cabildo, 5 December 1799, BA; *Recopilación de leyes de Indias*, leyes 1 and 3, titulo 8, Libro V.

6. Ibid.; Inspection of public books, weights, and measures by Governor Pedro de el Barrio Junco y Espriella, 14 May 1749, NA; "Autos hechos a representación de don Antonio Rodríguez Mederos, regidor decano de la villa de San Fernando en la provincia de Texas," 19 July 1749, BA; Proceedings in case of Cabildo versus Mederos, 21 July 1749, and 17 June 1750, ibid. As late as 1778 José Antonio Curbelo attempted to be named a lifelong councilman on the basis of his Isleño ancestry and the rights granted to the Isleños by the king—his efforts failed (Petition of José Antonio Curbelo, 9 January 1778, BA).

7. Peter Marzahl, "Creoles and Government: The Cabildo of Popayan," *Hispanic American Historical Review* 54 (November 1974): 636.

8. Mark A. Burkholder, "Bureaucrats," *Cities and Society in Colonial Latin America*, 82–83.

9. *Recopilación de leyes de Indias*, leyes 1 and 13, titulo 9, and ley 5, titulo 10, Libro 4.

10. Urrutia to Viceroy, 17 December 1740, in "Autos a consulta de don Toribio de Urrutia capitán del presidio de San Antonio de Béxar en la provincia de Texas," AGN: PI, vol. 32.

11. Cabildo meeting, 25 August 1745, BA.

12. "Autos practicados por el coronel don Domingo Cabello gobernador y comandante de las armas de la provincia de los Texas, contra la persona de Felipe Flores, de este vecindario, sobre ilícita amistad contraida con la mujer de Antonio de el Toro," 5 April 1783, BA.

13. "Diligencias practicadas en solicitud del alcalde don Vicente Amador por haberse ausentado de esta capital sin conocimiento del gobernador ni del ayuntamiento," Año de 1792, BA.

14. Cabello to Croix, 20 December 1779, BA.

15. Petition of don Juan José Flores de Abrego, [31] January 1758, BA; "Diligencias hechas por el gobernador capitán general de esta provincia don Antonio de Martos y Navarrete a pedimiento de don José Curbelo contenido en ellos," 8 July 1762, ibid.; Vicente Bernabeu to Governor, 11 January 1791, ibid.; Cabildo to Muñoz, 27 December 1794, ibid.; Muñoz to Cabildo, 29 December 1794, ibid.; Governor to Viceroy, 7 January 1792, NA.

16. Viceroy to Ripperdá, 10 February 1773, BA.

17. Viceroy to Ripperdá, 9 and 16 March 1774, BA; Viceroy to Ripperdá, 9 and 16 March 1774, in "Correspondencia con el gobernador de Texas, Barón de Ripperdá, en los años de 1774 hasta 1777" inclusive, AGN: PI, vol. 99; Ripperdá to Viceroy, 15 July 1774, nos. 1 and 2, ibid.

18. Viceroy to Ripperdá, 14 August 1772, BA; Ripperdá to Cabildo, 28 September 1772, ibid.; Order of Ripperdá, 9 and 14 October 1772, ibid.; "El ayuntamiento de la villa de San Fernando queja contra el Cura y a consecuencia se previene el modo en que se han de hacer las elecciones anuales de oficios concegiles, año de 1778," Archivo de Gobierno, Saltillo, legajo 5, expediente 270a, SM vol. 840.

19. "Testimonio de las diligencias practicadas por el gobernador de la provincia de los Texas sobre un oficio pasado al cabildo de la villa de San Fernando para que su vecindario concurriese a la reedificación de la guardia que sirve de cuartel de los soldados solteros de la compañía de caballería del presidio de Béxar y prisión de los reos que se apreenden por los alcaldes," 12 October 1785, BA.

20. Martínez to Viceroy, 9 March 1790, no. 1, BA.

21. Much of the Isleños' reputation may be traced to the writings of Fray Juan Agustín Morfi. As a Franciscan he no doubt looked with sympathy upon the

missionaries' complaints regarding the Isleños. The result is very unflattering portrayals of the families in his *History of Texas* 2: 286, 293, 337–38, 417. For an example of how historians have continued to apply Morfi's standards, see Jones, *Los Paisanos*, 50.

22. Hinojosa, *A Borderlands Town in Transition*, 5–16.

23. For instance, the act of possession for the town lots on 9 July 1731 states: "So that all may know who the original founding families of this villa were the following list is made of the fifteen families," "Repartimiento de solares," AGN: PI, vol. 163.

24. Almazán to viceroy, 1 December 1731, in "Autos sobre las providencias dadas por su excelencia al gobernador de la provincia de Texas para la pacificación de los Indios Apaches y sus aliados," 1731, AGN: PI, vol. 32.

25. Petition by the residents of the presidio, 3 February 1733, Dictamen de Juan de Rebolledo, 24 March 1733, and Viceroy's decree, 8 April 1733, all in ibid.

26. José Padrón v. Juan Leal Goraz, 25 June 1733, BA; Juan Leal Goraz v. Patricio Rodríguez, 29 August 1734, ibid.; Petition of Antonio Rodríguez, 27 February 1734, AGN: PI, vol. 163; "Testimonio de las disposiciones del virrey respecto a los vecinos y pobladores de la villa de San Fernando y del Real presidio de San Antonio de Béxar en las provincias de las Nuevas Filipinas, 1735," 13 April 1735, ibid.; Viceroy to Francisco de Lara, 4 August 1730, in "Carpeta de correspondencia . . . , AGN: PI, vol. 236; Petition of Martín Lorenzo de Armas, 14 February 1734, ibid.; Agreement between Querétaro Missions and the Town of San Fernando, 14 August 1745, GLO.

27. Petition of José Martínez, Alberto López, Bernabé de Carabajal, Gerónimo Flores, Ignacio Gómez, y José de Castro, 25 February 1734, AGN: PI, vol. 163.

28. Explanation of compromise, 5 September 1749, in "Inspection of public books, weights, and measures by Governor Pedro del Barrio Junco y Espriella," 14 May 1749, NA.

29. Ibid.

30. "Autos hechos a representación de don Antonio Rodríguez Mederos," 19 July 1749, BA: Proceedings in case of Cabildo v. Mederos, 21 July 1749, ibid.; Petition of Cabildo to Governor, [12 August 1749], ibid.; Case of Isleños v. Rodríguez Mederos, 17 June 1750, ibid.; Isleños v. Agregados, 16 June 1749, in "Inspection of public books, weights, and measures by Governor Pedro de el Barrio Junco y Espriella," NA; Agreement between Querétaro Missions and town of San Fernando, 14 August 1745, GLO.

31. Chabot, *With the Makers of San Antonio*, passim.

32. Ibid.

33. Ibid.

34. Ibid.

35. Representation of republicanos and *vecinos* 1 March 1790, BA.

36. Cabildo to Muñoz, 24 December 1793, BA.

37. The discussion for the following paragraphs on the San Fernando parish church are based on Castañeda, *Our Catholic Heritage in Texas* 3: 94–101, and Adán Benavides, "For God's and Man's Sakes: Building a Church in Eighteenth Century Texas," manuscript submitted for publication.

38. Castañeda, *Our Catholic Heritage in Texas* 3: 97, italics added.

39. Order of Alcalde Antonio Rodríguez Mederos, 2 October 1745, BA.

40. The importance of feasts celebrating a town's patron saint is discussed in Foster, *Culture and Conquest*, 158–226, passim.

41. Petition to be exempted from hauling stone for the erection of public buildings, 7 February 1771, NA; Papers relative to religious feasts, 12 February 1772, ibid.

42. Catherine Lugar, "Merchants," *Cities and Society in Colonial Latin America*, 67; Lyman Johnson, "Artisans," ibid., 232. See also George M. Foster, *Culture and Conquest*, 167, 225.

43. Ibid.

44. Auto of cabildo, 31 December 1771, in "Expediente promovido por Juan José Montes de Oca, sobre que se le devuelvan unas tierras que pobló en el paraje de la Candelaria," 3 January 1778, GLO.

45. Confession of Francisco Xavier Rodríguez, 3 June 1777, in "Causa formada por el gobernador de esta provincia Barón de Ripperdá, contra Francisco Xavier Rodríguez, Juan José Flores, y Nepomuceno Travieso, vecinos de la villa de San Fernando, sobre extracción de reses orejanas," 7 March 1777, BA.

46. "Diligencias practicadas por el coronel don Domingo Cabello," 22 September 1786, BA; Petition of Gavino Delgado, 18 August 1793, ibid.

47. Declaration of the cabildo with the governor and priest present, in "Papers relative to religious feasts," 12 February 1772, NA.

48. Receipt from Father Pedro Fuentes, 3 July 1783, BA.

49. Teja and Wheat, "Profile of a Tejano Community," 21–22.

50. Petition of Juan José Flores de Abrego, [31] January 1758, BA; Representation of the republicanos and *vecinos* of Béxar, 1 March 1790, ibid.; "El ayuntamiento de la villa de San Fernando queja contra el cura, Año de 1778," Archivo de Gobierno, Saltillo, legajo 5, expediente 270a, SM vol. 840.

51. Ibid.

52. A good brief synthesis of the literature on ritual kinship is Luis Berruecos, *El compadrazgo en América Latina: análisis antropológico de 106 casos* (Serie: Antropología Social, 15; Mexico: Instituto Indigenista Interamericano). Two anthropological works on which the compadrazgo literature is based are Sidney Mintz and Eric R. Wolf, "An Analysis of Ritual Co-parenthood (Compadrazgo)," *Southwestern Journal of Anthropology* 6 (1950): 341–68; and George M. Foster, "Cofradía and Compadrazgo in Spain and Spanish America," *Southwestern Journal of Anthropology* 9 (1953): 1–28.

53. Berruecos, *El compadrazgo*, a27.

54. Eighty-six clearly identified baptisms among the Hispanic residents of San

Antonio were studied for the years between 1719 and 1730, that is, before the arrival of the Canary Islanders; San Antonio de Valero Baptisms, 1703–1783, SF.

55. Ibid., entry no. 190.

56. San Fernando Church Baptisms, SF, book 2, entry nos. 434, 526, 661, 767, 818.

57. San Fernando Church Baptisms, SF, book 1 for the following dates: 19 February 1744, 12 August 1747, 18 November 1749, 12 March 1752, 31 January 1756, and 26 February 1758; Queja del presidio de San Antonio de Béxar contra Fray Mariano Francisco de los Dolores, 1742, SFG vol. 383.

58. Two hundred forty-four baptisms for the period were examined, with a gap for the years 1737–1743.

59. San Fernando Church Baptisms, SF, book 1 for the following dates: 23 February 1745, 9 March 1745, 13 March 1750, 14 September 1752.

60. Petition by vecinos of the presidio, 3 February 1733, in "Autos sobre las providencias dadas por su excelencia al gobernador," 1 December 1731, AGN: PI, vol. 32; Petition of Antonia Lusgardia Hernández, 9 August 1735, BA; Posting of bond by Miguel Núñez Morillo, 4 April 1736, ibid.; Petition of Captain Toribio de Urrutia, 7 May 1743, ibid.; Agreement to pay debt, 19 July 1757, ibid.

61. Petition of the cabildo, in "Superior despacho del ilustrísimo y excelentísimo señor arzobispo virrey de esta Nueva España," 24 January 1736, AGN: PI, vol. 32.

62. Order of Captain Toribio de Urrutia, 13 August 1743, BA.

63. Petition of María Egeciaca Rodríguez, 9 August 1770, BA; "Causa criminal formada de oficio por el gobernador contra Prudencio Barrón vecino del presidio de San Antonio de Béxar y villa de San Fernando," 12 March 1775, ibid.; "Diligencias practicadas sobre la presentasión de Juan José Flores, vecino de este presidio de Béxar, perteneciente a la extracción de cuatrocientas y cuarenta reses vacunas para transferirlas a la provincia de Coahuila," 26 April 1780, ibid.; "Autos practicados por el coronel don Domingo Cabello gobernador y comandante de las armas de la provincia de los Texas, contra la persona de Felipe Flores, de este vecindario, sobre ilícita amistad contraida con la mujer de Antonio de el Toro," 5 April 1783, ibid.; "Diligencias practicadas para la libertad de María Gertrudis de la Peña, natural de la Costa de Camargo," 25 January 1785, ibid.; Posting of bond, 5 January 1786, ibid.; "Testimonio de la certificación dada por el ilustre cabildo, justicia y regimiento de la villa de San Fernando y Real Presidio de San Antonio de Béxar al gobernador," 27 August 1787, ibid.

64. "Compromiso celebrado por el cabildo y vecindario de este presidio de San Antonio de Béxar de la provincia de Texas con las misiones de ella, sobre las recogidas de sus ganados, vacunos y caballares así herrados como orejanos, alzados y mostrencos," 8 January 1787, BA.

65. Proceedings concerning title to lot in Béxar, 23 March 1770, BA; Representation of republicanos and vecinos, 1 March 1790, BA.

66. Petition of cabildo, in "Superior despacho del ilustrísimo y excelentísimo

señor arzobispo virrey de esta Nueva España . . . ," 24 January 1736, AGN: PI, vol. 32.

67. Representation of the agregados in the case of Isleños v. Captain Urrutia, [1745], BA.

68. Petition of vecinos agregados, 16 August 1762, BA.

69. Donación de un solar a favor de José Martín de la Garza, n.d., 1778, Land Grants, BCSA.

70. Representation of Francisco Xavier Rodríguez, 4 May 1778, and representation of Joaquín Leal, 8 May 1778, in "Expediente promovido por el vecindario de la villa de San Fernando sobre pertenencias de tierras y ganados," [5 January 1778], GLO.

71. "Representación, apologia o escudo que la República de la Villa de San Fernando Real Presidio de San Antonio de Béxar," [1787], BA.

72. Muñoz to Viceroy, 7 January 1792, NA.

73. Auto of Governor Martos y Navarrete, 6 September 1762, BA.

74. Muñoz to the Viceroy, 7 January 1792, NA.

CONCLUSION

1. Chipman, *Spanish Texas,* 223–24; Hatcher, *The Opening of Texas to Foreign Settlement,* 102–26.

2. Chipman, *Spanish Texas,* 230–41; Elizabeth May Morey, "Attitude of the Citizens of San Fernando Toward Indpendence Movements in New Spain, 1811–1813" (M.A. thesis, The University of Texas at Austin, 1930), 38–39.

3. A useful discussion of Spanish-colonial self-identity is Anthony Pagden, "Identity Formation in Spanish America," in *Colonial Identity in the Atlantic World,* 1500–1800, ed. Nicholas Canny and Anthony Pagden (Princeton: Princeton University Press, 1987), 51–93.

Bibliography

ARCHIVES AND MANUSCRIPT COLLECTIONS

Archivo de San Francisco el Grande, Biblioteca Nacional de México, photostats, University of Texas Archives, Austin.

Archivo General de Indias, Seville, transcripts, University of Texas Archives, Austin.

Archivo General de la Nación de México, microfilm, University of Texas Nettie Lee Benson Latin American Collection, Austin.

Bexar Archives, manuscripts, University of Texas Archives, Austin.

Bexar County Spanish Archives, transcripts, Bexar County Clerk's Office, San Antonio.

Eberstadt Collection, manuscripts, University of Texas Archives, Austin.

Nacogdoches Archives, manuscripts, Texas State Archives, Austin.

San Fernando Parish Records, transcripts, University of Texas Institute of Texan Cultures, San Antonio.

Spanish Collection, manuscripts, Texas General Land Office, Austin.

Spanish Material from Various Sources, miscellaneous transcripts, University of Texas Archives, Austin.

PRINTED DOCUMENTS AND GUIDES

Beers, Henry P. "Part II: The Records of Texas." *Spanish and Mexican Records of the American Southwest: A Bibliographical Guide to Archive and Manuscript Sources.* Tucson: University of Arizona Press, 1979.

Benavides, Adán, Jr., comp. and ed. *The Béxar Archives (1717–1836): A Name Guide.* Austin: The University of Texas Press, 1989.

Bolton, Herbert E., comp. *Guide to Materials for the History of the United States in the Principal Archives of Mexico.* Reprint. New York: Karus Reprint Corp., 1965.

Castañeda, Carlos E., comp. *A Report on the Spanish Archives in San Antonio, Texas*. San Antonio, Texas: Yanaguana Society, 1937.

Chabot, Frederick C., trans. and ed., *Excerpts from the Memorias for the History of the Province of Texas by Juan Agustín Morfi*. Privately published, 1932.

Cruz, Gilberto and James A. Irby, comps. *Texas Bibliography: A Manual on History Research Materials*. Austin: Eakin Press, 1983.

"Diario de la conquista y entrada a los thejas." *Universidad de México* 5, 25–26 (1932): 58–69; 5, 27–28 (1933): 230–38.

Emory, William H. *Report on the United States and Mexican Boundary Survey*. 2 vols. in 3 pts. Reprint. Austin: Texas State Historical Association, 1987.

Florescano, Enrique. *Fuentes para la historia de la crisis agrícola de 1785–1786*. 2 vols. Mexico: Archivo General de la Nación, 1981.

Hodge, Frederick W., and Theodore H. Lewis, eds. *Spanish Explorers in the Southern United States, 1528–1543*. Reprint. Austin, Texas: Texas State Historical Association, 1984.

Kielman, William H., comp. *The University of Texas Archives: A Guide to the Historical Manuscript Collections in the University of Texas Library*. Austin: The University of Texas Press, 1968.

Lafora, Nicolás de. *Relación del viaje que hizo a los presidios internos situados en la frontera de la América Septentrional*. Mexico: Editorial Pedro Robledo, 1939.

Leutenegger, Benedict, trans. "Memorial of Father Benito Fernández Concerning the Canary Islanders, 1741." *Southwestern Historical Quarterly* 82 (January 1979): 265–96.

Morfi, Juan Agustín de, *Viaje de indios y diario del Nuevo México*. Reprint. Mexico: Manuel Porrua, 1980.

Naylor, Thomas H., and Charles W. Polzer, S.J., eds. and comps., *Pedro de Rivera and the Military Regulations for Northern New Spain, 1724–1729*. Tucson: The University of Arizona Press, 1988.

Pagés, Monsieur de. *Travels Round the World in the Years 1767, 1768, 1769, 1770, 1771*. London, 1791–1792.

Recopilación de leyes de los reinos de las Indias mandadas imprimir y publicar por la Magestad Católica del Rey Don Carlos. 4 vols. Madrid, 1841.

Reglamento e instrucción para los presidios que se han de formar en la linea de frontera de la Nueva España, 1772. Reprint, Mexico, 1790.

Relación de los méritos y servicios de Don Fernando Pérez de Almazán. Madrid, 1729.

Santos, Richard G., comp. and trans. *Aguayo Expedition into Texas, 1721: An Annotated Translation of the Five Versions of the Diary Kept by Br. Juan Antonio de la Peña*. Austin: Jenkins Publishing, 1981.

————. "Documentos para la historia de México en los archivos de San Antonio, Texas." *Revista de historia de América* 63–64 (1967): 143–49.

"Título de gobernador e instrucciones a Don Martín de Alarcón para su expedición a Texas." Archivo General de la Nación, *Boletín* 6 (1935): 530–40.

Velázquez, María del Carmen, comp. *La frontera norte y la experiencia colonial.* Mexico: Secretaría de Relaciones Exteriores, 1982.

West, Elizabeth H., trans. "Bonilla's Brief Compendium of the History of Texas, 1772." *Southwestern Historical Quarterly* 8, 1 (1904): 3–78.

BOOKS

Alessio Robles, Vito. *Coahuila y Texas en la época colonial.* 2nd ed. Mexico: Editorial Porrua, 1978.

Bancroft, Hubert Howe. *California Pastoral, 1769–1848.* San Francisco: The History Company, 1888.

Bannon, John Francis, ed. *Bolton and the Spanish Borderlands.* Norman: University of Oklahoma Press, 1964.

Barnes, Charles Merritt. *Combats and Conquests of Immortal Heroes Sung in Song and Told in Story.* San Antonio: Guessaz and Ferlet, 1910.

Barnes, Thomas C., et al. *Northern New Spain: A Research Guide.* Tucson: The University of Arizona Press, 1981.

Bender, Thomas. *Community and Social Change in America.* New Brunswick, N.J.: Rutgers University Press, 1978.

Berruecos, Luis. *El compadrazgo en América Latina: análisis antropológico de 106 casos.* Serie: Antropología Social, 15. Mexico: Instituto Indigenista Interamericano, 1976.

Bolton, Herbert Eugene. *Coronado: Knight of the Pueblos and Plains.* Reprint. Albuquerque: University of New Mexico Press, 1964.

_____. *Texas in the Middle Eighteenth Century: Studies in Spanish Colonial History and Administration.* Reprint. Austin: University of Texas Press, 1970.

Brading, D. A. *Miners and Merchants in Bourbon Mexico, 1763–1810.* London: Cambridge University Press, 1971.

Braudel, Fernand. *Civilization and Capitalism, 15th–18th Century, Volume 1: The Structures of Everyday Life.* New York: Harper and Row, 1981.

Buck, Samuel L. *Yanaguana's Successors: The Story of the Canary Islanders' Immigration into Texas in the Eighteenth Century.* Reprint. N.p., 1980.

Campa, Arthur L. *Hispanic Culture in the Southwest.* Reprint. Norman: University of Oklahoma Press, 1993.

Canny, Nicholas, and Anthony Pagden, eds. *Colonial Identity in the Atlantic World, 1500–1800.* Princeton: Princeton University Press, 1987.

Castañeda, Carlos E. *Our Catholic Heritage in Texas, 1519–1936.* 7 vols. Reprint. New York: Arno Press, 1976.

Chabot, Frederick C. *With the Makers of San Antonio.* San Antonio, Texas: private printing, 1937.

Chávez, John R. *The Lost Land: The Chicano Image of the Southwest.* Albuquerque: University of New Mexico Press, 1984.

Chevalier, François. *Land and Society in Colonial Mexico: The Great Hacienda.* Trans. Alvin Eustis, ed. with a forward by Lesley Byrd Simpson. Berkeley: University of California Press, 1963.

Chipman, Donald E. *Spanish Texas, 1519–1821.* Austin: University of Texas Press, 1992.

Cook, Sherburne F., and Woodrow Borah. *Essays in Population History: Mexico and the Caribbean,* vol. 2. Berkeley: University of California Press, 1974.

Corner, William, comp. and ed. *San Antonio de Bexar: A Guide and History.* San Antonio: Bainbridge and Corner, 1890.

Cruz, Gilbert R. *Let There Be Towns: Spanish Municipal Origins in the American Southwest, 1610–1810.* College Station: Texas A&M Press, 1988.

Davis, John L. *San Antonio: A Historical Portrait.* Austin: The Encino Press, 1978.

De León, Arnoldo. *The Tejano Community, 1836–1900.* Albuquerque: University of New Mexico Press, 1982.

Dobkins, Betty E. *The Spanish Element in Texas Water Law.* Austin: University of Texas Press, 1959.

Dobyns, Henry F. *Spanish Colonial Tucson: A Demographic History.* Tucson: University of Arizona Press, 1976.

Domínguez, María Esther. *San Antonio, Texas, en la época colonial (1718–1821).* Madrid: Ediciones de Cultura Hispánica, 1989.

Dunn, William Edward. *Spanish and French Rivalry in the Gulf Region of the United States, 1678–1702: The Beginnings of Texas and Pensacola.* Reprint. Freeport, N.Y.: Books for Libraries Press, 1971.

Espinosa, Isidro Félix. *Chrónica apostólica, y seráphica de todos los colegios de propaganda fide de esta Nueva España.* Madrid, 1746.

Fernández Duro, Césaro. *Don Diego de Peñalosa y su descubrimiento de Quivira.* Madrid, 1882.

Fisher, Lillian Estelle. *The Indendant System in Spanish America.* Berkeley: University of California Press, 1929.

Florescano, Enrique. *Origen y desarrollo de los problemas agrarios de México, 1500–1821.* 6th ed. Mexico: Ediciones Era, 1983.

———. *Precios del maíz y crisis agrícolas en México (1708–1810): Ensayo sobre el movimiento de los precios y sus consecuencias económicas y sociales.* Mexico: El Colegio de México, 1969.

Foster, George M. *Culture and Conquest: America's Spanish Heritage.* Chicago: Quadrangle Books, 1960.

Gallegos, Bernardo P. *Literacy, Education, and Society in New Mexico, 1693–1821.* Albuquerque: University of New Mexico Press, 1992.

Gerhard, Peter. *The North Frontier of New Spain.* Princeton: Princeton University Press, 1982.

Gibson, Charles. *Spain in America.* New York: Harper and Row, 1966.

Glick, Thomas. *The Old World Background of the Irrigation System of San Antonio, Texas.* The University of Texas at El Paso: Texas Western Press, 1972.

Guerra, Mary Ann Noonan. *The History of San Antonio's Market Square.* San Antonio: The Alamo Press, 1988.

Gutiérrez, Ramón A. *When Jesus Came the Corn Mothers Went Away: Marriage, Sexuality, and Power in New Mexico, 1500–1846.* Stanford: Stanford University Press, 1991.

Habig, Marion A. *The Alamo Chain of Missions: A History of San Antonio's Five Old Missions.* Revised ed. Chicago: Franciscan Herald Press, 1976.

_____. *San Antonio's Mission San José: State and National Historic Site, 1720–1968.* Chicago: Franciscan Herald Press, 1968.

Haggard, J. Villasana. *Handbook for Translators of Spanish Historical Documents.* University of Texas as Austin, 1941.

The Handbook of Texas. 2 vols. Walter Prescott Webb, ed. Austin: Texas State Historical Association, 1952.

Haring, C. H. *The Spanish Empire in America.* New York: Harcourt, Brace & World, Harbinger Book, 1963.

Harris, Charles H., III. *A Mexican Family Empire: The Latifundio of the Sanchez Navarros, 1765–1867.* Austin: The University of Austin Press, 1975.

Hatcher, Mattie Austin. *The Opening of Texas to Foreign Settlement, 1801–1821.* Reprint. Philadelphia: Porcupine Press, 1976.

Hine, Robert V. *Community on the American Frontier: Separate But Not Alone.* Norman: University of Oklahoma Press, 1980.

Hinojosa, Gilberto Miguel. *A Borderlands Town in Transition: Laredo, 1755–1870.* College Station: Texas A&M University Press, 1983.

Hoberman, Louisa Schell, and Susan Migden Socolow, eds. *Cities & Society in Colonial Latin America.* Albuquerque: University of New Mexico Press, 1986.

Ivey, James, and Anne Fox, *Archaeological Survey and Testing at Rancho de las Cabras, Wilson County, Texas.* San Antonio: Center for Archaeological Research, University of Texas at San Antonio, Archaeological Survey Report No. 104, 1981.

Jackson, Jack. *Los Mesteños: Spanish Ranching in Texas, 1721–1821.* College Station: Texas A&M University Press, 1986.

John, Elizabeth A. H. *Storms Brewed in Other Men's Worlds: The Confrontation of Indians, Spanish, and French in the Southwest, 1540–1795.* Reprint. Lincoln: University of Nebraska Press, 1981.

Jones, Oakah L. Jr. *Los Paisanos: Spanish Settlers on the Northern Frontier of New Spain.* Norman: University of Oklahoma Press, 1979.

Kicza, John E. *Business and Society in Late Colonial Mexico.* Albuquerque: University of New Mexico Press, 1983.

Kutsche, Paul, ed. *The Survival of Spanish American Villages.* The Colorado
  College Studies No. 15. Colorado Springs: The Colorado College, 1979.
Lafaye, Jacques. *Quetzalcoatl and Guadalupe: The Formation of Mexican National
  Consciousness, 1531–1813.* Trans. by Benjamin Keen. Chicago: University of
  Chicago Press, 1976.
MacLachlan, Colin M. and Jaime E. Rodríguez O. *The Forging of the Cosmic
  Race: A Reinterpretation of Colonial Mexico.* Berkeley: University of
  California Press, 1980.
McGraw, A. Joachim, and Kay Hindes. *Chipped Stone and Adobe: A Cultural
  Resources Assessment of the Proposed Applewhite Reservoir, Bexar County, Texas.*
  San Antonio: Center for Archaeological Research, University of Texas at
  San Antonio, Archaeological Survey Report No. 163, 1987.
McWilliams, Carey. *North From Mexico: The Spanish-Speaking People of the
  United States.* New ed. New York: Praeger, 1990.
Meyer, Michael C. *Water in the Hispanic Southwest: A Social and Legal History,
  1550–1850.* Tucson: University of Arizona Press, 1983.
Monroy, Douglas. *Thrown Among Strangers: The Making of Mexican Culture in
  Frontier California.* Berkeley: University of California Press, 1990.
Moorhead, Max L. *The Presidio: Bastion of the Spanish Borderlands.* Norman:
  University of Oklahoma Press, 1975.
Morfi, Juan Agustín. *History of Texas, 1673–1779.* 2 vols. Trans. and annotated
  by Carlos Eduardo Castañeda. Albuquerque: Quivira Society, 1935.
Mörner, Magnus. *Race Mixture in the History of Latin America.* Boston: Little,
  Brown and Company, 1967.
Muñoz, Virgilio and Mario Ruiz Massieu. *Elementos jurídico-históricos del
  municipio en México.* Mexico: Universidad Nacional Autónoma de México,
  1979.
Myres, Sandra L. *The Ranch in Spanish Texas, 1691–1800.* The University of
  Texas at El Paso: Texas Western Press, 1969.
Navarro García, Luis. *Don José de Gálvez y la Comandancia General de las
  Provincias Internas del norte de Nueva España.* Seville: La Escuela de
  Estudios Hispano-Americanos, 1964.
———. *Intendencias en Indias.* Seville: Escuela de Estudios Hispano-Americanos,
  1959.
Newcomb, W. W., Jr. *The Indians of Texas: From Prehistoric to Modern Times.*
  Austin: University of Texas Press, 1961.
Orozco, Wistano Luis. *Legislación y jurisprudencia sobre terrenos baldíos.* 2 vols.
  Mexico, 1895.
Pérez Herrero, Pedro. *Plata y libranzas: la articulación comercial del México
  borbónico.* México: El Colegio de México, 1988.
Plant, Raymond. *Community and Ideology: An Essay in Applied Social Philosophy.*
  London: Routledge and Kegan Paul, Ltd., 1974.

Poyo, Gerald E., and Gilberto M. Hinojosa, eds. *Tejano Origins in Eighteenth-Century San Antonio.* Austin: University of Texas Press, 1991.

Powell, Philip W. *La guerra chichimeca (1550–1600).* Trans. by Juan José Utrilla. Mexico: Fondo de Cultura Económica, 1977.

Ríos-Bustamante, Antonio. *Los Angeles, pueblo y región, 1781–1850: continuidad y adaptación en la periferia del norte mexicano.* Mexico: Instituto Nacional de Antropología e Historia, 1991.

Saint-Lu, Andre. *Condición colonial y conciencia criolla en Guatemala (1524–1821).* Trans. by Pierrette de Villagran. Guatemala: Editorial Universitaria, 1978.

Sayles, John, and Henry Sayles. *A Treatise on the Laws of Texas Relating to Real Estate, and Actions to Try Title and for Possession of Lands and Tenements.* 2 vols. St. Louis, 1890.

Simmons, Marc. *Albuquerque: A Narrative History.* Albuquerque: University of New Mexico Press, 1982.

———. *Spanish Government in New Mexico.* Reprint. Albuquerque: University of New Mexico Press, 1990.

Spicer, Edward H. *Cycles of Conquest: The Impact of Spain, Mexico, and the United States on the Indians of the Southwest, 1533–1960.* Tucson: The University of Arizona Press, 1962.

Swann, Michael M. *Tierra Adentro: Settlement and Society in Colonial Durango.* Boulder, Colorado: Westview Press, 1982.

Thonhoff, Robert H. *El Fuerte del Cíbolo: Sentinel of the Bexar-La Bahia Ranches.* Austin: Eakin Press, 1992.

Timmons, W. H. *El Paso: A Borderlands History.* El Paso: Texas Western Press, 1990.

Tuan, Yi-Fu. *Space and Place: The Perspective of Experience.* Minneapolis: University of Minnesota Press, 1977.

Van Ness, John R. *Hispanos in Northern New Mexico: The Development of Corporate Community and Multicommunity.* New York: AMS Press, 1991.

Van Young, Eric. *Hacienda and Market in Eighteenth-Century Mexico.* Berkeley: University of California Press, 1981.

Wall, Helena M. *Fierce Communion: Family and Community in Early America.* Cambridge, Mass.: Harvard University Press, 1990.

Weber, David J. *Myth and the History of the Hispanic Southwest: Essays by David J. Weber.* Albuquerque: University of New Mexico Press, 1988.

———, ed. *New Spain's Far Northern Frontier: Essays on Spain in the American West, 1540–1821.* Reprint. Dallas: Southern Methodist University Press, 1989.

———. *The Spanish Frontier in North America.* New Haven: Yale University Press, 1992.

Weddle, Robert S. *The French Thorn: Rival Explorers in the Spanish Sea, 1682–1762.* College Station: Texas A&M University Press, 1991.

_____. *The San Sabá Mission: Spanish Pivot in Texas.* Austin: University of Texas Press, 1964.

_____. *Spanish Sea: The Gulf of Mexico in North American Discovery, 1500–1685.* College Station: Texas A&M University Press, 1985.

_____. *Wilderness Manhunt: The Spanish Search for La Salle.* Austin, Texas: The University of Texas Press, 1973.

Weddle, Robert S., and Robert H. Thonhoff. *Drama and Conflict: The Texas Saga of 1776.* Austin: Madrona Press, 1976.

ARTICLES

Arneson, Edwin P. "Early Irrigation in Texas." *Southwestern Historical Quarterly* 25 (October 1921): 121–30.

Austin, Mattie Alice. "The Municipal Government of San Fernando de Béxar, 1730–1800." *Southwestern Historical Quarterly* 8 (April 1905): 277–352.

Bishko, C. J. "The Peninsular Background of Latin American Cattle Ranching." *Hispanic American Historical Review* 32 (November 1952): 491–515.

Brading, David A. "Grupos étnicos, clases y estructura ocupacional en Guanajuato (1792)." *Historia mexicana* 21 (1972): 460–80.

Bronner, Fred. "Urban Society in Colonial Spanish America: Research Trends." *Latin American Research Review* 21 (1986): 7–72.

Chance, John K., and William B. Taylor, "Estate and Class in a Colonial City: Oaxaca in 1792." *Comparative Studies in Society and History* 19 (1977): 454–87.

_____, "Estate and Class: A Reply." *Comparative Studies in Society and History* 21 (1979): 434–42.

Clark, R. C. "The Beginnings of Texas." *Southwestern Historical Quarterly* 5 (January 1902): 189–201.

Din, Gilbert C. "The Immigration Policy of Governor Esteban Miró in Spanish Louisiana." *Southwestern Historical Quarterly* 83 (October 1969): 155–75.

Dunn, William E. "The Apache Mission on the San Saba River; Its Founding and Failure." *Southwestern Historical Quarterly* 17 (1914): 379–414.

Foster, George M. "Cofradía and Compadrazgo in Spain and Spanish America." *Southwestern Journal of Anthropology* 9 (1953): 1–28.

Hillery, George A., Jr. "Definitions of Community: Areas of Agreement." *Rural Sociology* 20 (1955): 111–23.

Hutchins, Wells A. "The Community Acequia: Its Origin and Development." *Southwestern Historical Quarterly* 31 (January 1928): 261–84.

Jones, O. Garfield. "Local Government in the Spanish Colonies as Provided by the *Recopilación de leyes de los reinos de las Indias.*" *The Southwestern Historical Quarterly* 19 (July 1915): 65–90.

Marzahl, Peter. "Creoles and Government: The Cabildo of Popayan." *Hispanic American Historical Review* 54 (November 1974): 636–56.

McCaa, Robert, Stuart B. Schwartz and Arturo Grubessich. "Race and Class in Colonial Latin America: A Critique." *Comparative Studies in Society and History* 21 (1979): 421–33.

Mecham, J. Lloyd. "The *Real de Minas* as a Political Institution." *Hispanic American Historical Review* 7 (February 1927): 45–83.

Mintz, Sidney, and Eric R. Wolf, "An Analysis of Ritual Co-parenthood (Compadrazgo)." *Southwestern Journal of Anthropology* 6 (1950): 341–68.

Morse, Richard M. "Urban Development." *Colonial Spanish America*. Leslie Bethell, ed. Cambridge: Cambridge University Press, 1987.

Pagden, Anthony. "Identity Formation in Spanish America." *Colonial Identity in the Atlantic World*, 1500–1800, Nicholas Canny and Anthony Pagden, eds. Princeton: Princeton University Press, 1987.

Palerm, Angel. "Sobre la formación del sistema colonial: Apuntes para una discusión." *Ensayos sobre el desarrollo económico de México y América Latina* (1500–1975), Enrique Florescano, comp. Mexico: Fondo de Cultura Económica, 1979.

Poyo, Gerald E., and Gilberto M. Hinojosa. "Spanish Texas and Borderlands Historiography in Transition: Implications for United States History." *Journal of American History* 75 (September 1988): 393–416.

Robinson, Willard B. "Colonial Ranch Architecture in the Spanish–American Tradition." *Southwestern Historical Quarterly* 83 (October 1979): 123–50.

Seed, Patricia "Social Dimensions of Race: Mexico City, 1753." *Hispanic American Historical Review* 62 (November 1982): 569–606.

Schuetz, Mardith K. "The People of San Antonio, Part I: In the Period 1718–1731." *San Antonio in the Eighteenth Century*. San Antonio: San Antonio Bicentennial Heritage Committee, 1976.

Spell, Lota M. "The Grant and First Survey of the City of San Antonio." *Southwestern Historical Quarterly* 66 (July 1962): 73–89.

Teja, Jesús F. de la. "El Camino Real: Lifeline of Colonial Texas." *Gulf Coast Historical Review* 8 (Fall 1992): 64–72.

_____. "Indians, Soldiers, and Canary Islanders: The Making of a Texas Frontier Community." *Locus* 3, 1 (Fall 1990): 81–96.

_____. "Sobrevivencia económica en la frontera de Texas: los ranchos ganaderos del siglo XVIII en San Antonio de Béxar." *Historia Mexicana* 42 (April—June 1993): 837–66.

Teja, Jesús F. de la, and John Wheat. "Béxar: Profile of a Tejano Community, 1820–1832." *Southwestern Historical Quarterly* 89 (July 1985): 7–34.

Tjarks, Alicia V. "Comparative Demographic Analysis of Texas, 1777–1793." *Southwestern Historical Quarterly* 77 (January 1974): 291–338.

_____. "Demographic, Ethnic and Occupational Structure of New Mexico, 1790." *The Americas* 35 (July 1978): 45–88.

Van Young, Eric "Mexican Rural History Since Chevalier: The Historiography of the Colonial Hacienda." *Latin American Research Review* 18 (1983): 5–61.

UNPUBLISHED MATERIALS

Benavides, Adán. "For God's and Man's Sakes: Building A Church in Eighteenth Century Texas." Manuscript submitted for publication.

Cuello, José. "Saltillo in the Seventeenth Century: Local Society on the North Mexican Frontier." Ph.D. dissertation, University of California, Berkeley, 1981.

Gutiérrez, Ramón Arturo. "Marriage, Sex and the Family: Social Change in Colonial New Mexico, 1690–1846." Ph.D. dissertation, University of Wisconsin–Madison, 1980.

McReynolds, James Michael. "Family Life in a Borderland Community: Nacogdoches, Texas, 1779–1861." Ph.D. dissertation, Texas Tech University, 1978.

Morey, Elizabeth May. "Attitude of the Citizens of San Antonio Toward Independence Movements in New Spain, 1811–1813." M.A. thesis, University of Texas at Austin, 1930.

Offutt, Leslie Scott. "Urban and Rural Society in the Mexican North: Saltillo in the Late Colonial Period." Ph.D. dissertation, University of California, Los Angeles, 1982.

Pickman, Susan Lois. "Life on the Spanish American Colonial Frontier: A Study in the Social and Economic History of Mid Eighteenth Century St. Augustine, Florida." Ph.D. dissertation, State University of New York, Stony Brook, 1980.

Schuetz, Mardith Keithly. "The Indians of the San Antonio Missions, 1718–1821." Ph.D. dissertation, The University of Texas at Austin, 1980.

Stern, Peter Alan. "Social Marginality and Acculturation on the Northern Frontier of New Spain." Ph.D. dissertation, The University of California, Berkeley, 1984.

Index

Adaesanos: described, 21; access to farmland at Béxar, 84–86

agregados: excluded from first town lot grants in San Fernando, 34; efforts to gain grants of farmland, 77–78, 80; purchase farmland from Canary Islanders, 79; interest in upper farm, 81; participation in municipal government, 140, 144–46; efforts to become full citizens, 144–46; use of *compadrazgo* to form social bonds with Canary Islanders, 151–52; early families of and Canary Islanders as social equals, 153–54; *see also* San Fernando de Béxar

agriculture, 32, 46–47: *huertas*, 32; communal farming in early Béxar, 76; first crops planted by Canary Islanders, 76; early efforts at commercialization, 89–90; exports from Béxar area, 90; absence of wheat culture, 91; preference of maize over wheat, 91; obstacles to commercialization, 91–92; absence of fodder crops, 92; annual agricultural cycle described, 92; maize prices, 92–95; effects of climate on, 93–94; labor, 120–21; *see also* land, livestock

Aguaverde, Presidio de: commercial link with Béxar, 116

Aguayo, Marqués de San Miguel de: *see* San Miguel de Aguayo, Marqués de

Alamo: *see* San Antonio de Valero

Alarcón, Martín de (Governor), 3, 129: orders for settlement of San Antonio area, 7, 32; problems with Franciscans, 8; expedition to Texas, 17–18; expedition of forgotten, 154

Almazán, Fernando or Juan Antonio Pérez de: *see* Pérez de Almazán

Alvarez Travieso, Vicente: *see* Travieso, Vicente Alvarez

Amador, Vicente, 27, 86, 88, 141

Amangual, Francisco, 43, 87, 90, 131

American Indians: *see* under tribal names

Anglín, Pedro, 81

Angulo, Juan de, 129–30, 136

Apaches, 14, 19, 20, 39, 76, 128, 148: first appearance at Béxar, 8; displaced by Comanches, 8–9; expeditions against, 9, 19; hostilities at Béxar, 9–10; peace treaty with, 11–13; obstacle to ranching, 100–101; raids on Béxar horse herds, 113; as captive labor, 123; Mescaleros, 133